PENNIES FOR HEAVEN

Karen

Thank you so
much & please
enjoy this book

David John

Brandeis Series in American Jewish History, Culture, and Life

Jonathan D. Sarna, Editor | *Sylvia Barack Fishman*, Associate Editor

For a complete list of books that are available in the series, visit www.upne.com

Daniel Judson
*Pennies for Heaven: The History of
American Synagogues and Money*

Marc Dollinger
*Black Power, Jewish Politics:
Reinventing the Alliance in the 1960s*

David Weinstein
*The Eddie Cantor Story: A Jewish
Life in Performance and Politics*

David G. Dalin
*Jewish Justices of the Supreme Court:
From Brandeis to Kagan*

Naomi Prawer Kadar
*Raising Secular Jews: Yiddish
Schools and Their Periodicals for
American Children, 1917–1950*

Linda B. Forgosh
*Louis Bamberger: Department Store
Innovator and Philanthropist*

Gary Phillip Zola and
Marc Dollinger, editors
*American Jewish History:
A Primary Source Reader*

Vincent Brook and
Marat Grinberg, editors
*Woody on Rye: Jewishness in the
Films and Plays of Woody Allen*

Mark Cohen
*Overweight Sensation: The Life
and Comedy of Allan Sherman*

David E. Kaufman
*Jewhooing the Sixties: American
Celebrity and Jewish Identity —
Sandy Koufax, Lenny Bruce, Bob
Dylan, and Barbra Streisand*

Jack Wertheimer, editor
*The New Jewish Leaders: Reshaping
the American Jewish Landscape*

Eitan P. Fishbane and
Jonathan D. Sarna, editors
*Jewish Renaissance and Revival
in America*

Jonathan B. Krasner
*The Benderly Boys and
American Jewish Education*

Daniel Judson

Pennies *for* Heaven

THE HISTORY OF AMERICAN SYNAGOGUES AND MONEY

Brandeis University Press | Waltham, Massachusetts

Brandeis University Press
An imprint of University Press of New England
www.upne.com
© 2018 Brandeis University
All rights reserved
Manufactured in the United States of America
Designed by Mindy Basinger Hill
Typeset in Arno Pro

For permission to reproduce any of the material in this book,
contact Permissions, University Press of New England,
One Court Street, Suite 250, Lebanon NH 03766;
or visit www.upne.com

Library of Congress Cataloging-in-Publication Data

Names: Judson, Daniel, author.
Title: Pennies for heaven : the history of American synagogues
    and money / Daniel Judson.
Description: Waltham, Massachusetts : Brandeis University Press, [2018] |
Series: Brandeis Series in American Jewish History, Culture, and Life |
    Includes bibliographical references and index.
Identifiers: LCCN 2018003594 (print) | LCCN 2018005609 (ebook) | ISBN
    9781512602760 (epub, pdf, & mobi) | ISBN 9781512602746 (cloth : alk.
    paper) | ISBN 9781512602753 (pbk. : alk. paper)
Subjects: LCSH: Synagogues—United States—History. |
Synagogues—Finance—United States—History. | Judaism—United
    States—History.
Classification: LCC BM205 (ebook) | LCC BM205.J83 2018 (print) |
    DDC 296.6/50973—dc23

LC record available at https://lccn.loc.gov/2018003594.

5   4   3   2   1

Contents

Acknowledgments

In the Orach Chaim synagogue, a modern orthodox shul in the Upper East Side of Manhattan founded in 1879, there is a small plaque above the entranceway to the sanctuary that reads "In honor of Abraham Daniel Cohen, Vice-President of the congregation, for 37 years of service." Family lore says that my grandfather, Abraham Daniel, for whom I was named, spent 37 years as synagogue vice-president but never became president because his father was never president of his synagogue. Commitment to synagogues is in my genes.

This project has been long in the making, but from start to finish it has continuously felt like a gift. I am grateful to many people for their support. The archivists and librarians I consulted are chief among those to whom I am indebted. Harvey Sukenic, the Hebrew College librarian is a model of research acumen and unfailing helpfulness. Martha Berg, the archivist at Rodeph Shalom in Pittsburgh, and Lindsay Sprechman, the archivist at Temple Israel in Boston, were both supremely helpful in locating important documents. The American Jewish Archives — with particular gratitude to Elisa Ho, Kevin Proffitt, and Gary Zola — is a scholar's dream. Yehuda Halevi likened a library to an orchard and spending time at the Archives brings this sentiment to life.

James Hudnut-Beumler's work on the history of Protestant church finance was a model and inspiration for this book and I was honored and appreciative of his help in this project.

I am grateful to the leadership of Hebrew College and the Hebrew College Rabbinical School — Sharon Cohen-Anisfeld, Art Green, and Danny Lehmann — for encouraging me at every step of this process, and for creating an atmosphere that nurtures faculty. My colleagues at the rabbinical school have also been a tremendous resource for all manner of help and questions, my thanks to: Rachel Adelman, Harvey Bock, Jane Kanarek,

Daniel Klein, Ebn Leader, Allan Lehmann, Nehemia Polen, Shayna Rhodes, Micha'el Rosenberg, and Laurena Rosenberg.

I am deeply indebted to Brandeis' Department of Near Eastern and Jewish Studies. Eugene Sheppard, ChaeRan Freeze, and Jonathan Decter were enormously generous with their time and I was privileged to have had the opportunity to study with them.

It is wonderful to have friends who are scholars in diverse fields whom I could tap for advice. Richard Grossman, an economic historian, and Jed Shugerman, a legal historian, gave essential help with some of the economic and legal issues that appear in the book.

My Yiddish teacher, Lillian Leavitt, communicates a love and passion for the language that has inspired my own love of Yiddish.

I am grateful to Phyllis Deutsch, editor-in-chief of University Press of New England and Sylvia Fuks Fried, Director of the Brandeis University Press for their suggestions and encouragement in this process.

As has happened many times in my life, my wife knew what I needed and wanted before I even did. It was her suggestion and encouragement that I should start a doctoral program despite having a job and three children. Even when I was not sure I could get this book done, it was her constant feeling that I could and I should do this, which allowed me to complete this project. I am grateful for her ongoing love and support as well as her keen editing.

I tried very hard not to let this work get in the way of being a father to Tali, Maayan, and Revaya, but I am sure they knew there were times when I was reading them Harry Potter when I was really thinking about the cost of synagogue seats at Mikveh Israel in 1845. I trust they will forgive me for this. I hope that this work will be an inspiration for them to care about Jewish institutions, as their great-grandfather's plaque is a legacy for me.

Finally and very simply, this book only came to fruition because of Jonathan Sarna. Jonathan's continual encouragement and belief in the value of this work has made all the difference. In the years that I have been working on this project, I cannot remember a single time when a question I had was not responded to within the day, or more likely within the hour of the email being sent. It's a little daunting if it were not so remarkable. His erudition and scholarship are of course immense, only topped by his *menschlichkeit*.

PENNIES FOR HEAVEN

Introduction

The archivist at the American Jewish Archives in Cincinnati was not completely sure what to do either. I had requested the two-hundred-year-old ledger books for a prominent synagogue and the documents she brought out were knotted in what looked like their original string and sealed in their original box. I was not sure whether I could just cut two-hundred-year-old string or whether that needed to be preserved along with the documents. "Nobody has ever looked at these?" I asked the archivist with surprise, as many articles and books have focused on this synagogue's history. The archivist responded with some bemusement as she cut the string off, "Well, rabbinic sermons attract historical interest, but synagogue ledger books . . . they are not everyone's cup of tea."

As this was the not the last time I had the opportunity to cut the string off a dusty box of unread synagogue ledgers, I can attest to the fact that congregational finances have generally not been every scholar's cup of tea.[1] This lack of interest in synagogue economics is part of a broader pattern of indifference to financial matters in Jewish scholarship. The field of Jewish studies has been criticized for its focus on intellectual and spiritual achievement while ignoring material and economic experience. No doubt the historical baggage associated with Jews and money partly explains the trend. As one historian described the issue recently, "Shylock has cast a long shadow of defensiveness over Jewish self-perception."[2]

But this has been a loss for our knowledge of Jewish history in general and synagogues in particular. An economic perspective does not aim to reduce the complex experience of religion to financial concerns; rather, as James Hudnut-Beumler writes in his history of American Protestant churches and money, looking at religion from an economic perspective allows us "to see some things in the history of religious life to which we are typically blind."[3] This book seeks to overcome this "blindness" by examining how synagogues raised income, financed buildings, and paid clergy. A focus on congregational finances sheds light not just on the historical development of synagogues but also on the values and beliefs of the Jews who worshipped within them.

If you ask American Jews today about the financial system of synagogues, most will likely presume that the system of collecting dues was given with the Torah at Mt. Sinai. It feels completely engrained in synagogue life. But dues are actually a twentieth-century innovation, and this book, perhaps surprisingly, has change, experimentation, and adaptation as central themes.

The establishment of synagogues in America called for a new form of synagogue finance and governance. The model of synagogue life that Jews brought from Europe did not fit in an American context. In Europe, Jewish communal institutions were funded by a compulsory tax levied by the country or municipality. In America, Jewish communities needed to survive on a purely voluntary basis. As immigrant rabbi Moses Weinberger noted in 1887: "In all other lands a man is required by the government to belong to the kehila [community] of the area where he lives, and like it or not it levies taxes upon him. In America any man may cut himself off from his community, taking no part in it whatsoever. One who remains loyal to his community and faith is deemed meritorious."[4]

In adapting to the American context, American synagogues often looked to their Christian neighbors for examples. Following the lead of Protestant churches, synagogues in the eighteenth and nineteenth centuries primarily financed themselves by selling seats. Members bought seats that became the individual's legal property. A percentage of the total price of the seats was paid to the congregation on a yearly basis. Like Broadway tickets, seats were valued according to their comfort and proximity to the worship service. No one could sit in a seat at any time except the owner. If a seat owner wanted to sell his seat, he/she could do so to other members or prospective members, creating a kind of synagogue seat market. If members could not afford the upfront cost of seats, synagogues would loan money to individual members to pay for a seat, and each synagogue had rules about how much one needed to pay up front and how much one could take out on loan. Contemporary synagogues today often encourage their members to take ownership of the congregation and to feel invested in its future, but for eighteenth- and nineteenth-century synagogues, this was a literal truth: members owned and were invested in the synagogue.

In the post–World War I era, however, the selling of seats went out of fashion and the dues system was introduced. This change came about as a result of cultural and economic trends. The selling of seats, with the wealthier being able to afford better seats, became a problem in an era that was suffused with rhetoric about democracy and egalitarianism. As the president of Adath Israel in Louisville, Kentucky, argued to his congregation in 1919, the time had come to give up on selling seats: "You hear much about democracy these days; democracy everywhere, but it occurs to me that there is no place on earth where there should be so much of democracy as in the house of God. There should be in the Temple no distinction of wealth or class; there should be no rich men's section and no poor man's corner . . . Every man should be permitted to enter a Temple and take whatsoever seat he may desire that may be unoccupied at the time of his entrance."[5]

Rabbi Leo Franklin, another early proponent of eliminating seat ownership, argued in a similar vein that in synagogues "there must be no aristocracy and no snobocracy."[6]

Synagogues moved away from seats not only because of cultural forces advocating democracy but also because of economic changes within the Jewish community. The Jewish community in the post–World War I era was more entrenched in American life and more prosperous than in previous eras. Congregations sought to build new buildings with expanded missions, "the shul with a pool" phenomenon that was prevalent in every city with a sizable Jewish population. But having membership revenue tied to seat ownership meant congregations were effectively limited in their revenue and their membership by the number of seats they had. Synagogues were anxious to find ways to broaden their financial base. Moving to dues and away from seats would quite simply allow congregations to have more members.

The move may seem obvious in retrospect, but there was significant anxiety at the time that without the lure of a nice seat, wealthier members would not choose to join a synagogue. Rabbi Harry Levy of Temple Israel in Boston, however, urged his congregation to eliminate paying for seats and move to dues: "Increased membership means larger strength, larger influence, larger possibilities. And there is no limit to the number of members we can secure."[7]

Slowly but steadily over the next two decades, congregations of all denominations would abandon selling seats and turn to the dues model we know from synagogues today. This story of transition gives us a picture of a Jewish community after World War I that is both ever more attuned to broader American values like democracy, while also seeking a bolder and more influential presence on the American landscape. The story is also illustrative of the ways in which an economic perspective opens up a window into the development of American synagogues.

The change from selling seats to dues marks one significant transition in synagogue finance and will receive detailed attention in chapter 4. This book also explores a number of other important experiments and transitions that have heretofore received little scholarly attention, including the free synagogue movement of the early twentieth century pioneered by Rabbi Stephen Wise that eliminated both buying seats and dues;[8] the creation of "mushroom synagogues," for-profit High Holiday experiences held in Yiddish theaters that attracted hundreds of thousands of immigrant Jews before being outlawed by the New York State Legislature;[9] the synagogue-center movement of the 1920s, which saw the financial costs of synagogues skyrocket as new synagogues were built with pools, gymnasia, social halls, and other amenities;[10] and the "hazan craze" that took place in the late 1880s in which famous hazanim (cantors) were quite suddenly paid ever more exorbitant salaries until the "cantor bubble" burst as quickly as it started.[11]

While change and experimentation comprise one thread in the story of American synagogue finance, another thread is the extent to which congregations aligned their financial system with their religious ideals and values, what is called by some scholars "ecclesiastical economics."[12] For the most part, synagogues were highly pragmatic and generally did not approach their finances from a religious perspective. Synagogues typically did not turn to biblical or religious sources to ground their financial decisions, as their Protestant neighbors did; most often, they simply acted in the most expedient way to pay their bills. Synagogues also developed no theological language around the support of congregations; there was and is no Jewish equivalent to what in the Protestant world is known as "stewardship" or "systematic benevolence."

Just as congregations were pragmatic, rabbis, in turn, were also pragmatic. They understood themselves to be part of the professional class and wanted compensation commensurate with this status. The earliest board minutes of the first congregation in America, Congregation Shearith Israel, confirm that Jewish spiritual leaders even prior to the colonial era thought there was no issue with demanding more money from their congregation, threatening to strike, or leaving if better opportunities arose.[13] Beginning in the late nineteenth century, rabbis formed unions that effectively served to maintain the rabbinate as a professional class.

The pragmatism of rabbis stood in contrast to Christian clergy, who often saw money in the religious realm as inherently problematic. As frontier preacher Elijah Goodwin wrote in 1825, "I did not think it was right to preach for money; still, I thought a little money was very convenient when it came to paying ferries at the rivers."[14] For some Christian clergy, the religious template of Jesus overthrowing the money changers made them wary of mixing God and money. A result of the ministerial anxiety around money meant that by the late nineteenth century, Protestant ministers, who had at one time been part of the professional class, had effectively de-professionalized themselves and by the mid-twentieth century lagged significantly behind rabbis in terms of salaries.[15]

The pragmatism of rabbis and synagogues reflected Jewish tradition that long understood that rabbis should receive compensation for their work and saw money in religion as instrumental, neither good nor bad in and of itself.[16] But pragmatism had its limits. In 1790, Congregation Mikveh Israel in Philadelphia needed to retire its building debt or face foreclosure. Following the lead of some prominent churches and under the auspices of the city, they held a lottery to raise money. Quaker churches in Pennsylvania had come out against the holding of lotteries to finance religion, but the synagogue believed itself to have no recourse other than to utilize the lottery. Pragmatism trumped any religious qualms the congregation might have had. This situation would reemerge in the twentieth century when "bingoitis" struck America during the Depression, and Americans flocked to churches to play bingo.

When bingo came to synagogues, all of the Jewish denominations rejected it as an inappropriate way to raise money; however, in the Conservative movement the issue became contentious. The movement flipped its position on the propriety of using bingo to fund synagogues multiple times. First the movement decried bingo as not in keeping with Jewish values and threatened to expel any congregations that used it. A few years later, it reversed positions and deemed it acceptable, although not ideal, for synagogues to raise money in this way. This led to numerous Conservative synagogues across the country holding bingo nights. Later the movement reversed positions yet again and went back to saying it was not in keeping with Jewish values.[17]

The multiple reversals reflect the tension between a pragmatic approach and a values-based approach to congregational finance. On the one hand, bingo allowed for congregations to tap nonmembers for money, and for many congregations the revenue from bingo was the difference between a surplus and a deficit budget. On the other hand, some perceived that bingo synagogues were simply aiding and abetting gambling. The debate over bingo was often fierce and contested, but it was only one of a number of issues where congregations oscillated between a pragmatic and a religious outlook to their finances.

The final theme that emerges from a broad look at synagogue finance is the extent to which the forces of competition and a religious marketplace shaped and continue to shape American Jewish life.[18] The establishment in 1825 of alternative synagogues in Charleston, South Carolina, and New York City marks the beginning of competition among synagogues. Prior to this year, most cities effectively just had one synagogue. Jonathan Sarna has written that this development was crucial to the history of American synagogues because it forced congregations to become responsive to their members as congregants now had a choice of synagogues.[19]

Religious competition had beneficial effects in driving creativity as congregations competed for the attention of prospective members. Competition also put a check on the cost of being a member (if the membership fee was too high, one might walk down the street to a cheaper synagogue). But competition has also limited synagogue cooperation and the sharing of resources, an issue that becomes even more significant in the present day.

The invisible hand of the market is often just that in religion — invisible — as we ignore the extent to which it impacts the structure of religion. But as we will discover, the American embrace of free market principles in religion has influenced almost every aspect of synagogue life, from the pay and quality of rabbis, to the size and architecture of synagogues, to even, as we will discover, Jewish ritual itself.

This book is first and foremost a work of critical history written primarily for academics and lay readers interested in deepening their understanding of American Jewish history. But one cannot write about synagogue funding of the past without having one eye on the present. And many contemporary synagogues are, to put it bluntly, in trouble. Since the recession of 2007–2008, synagogue membership at non-Orthodox synagogues has been declining significantly. One recent study of the Boston Jewish community cited an 11 percent decline in the number of families that pay dues at traditional "brick and mortar" synagogues from 2006 to 2015.[20] Reasons cited for the membership decline include the re-urbanization of the Jewish community away from suburban synagogues and the disinterest among millennials in joining Jewish institutions. The dues system itself has been cited as a reason Jews are staying away. The need for members to work out a special arrangement if they cannot meet the dues obligations is felt by some to be embittering and embarrassing. The dues fee is also beyond the reach of many younger families and creates a large barrier to entry.

The result for this book is that an odd thing happened on the way to its publication, which is that it became relevant and even part of the story to some degree. As synagogues suffered a downturn in their finances and membership, some synagogues began casting about for new models to finance themselves. Based in part on the research for this book into Stephen Wise's Free Synagogue, synagogues began to explore the Free Synagogue model as a response to fiscal difficulties and moved to adopt Wise's vision of a synagogue free of compulsory dues. This move by some synagogues to eliminate dues garnered a good deal of attention in the Jewish world and even beyond as the *New York Times*,[21] the *Boston Globe*,[22] and the *Washington Post*[23] all published articles on the move to eliminate dues. To date, over sixty synagogues have now adopted this model in the past few years.[24]

This is not to say that every historical funding idea should be resurrected. It seems unlikely that congregations will bring back fining members who cause trouble during services or refuse to serve as an officer of the congregation if asked (true for most nineteenth-century congregations). But for readers who are picking up this book because they care about the future of synagogues, the historical debates and ideas presented here should broaden our sense of what is possible in contemplating how to solve the problem of synagogues today. Recognizing the extent of change and adaptation that has taken place over the history of synagogue financing could inspire old-new thinking about the perennial problems of financing congregations. While the context continues to change, the fundamental issue of raising money in a market-driven, voluntary religious community remains the same.

Note to the Reader Regarding Historical Values

Throughout this book I have tried to give the reader a sense of how past costs translate into contemporary dollars. Where I have provided historical data on costs, I have placed the contemporary value in brackets next to it. However, translating from historical values is a complicated endeavor. The colonial period is the most problematic because each state had a different currency, so £100 in Pennsylvania in 1770 was not equivalent to £100 in New York. Because of the difficulty of translating historical values into contemporary dollars, the reader should understand the contemporary values only as a broad approximation. For the colonial period, I calculated contemporary values using the standard work on the subject of historical pricing, John McCusker's *How Much Is That in Real Money?: A Historical Commodity Price Index for Use as a Deflator of Money Values in the Economy of the United States*.[25] For prices in the nineteenth and twentieth centuries, I have used an inflation calculator found online at www.westegg.com/inflation/infl.cgi.

ONE

"The Foundation Stones Are Now for Sale"
[1728–1805]

In the fall of 1790, Congregation Mikveh Israel, the first synagogue in Philadelphia, had just come through years of perilous economic conditions. Two years earlier the congregation had faced bankruptcy and foreclosure after they accrued £2200 [$44,000] in debt to pay for a building, a mikvah, and a schoolhouse. Through pleas to the general public, and a successful lottery, it staved off its creditors and retired its debt.[1] But fiscal trouble loomed again. Members were not contributing the requisite amount to keep the congregation functioning.

At Rosh Hashanah services that year, the leader of the adjunta (the board of the congregation) was so incensed at the lack of financial support that he made a special announcement at morning services. Any member not contributing to the synagogue would not only no longer receive the standard benefits of membership, like kosher meat, but if they or their family members died, the synagogue would forbid anyone from attending the funeral or help them in any way. Not giving to the synagogue, he said, in what was probably the first "High Holiday Appeal" in American Jewish history, was consigning yourself to die alone.[2]

The finances of colonial congregations were not always quite so desperate, but they were often in flux. New York's Congregation Shearith Israel, America's first synagogue, cycled through a number of different funding models looking for the best way to raise money. Similar to the country itself, synagogues were new endeavors without inherited traditions as to how they should be administered. As a result, synagogue funding was a mix of traditional Jewish methods, like paying the synagogue for Torah honors, and methods learned from the American environment, like the lottery that helped save Mikveh Israel. This mix of tradition, adaptation, and experimentation would come to define synagogue finance in the colonial era.

The other defining feature of colonial finance is the transition from the humble synagogue, which Shearith Israel built in the 1730s in New York City, to the much more grandiose synagogue, which Kahal Kadosh Beth Elohim (KKBE) would build some fifty years later in Charleston, South Carolina. Whereas Shearith Israel's synagogue was meant to be indistinguishable from its surroundings, KKBE employed one of Charleston's most well-known (non-Jewish) architects to create a building that purposefully rivaled the most prominent church in the city. While the transition reflected a changed cultural value around announcing a Jewish presence, it also had economic ramifications. The Charleston building was five times the cost of the New York City synagogue in today's money. It also led the congregation into debt. This was the first time, but certainly not the last time, a synagogue built an impressive building to demonstrate a Jewish presence even if it meant sending the congregation into the red. The large new building also meant the need for greater resources to keep up that building, a challenge with which contemporary synagogues are quite familiar.

The Dutch Synagogue-Community Model

The original Jews who landed in New York City in 1654 from Recife, Brazil, were coming from a synagogue community where the Jewish leaders held significant power over the lives of its members. The mahamad (community leaders) had the power to tax, fine, and adjudicate civil and criminal matters among its members. Every Jew in Recife, indeed every Jew in Brazil, was considered a member of the synagogue and subject to the decisions of the mahamad. This communal structure mirrored the structure of the Amsterdam Jewish community, as Recife was a Dutch colony until recaptured by Portugal. The Dutch model of synagogue life was the central model for Jewish communities throughout the West Indies as well as London.[3] And as the model with which early American Jews were most familiar, it would have a significant influence on Congregation Shearith Israel, the first American synagogue and itself the model for subsequent colonial synagogues.

The financing for synagogues in the Dutch model came from a tax that each member paid to the Jewish community. The synagogue of Recife,

Zur Yisrael, was primarily financed out of the Imposta tax. The Imposta, a tax on every Jew living in Brazil, was primarily a tariff on goods being imported and exported, but also included currency exchange fees, taxes on government bonds, fees on housing sales, and other items. In 1648, the tax on all dry and wet goods imported was 75 percent of the value of the goods. For slaves, the Imposta tax was 5 soldos per slave, while the tax for a case of high-quality white sugar was 8 soldos. Every Jew was obligated to show his or her financial books to the mahamad twice a year, and the Imposta tax itself was due in two payments — one just before Rosh Hashanah and the other just before Passover.[4]

Additional funds for the community were raised in a few ways. Members would donate to funds set aside for a variety of charitable causes: caring for the Jewish poor, redeeming captives, marrying indigent orphans, and aiding needy Jews in Israel. Members could also be fined for various infractions. Those who refused to serve on the mahamad, or who were guilty of improper conduct during services, or who changed seats without permission, or who gambled on Friday afternoon instead of preparing for Shabbat, were all subject to fines. And if all of these sources still did not meet communal needs, a special tax called a Finita could be levied.[5]

Many of the features of the Dutch system were then transferred to American shores. The parnas (president) was an elected official at Shearith Israel who, like the mahamad, held ultimate authority within the synagogue. He had the power to levy fines, collect offerings, adjudicate synagogue disputes, and determine salaries of synagogue employees, and was generally responsible for the welfare of the synagogue community. Aided by the fact that there were no rabbis or hahamim (Sephardic title for spiritual leader) in colonial America (the first rabbi would not come to America until the 1840s), and thus no other clerical figures of authority, the parnas was the undisputed center of communal power.

What was not transferrable from the Dutch model was the full extent of the mahamad's authority. The powers of the board of Shearith Israel were circumscribed to the synagogue. As Jonathan Sarna notes in *American Judaism*, "Synagogue communities, as they developed in the major cities of colonial America, bespoke the growing compartmentalization of eighteenth-century American Jewish life into Jewish and worldly domains. This distinction was unknown . . . to most European Jews of the day, but it was characteristic of American Judaism almost from the beginning."[6] In terms of synagogue finance, this meant that in America there would be no Imposta. Synagogue leaders in America were not empowered to tax the commercial activity of their members like in Recife or Amsterdam, so their funding mechanisms were confined to the synagogue. Shearith Israel initially funded itself by selling synagogue honors, collecting donations, and, starting in 1728, imposing an annual tax on synagogue seats.

Ultimately, colonial American synagogues settled on a blend of models for their governance. From the Dutch model they took the necessity for strong central authority, but to fund themselves they would rely on a succession of changing models and schemes throughout the eighteenth century, some inherited from Jewish tradition, some adapted from their Christian neighbors.

Those neighboring churches were financed in two different ways. The Anglican churches around Shearith Israel were established churches, where the minister's salary was set by the state and paid for by tax.[7] With the exception of Rhode Island, Delaware, New Jersey, and Pennsylvania, all of which had significant populations of dissenters, the remaining colonies had some form of tax support for an established church. In Virginia, for example, Anglican ministers received a salary of 16,000 pounds of tobacco, as well as a glebe — 200 or more acres of land purchased by the state — which the minister either farmed himself or received rental value from.[8] In the New England colonies, each citizen of a town, because they paid a tax to support the Congregational church, had rights in their local church. This led to the unusual circumstance of individuals who might not have even been professing Christians voting on a new pastor.[9] In New York, the 1703 Act for the Better Establishment of the Maintenance for the Ministers of the City of New York made it possible for the city constable to confiscate and sell the goods of anyone refusing to pay the tax to support the Anglican ministry.[10]

The nonestablished churches of the colonial era — Lutheran, German and Dutch Reform, Quakers, Methodists, Baptists, Presbyterians, and so on — were for the most part left to fund themselves, although on occasion some churches made the case that they should receive the support due the established church.[11] Some denominations, like Methodism under John Wesley, sought national financial standards for their churches. Wesley wished to pay all Methodist ministers the exact same salary regardless of where they lived or how large their parish was. Donations would be received from parishioners and then funneled to the national level, where they would be sent back out to pay local ministers.[12] But more common was that each church set its own course to fund itself and determine ministerial salaries.

The method employed most often for funding was to sell or rent pews. Seats were either assessed a value and then sold, or put on auction and awarded to the highest bidder.[13] As we will see in the next chapter when this became the standard practice among synagogues, the selling of seats sometimes led to complex problems. Buying a seat meant that it became one's personal property that could then be transferred to heirs upon death. Complications naturally arose when people moved cities and wanted to sell their seats, or when the synagogue built a new building, or when children wanted the seats but were unable to keep up with the yearly assessments.[14] The rental of pews also introduced into American houses of worship what Stephen Wise would later call "the unlovely differentiation of the outside world"[15] — that is, differentiation based upon wealth. Typically the well-to-do bought seats closer to the front of the church/synagogue, with back rows being reserved for the poor. In both church and synagogue, criticism of the system's inequity was frequent throughout the nineteenth century and ultimately led to its abandonment. The democratizing element of the Second Great Awakening would inspire figures like Charles Grandison Finney to decry the system as unworthy of Christian virtues.[16] But in colonial America, where distinctions between class and gender were accepted in general society and in houses of worship, the system made financial sense.

The Colonial Synagogue Budget: Expenses

The expenses associated with running a synagogue have not changed very much historically. Just as salaries and building costs make up the bulk of the budget now, so it was in the first American synagogue. In 1733, the salaries of the hazan (prayer leader), the shochet (kosher butcher), and the shamas (sexton) together equaled roughly 65 percent of the budget. The remaining 35 percent of budget expenses were primarily for keeping the synagogue functioning — wax for candles, oil for the eternal flame, and various sundries amounting to £30 [$2,310]. The only other expenditure was "cash given to ye poor," which came to around £20 [$1,440].[17]

The hazan, Moses Lopez de Fonseca, was paid £50 [$3,850], while the kosher butcher's salary was £20 [$1,540]. In 1733, the butcher petitioned the adjunta for another "augmentation of salary," which they unanimously consented to "in consideration of his indefatigable Pains." The salary increase, though, came not in the form of money; rather, the amount of wood he was given was increased to eight cords, and the congregation agreed to pay for "Passover cakes" for his whole family.[18] The shamas (sexton) was paid £18 [$1,296] with an additional £1.10 [$22] for "his negro's wages for cleaning the Synagog [sic]."[19]

While the salaries of the sexton and butcher were modest, the salary of the hazan was quite noteworthy. His £50 salary, when translated into today's dollars, seems like he was being paid a pittance, $3,850, but in fact just the opposite may be the case. As a point of comparison, New England clergy were paid in the 1730s an average of £60 [$2,310].[20] Because of the differing value of the pound in New York versus Massachusetts, the hazan was actually being paid roughly 50 percent more than the average New England minister.[21] His salary also compares well to other kinds of basic trades. A New York City carpenter working on a ship in 1733 made £33 a year, while an unskilled laborer in New York might make £20 to £30.[22] Given that it cost between £20 and £30 to rent a house in New York City during this period,[23] and £1 to buy a new suit,[24] we have some sense, then, that the hazan was paid well enough to have led what we might call today a solid middle-class existence.[25] The relatively high salary of the hazan is surprising considering he was not even ordained clergy. It underscores that American Jewish communities from their earliest incarnation would pay their leadership significant salaries. Perhaps out of traditional respect for the leadership or out of a sense that it would be an embarrassment to have religious leaders in need of handouts, Jewish religious leaders by and large throughout American history would command a higher salary than their Protestant counterparts.

The congregation may have had a feeling that they were overpaying their hazan; when he left the position in 1737 to become the hazan of the synagogue in Curaçao, they hired his replacement at only £40 [$2,880] a year — £10 less than what Lopez de Fonseca made. They did, however, add a proviso stating that if there were unspent money in the charity fund, the congregation would pay him up to an additional £10 from that money.[26]

When in 1768 the congregation hired Gershom Seixas, who would become the most well-known Jewish religious leader in the colonial era, they paid him a salary of £80 [$4,300] plus wood and use of a house the congregation owned.

His salary was soon increased to £100 [$5,474], but in 1775 there was the first (but not the last) salary dispute between congregation and religious leader. The adjunta received a letter from Seixas saying that the "perquisites of his office, was verry [sic] Inconsiderable & his time entirely taken up with the Duties . . . he was under the Disagreeable necessity of applying for an additional Salery [sic]," of £140 [$6,648]. The board responded after a three-month delay that they could not offer more than his present £100. Seixas said he needed to receive at least £120 and subsequently resigned. The showdown between Seixas and the board ended a few days later when the adjunta declared that Seixas would be paid the additional £20, with the money to come from the synagogue tzedakah fund or, if that was spent, the adjunta itself would put up the funds.[27]

The amicable resolution of the salary dispute had seemingly no negative effects on the career of Seixas — he would go on to serve the congregation for thirty-two years after the Revolution. This suggests that both congregation and religious leader took a very pragmatic approach to the salary spat. While the history of American synagogue finance is replete with disputes over money between rabbi and synagogue, there is rarely a sense that it was unseemly for Jewish clergy to be seeking raises. In contrast, there often existed a tension for Protestant clergy around charging people for their services. Hudnut-Beumler cites a frontier preacher named Elijah Goodwin who in 1825 wrote, "I did not think it was right to preach for money; still, I thought a little money was very convenient when it came to paying ferries at the rivers."[28] American Jews inherited a tradition that, for the most part, was free from such tension, as Judaism historically understood the need to pay its rabbis and scholars.[29]

"Cash Given to Ye Poor"

The seventh paragraph of the 1706 Shearith Israel constitution, revised in 1728, stated, "Those poor of this Congregation that shall apply for Sedaka shall be assisted with as much as the Parnaz and his assistants shall think fit."[30] In practice, this meant the congregation spent between 10 and 20 percent of the total budget of the congregation on charity throughout the colonial era. In 1731, for example, "cash given to ye poor" was £20 [$1,540] or one-seventh of the total budget of the congregation, while in 1748, the congregation gave over £76 [$4,517] "to the poor and for their use," which represented almost 20 percent of the total budget.

Shearith Israel's congregational minutes frequently noted individuals and families asking for financial assistance. The most common notations were for the support of widows. Typical was the note from 1763, where the parnas "agreed to allow the Widdow [sic] Solomons Five Pounds [$292], towards house rent, to commence the first day of May."[31] In 1753, "It was unanimously agreed to allow Rachel Campanel, the sum of Twenty Pounds Currt money [$1,213] per annum in consideration of her age and infermities [sic]."[32] Rachel was the widow of the former shamas and, fifteen years later, her annual pension rose to £25. Her pension was again increased in 1770, and in 1771 a note was made of the congregation paying £5 to Dr. Anderson for attending to her in her final days. Although the giving of pensions to former employees and their widows was not the norm for New York society at the time, Shearith Israel provided monthly stipends, wood, matzah, medical care, and money for rent and covered funeral experiences and cemetery plots. Hyman Grinstein in his comprehensive history of the Jews of New York wrote that the giving of pensions and the sustaining of elderly members who had fallen on hard times "reveals a breadth of social view hardly paralleled until the rise of state social security laws in more recent times."[33]

Some of the board minutes, though, reflect the tension between the charitable commitment to widows and limited synagogue funds. Judith Myers, wife of the deceased shochet, had been receiving £30 [$1,993] per year plus wood, but in 1747 this was decreased to £20 per year plus wood, as the congregation needed the remaining £10 to supplement the salary of the hazan.[34]

One of the ongoing expenses the congregation bore was to assist the transient poor. The congregation distinguished between members of the community in need and those who were transient. The transients were small in number compared to the numbers of Jewish itinerants in Europe, but they came from all over the world, and "made a sort of circuit of the New World," moving from one city to the next when their assistance was cut off.[35]

The 1728 synagogue constitution read, "If any poor person should happen to come to this place and should want the assistance of the Sinagog the Parnaz is hereby impowered to allow every poor person for his maintenance the sum of Eight Shillings per week [$30] and no more Not Exceeding the term of twelve weeks. And the Parnaz is also to use his utmost endeavors to despatch them to sum othere place as soon as Possible assisting them with necessarys, for their Voyage."[36] The expense for assisting them on a journey was limited to 40 shillings [$150] for a single person, while for a family the parnas would make an individual decision.

The desire to push transient Jews to another city reflects the fear that such ongoing poverty would be a drain on the synagogue's limited resources. It may have also reflected a wariness of the Jewish poor coming to the attention of the civil authorities. The West India Company in 1655 granted the Jews a charter to settle in New Netherland as long as "the poor among them shall not become a burden to the Company or to the community, but be supported by their own nation."[37] Although the Jews were no longer living under this charter, the culture of New York City was for religious groups to take care of their own poor. In 1693, the New York Ministry Act had created some relief from the government in the form of clothing, fuel, food, or cash for "the deserving poor" — those who had fallen on hard times through no fault of their own. But aid from the city government went to relatively few, as the definition of "deserving poor" was restricted and only open to citizens of New York.[38]

There was a significant difference between the transient Jewish poor in America versus Europe. As Jacob Rader Marcus notes in *The Colonial American Jew*, "There were thousands of Jews constantly on the road in the Old World; they were victims of wars and persecutions, penniless, true paupers broken on the wheel of fortune. Fed for a night, they were housed in a *hekdesh*, a dirty hospice, and then carried by cart to the next village which sheltered a Jewish community."[39] In America, by contrast, there were few transient poor, and the community apparently gave all who applied some degree of support. But the support had its limits, and Shearith Israel made significant efforts to remove the transient poor.

In 1740–1741, the congregation paid for the passage of four families to Barbados and other locations at a cost of almost £18 [$1,137], which was more than twice what the congregation spent on "regular" charity. In 1748, twice that amount was spent to relocate two families to Curaçao and Barbados. Between paying for passage on ships, sustaining them until the ship left, and giving them kosher food, dealing with the transient poor was a significant expense.

In Philadelphia, Mikveh Israel set up an autonomous organization, Ezrath Orechim (Society for Destitute Strangers), just to deal with itinerant Jews who had come to the city after the Revolution. Itinerants were given between 15 shillings [$33] and 1 pound [$44]. The money was considered a loan, though, and the recipients promised to repay the money when it was in their power to do so.[40]

Another type of charitable case that came before colonial congregations were the rabbis who came through America collecting on behalf of Jewish communities in Palestine or in another part of the world where Jews were suffering. Colonial congregations did not generally give significant amounts to these figures but did pay for them to move to the next city. Isaac Carigal from Palestine stayed for several months with Shearith Israel before they paid for his travel to Newport. In 1775, the congregation received a letter from the hacham (spiritual leader) Samuel Cohen requesting assistance for the "distressed brethren of the Hebron." The congregation joined with the Newport synagogue to pay for him to travel to London at a cost of £31 [$1,801].

Shearith Israel also received requests for support from other synagogues around the world. In 1775, the congregation received letters requesting aid for the Jewish community of Smyrna, which had suffered from a disastrous fire, and a request from the Jews of Charlestown to send a donation toward the building of a new synagogue. Both of these requests were rejected, as the adjunta resolved that it "is not in the Power of this Congregation at Present to Give any moneys toward any of those uses."[41] It is not clear why the congregation refused a donation to the Charlestown synagogue. It had been over forty years since they themselves reached out to Jewish congregations around the world seeking donations for their first building. Perhaps the congregational budget had been exhausted by other charitable requests as the economy tumbled with the growing agitation that would shortly lead to war.

After the Revolution, the congregation continued to provide relief to poor Jews, but also began a series of autonomous philanthropic organizations. In 1785, the congregation organized the *Hebra Gemilut Hasadim*

(Society for Dispensing Acts of Kindness), which existed for five years and provided financial help in the form of money for rent and medical care; its members also performed religious acts like visiting the sick and aiding the bereaved.[42] In 1798, when an epidemic of yellow fever raged and most people escaped the city, Gershom Seixas established a fund "to assist such poor or such persons as might be in want during the time our trustees should be absent from the city." The *Kalfe Sedaka Mattan Basether* (Collection of Charity Given Secretly) continued its work after the epidemic passed, helping those in poverty until 1816, when Seixas passed away. The creation of autonomous philanthropic organizations presaged the growth of Jewish communal organizations that would tend to the needs of the Jewish poor. After the colonial period, synagogue expenditure on tzedakah would drop as a percentage of total budget as other Jewish organizations specifically devoted to tzedakah would take over that role.[43]

The Colonial Synagogue Budget: The Income Side

While the expense side of the budget may look similar to today, the income side is barely recognizable. The earliest records of Shearith Israel Congregation from 1720 to 1721 show that the primary source of income were offerings made by members when called to the Torah. Members also made gifts to the congregation on Rosh Hashanah, Yom Kippur, and the three Pilgrimage Festivals. Jacob Franks, for example, an active and wealthy member of the congregation, gave ten different offerings to the congregation over the course of the year for a total of £15.13 [$1,155]. Moses Mickell, less well off than Jacob Franks, gave nine different offerings to the congregation totaling £3.5 [$270].[44] The congregation's total revenue was around £90 [$6,930]. Jacob Rader Marcus, the great scholar of colonial American Jewry, suggests that this income reflects the relative poverty of New York Jews compared to European Jews: "People of wealth did not commonly leave Europe to settle a frontier land, and while there were pioneers who acquired some wealth in America and others of substance, eleemosynary standards were low. . . . It is an adequate commentary on the frontier character of Shearith Israel to note that its total income in 1732 was less than £180 New York currency while the income of London's Bevis Marks synagogue less than a decade earlier in 1726 had been £6,742, sterling!"[45]

While Marcus is certainly correct in the relative comparison of New York to London, it does not mean the congregation was impoverished. As noted above, the congregation was paying their hazan a middle-class wage, and more notably, the congregation had just raised over £350 [$26,950] for the construction of their new building (discussed below). While it was not Bevis Marks, neither was it a backwater.

In 1728 the congregation amended the constitution that had been in place since 1706, and one of the changes they made regarded synagogue funding. The constitution of the synagogue stated that because the selling of mitzvot are not convenient, "It's Resolved for the future that . . . the Parnaz with his assistants shall tax the men's Seats in the Sinagog [sic], as they are now seated But not exceeding Fifteen Shillings [$57.75] each Seat per annum, nor less than five Shillings."⁴⁶ As noted above, the renting of seats was the practice in nonestablished churches, and one presumes the adoption of this method was a result of this influence.

The money raised from this move was quite small, as the primary funding source for the synagogue was offerings. In 1733, for example, the congregation received a total of £130.13 [$10,010] in offerings, which accounted for over 95 percent of the budget. But offerings were not without contention. The board minutes note that the leaders of the adjunta

> decided for the peace and harmony of the Kahal and of the holy
> synagogue that any person who may be called to the Sepher Torah
> be obliged to offer at least three blessings for the health of the Parnas,
> Presidente and the Kahal Kados, and it shall be the duty of the Hazan to
> advise such person, and if he refuse, his offering shall not be accepted, and
> he shall be fined to the full extent with Thirty Shillings for the Sedaka;
> and in case he wishes to make an offering to the Kahal Kados other than
> at the Sepher, it shall not be accepted without naming the Parnas first, and
> if he insists he shall incur the above said punishment; Peace be on Israel,
> Amen.⁴⁷

This small piece of synagogue disputation tells us a great deal about money and power in eighteenth-century synagogues. The reading of Torah is traditionally the place in the liturgy where various blessings are offered, but one had to offer blessings for the leaders of the community if they wanted the honor of being called to the Torah. This presumably was to signify their control of the community. But it also appears that the adjunta's desire to assert control was often being met with rebellion.

In 1768, the issue had changed very little when the adjunta upped the ante, and resolved that anyone being called to the Torah had to offer at least sixpence in honor of the parnas, and anyone, "making an Offering otherwise then the True Intent and meaning of this Resolve, he or they so offending Shall no longer be deemed a member of this K.K. [holy congregation]."⁴⁸ We hear little in the synagogue board minutes about the reasons for the rebellions, which must have spurred this new rule, but it is significant that members were willing to so openly chafe at the adjunta's leadership. In an American context where the authority of the adjunta was more limited than in the Dutch model, and perhaps within a general culture where authority was openly questioned, challenges to the adjunta would increase and ultimately spell the demise of this form of synagogue governance. In 1824, the congregation finally abolished the need to make an offering in honor of the parnas, a result of a major squabble that would lead to a congregational schism and the creation of an entirely new synagogue.⁴⁹

In 1737, the congregation seems to have reached a turning point in its finances. It found that it could not meet its budget through offerings and began a few decades of tinkering with the way it was going to raise funds. The budget for that year came to £134 [$10,318]. The adjunta determined that they could not afford their expenses "without the help & assistance of our brethren dwelling in the Country, and do by the consent of the majority of this K.K., order that every family that carries on trade in the Country . . . shall pay yearly for the use of this K.K . . . the Sum of forty shillings [$144]."⁵⁰ Those who refused to pay on time would be excluded from being a member of the synagogue and receive no benefit from the synagogue until they paid. The congregation did make allowances for those unable to afford the payment.

The imposition of a tax on every Jew dwelling in the region may strike us today as odd given the localization of synagogue support. But at this point in time Shearith Israel was the only synagogue in North America, and it would take almost a century before another congregation in New York was founded. The tax is clarified when considering the Dutch model. The synagogue in Recife, for example, considered every Jew in Brazil a member of the synagogue, and excommunication was the threat if orders were not followed. The adjunta understood it could not threaten excommunication in the American milieu — there would be no mechanism for carrying out such a threat — so the adjunta threatened with the power they had, which was to exclude someone from the synagogue.

The tax, however, did not raise sufficient revenue to cover the synagogue budget and as the congregation increased, its budget increased accordingly. By 1747, the budget had grown to £308 [$20,651], roughly double the value of what it had been ten years earlier. In response, the congregation changed its funding mechanism entirely, instituting an income tax. Every member of the congregation was assessed a tax to pay over eighteen months. Offerings were counted as part of paying the tax. Threats of synagogue exclusion were given for those who failed to pay the tax. Mordecay Gomez and Jacob Franks, two of the wealthiest members of the congregation, were taxed at £14 [$940], another eight members charged between £7 and £11, and the rest of the membership — forty members — paying between £1 and £5.[51] The rest of the budget was to be made up by voluntary donations.

But voluntary offerings were problematic both politically and financially. We have already noted that offerings were the locus of contention and rebellion against the parnas. But offerings were also an uncertain source of income because they could not be accurately budgeted for. One of course cannot know how much members will be moved to give of their heart a year in advance. So in 1750, on top of the recently imposed taxes, the congregation again returned to valuing seats. Each seat in the congregation was given a value and members were obliged to pay a yearly fee for that seat.[52] In 1766, the congregation made the renting of seats their primary fund-raiser, raising £300 [$16,200] from the selling of seats and eliminated the income tax.[53] The selling of seats would be the funding mechanism for the congregation for well over one hundred years.

The congregation's move away from an income tax may have reflected an overreach into the secular realm that members of the congregation ultimately found distasteful. The 1805 constitution of Shearith Israel makes this abundantly clear. The sixth article of the constitution and the only article dealing with finances states, "The support of the congregation shall forever be from the sale or taxation of seats and from free-will offerings, and no poll or income tax shall ever be assessed on its members."[54]

The Colonial Synagogue Budget: Widening the Bench, Fines, Bequests, and Other Sources of Revenue

If one were to read through the minutes of Congregation Shearith Israel in the colonial period and take note of every threat of a fine issued by the adjunta, one might suppose the congregation would need no other source of funding than this. Fines were threatened for all manner of things. Ultimately, the amount of money raised by the fines was rather small, as the threats were far more numerous than the actual fines.

The 1728 congregational constitution article three said that should any person "give any affront or abuse, Either by words or action to any person or persons within the said Sinagog [sic], he or they so offending shall be obliged to pay the Parnas . . . the Sum of Twenty Shillings [$77]." It also said that anyone elected parnas and refused to serve would be fined £3 [$231], while anyone elected to serve as hatanim (assistants to the parnas) and refusing to serve would be fined 40 shillings [$144]. The fifth article dealing with employees says that the officers have the right to fine the hazan, shochet, and shamas up to £3 for failure to do their jobs.[55]

In 1748, congregational meetings were obviously the site of discord, as the parnas declared that any person at a congregational meeting "presuming to make a disturbance or speak otherwise then in their proper turn or place" would be fined 20 shillings [$59]. The congregation must have also been having trouble making sure that those elected parnas would serve, as the fine that was £3 twenty years earlier was upped to £10 [$590][56] — certainly a significant sum that might dissuade someone from turning the office down. However, those elected parnas were usually among the wealthy of the congregation, so we find two years later that David Gomez of the well-to-do Gomez family paid the fine and chose not to serve.[57]

Members of the congregation were fined 20 shillings for taking kosher meat on a "fryday or Hereb Yomtob" (Friday or prior to a holiday) and selling it, thus limiting the supply of meat for the congregation.[58] Anyone found quarreling or causing disturbances in the synagogue courtyard or even in the street outside the synagogue could be fined at the discretion of the parnas.[59] Anyone called for an aliyah and refused would be fined, and any elder of the congregation who was summoned to help determine a synagogue matter and did not show up could be fined.[60]

A rather dramatic case of dispute and fining occurred in 1760, when two members got into a tussle regarding seats in the women's section. Judah Hays complained to the parnassim that Judah Mears had gone into the women's gallery and forced Judah Hays's daughter, Josse Hays, out of a seat next to her mother because he claimed the seat was the property of his daughter. Unlike the men's seats, which were specifically parceled out and sold, the women's gallery at this time was limited, and the seats were not as clearly delineated. The parnas fined Judah Mears 40 shillings and told both young women to go back to their original seats.

Judah Hays, however, was not satisfied with this result and must have been making trouble as the parnassim met "to procure some method to pacify Mr. Judah Hays in respect to a Seat for his Daughter." The Solomonic decision of the parnassim was to build an extension to the bench to allow the daughter to sit next to her mother. The carpenter was called and the bench extended, but Judah Hays was still not pacified. The whole congregation met to discuss the matter and there was a unanimous vote that the decision of the parnassim was correct. Judah Hays would still not relent, claiming he would not sit his daughter on the extended bench. This time it was he who was fined 40 shillings for being in contempt of the order of the parnassim. They decreed that until he both paid up and sat his daughter in her newly appointed seat he was not to be looked upon as a member of the synagogue.[61]

This was by no means the only dispute involving seats in the women's gallery. In 1786, the adjunta met to determine regulations for seating in the women's gallery as a result of "many inconveniences . . . & much Dissatisfaction . . . , for the want of proper regulation in the woman's Seats."[62] The congregation decided that front row seats should preferably be given to married women. However, on Rosh Hashanah two months later, three unmarried sisters took front row seats. Various mediators, including Gershom Seixas, tried to settle the dispute but ultimately the adjunta took the sisters to court, where the judge found the congregation had the right to administer the seats in the manner they saw fit and fined the sisters sixpence. In 1818, the issue of front row seating in the women's gallery again became an issue when the congregation had to summon a policeman to the synagogue to forcibly remove a woman from the front row and place her in her rightful seat.[63]

A less contentious way of raising revenue for the synagogues than fining people was the bequests the congregation received. This amounted to a small but steady revenue stream. The typical bequest throughout the colonial period was £5 or £10. Manuel Myers, a merchant and distiller as well as former parnas of the congregation, instructed in his 1799 will that £10 [$325] be given to the trustees of Shearith Israel "for an *Escava* in the Synagogue according to custom after my decease *[sic]*."[64] An *escava* (alternatively, *hashkavah*) was a memorial prayer said annually on Yom Kippur, holidays, and the deceased's yahrzeit.[65] In 1751, the congregation had set a specific price of £5 for a perpetual *hashkavah*.

Occasionally, the congregation received a more generous bequest, like Jacob Franks's bequest of £25 [$1,350] in 1769.[66] And some of the bequests were made with specific projects in mind. Rachel Luis left the congregation £10 in 1737 for the purpose of buying a Torah scroll. In 1744, Joshua Isaacs, who otherwise did not play a prominent role in the history of the congregation, gave one of the largest bequests the synagogue received in the colonial era, leaving £50 [$4,324] specifically "for support of our Hebrew school at [Congregation Shearith Israel] to teach poor Children the Hebrew tongue."[67]

Given the centrality of the congregation to the life of the community, it is almost surprising that members were generally not more generous in their bequests. Typically, the donation to the synagogue represented just a small percentage of the total estate. As is custom today, the vast majority of people's wealth was transferred to family first, with charitable and communal gifts second.

The First Capital Campaigns

On October 28, 1728, the parnas of congregation Shearith Israel called a public meeting to discuss the purchase of land for the first synagogue building in America. David de Sola Pool, historian of the congregation, suggests two possibilities for the timing. First, in the wake of King George's death in 1727, New York governor William Burnett permitted Jews to omit the words "upon the true faith of a Christian" in taking their oath of naturalization, suggesting a growing level of societal openness to Judaism.[68] Second, in 1727–1728, a church building boom took hold in New York City. The Dutch church, the Lutheran church, and the Baptist congregation all built new edifices to accommodate growing congregations. The new buildings presumably did not go unnoticed by the Jewish community, who soon began planning for their own structure.[69]

A third reason might be added as to the timing of the building: the increasing wealth of New York City as a whole and the Jewish community in particular during the first half of the eighteenth century. According to Michael Kammen in his book *New York: A Colonial History*, New York's economy "underwent a striking period of growth from 1713 until 1728."[70] This period saw a large increase in commercial activity as New York City became a major trading post rivaling Boston. The sugar trade with London and the West Indies was at the center of this expansion. New Yorkers shipped food — corn, beef, flour, and pork — to the West Indies and in return received sugar, rum, molasses, cotton, and other commodities, which were then shipped to markets in London. The profitability of this trade gave rise to an expansion in ship building and trading merchants in the city, which in turn gave rise to a vast expansion of auxiliary businesses to support the trade — coffee houses, lawyers, bankers, underwriters — and all flourished during this period.[71]

Jews who participated in this trade benefited enormously. Nathan Simson, the wealthiest Jewish merchant in New York and president of Shearith Israel in 1720–1721, participated in the West Indian trade and retired at the end of the 1720s with an estate valued at £60,000 [$4,620,000].[72] The economic boom in the city is reflected in Shearith Israel's budget. Total expenditures in 1721 amounted to £132 [$10,170], in 1729 it rose to £175.10 [$12,119], and by 1738 it was £235 [$19,059].[73] The growing wealth of the community and of the city no doubt pushed the congregation toward building a synagogue. The positive correlative relationship between general economic trends and the growth of synagogues is an ongoing theme in American Jewish history, but one that is often overlooked. The few scholars that have written about this period in the history of Shearith Israel have failed to note that synagogue building comes into being at the height of an economic boom.

In December 1728, a lot was purchased for £100 [$7,700], plus one loaf of sugar and a pound of Bohea tea.[74] The purchase of the lot was roughly equal to the amount the congregation spent on salaries that same year. Because it was not incorporated and thus could not purchase land as a congregation, four of the most prominent members of the synagogue purchased the land on behalf of Shearith Israel. Having secured the property, the synagogue faced the much larger challenge of financing the building.

The first American synagogue capital campaign began with the solicitation for contributions from members of Shearith Israel, but the campaign very quickly turned to other sources of funding outside the congregation, specifically other Jewish communities in the New World. Although New York was experiencing an economic boom, the financing of a synagogue building represented an enormous jump in expenditures, and there was not any history of philanthropy of this magnitude, so the turn to outside sources was necessary. Ultimately, £223.17.9¼ [$17,185], representing roughly 40 percent of the total cost of the building, came from international sources. The following letter to the "illustrious gentleman ... of the Mahamad of the Holy K.K. of the Island of Jamaica" is an example of their international efforts:

Most Benevolent Gentleman,

We the undersigned appointed Parnasim and Adjuntos of this holy K.K. of Shearith Jacob[75] for the present year 5489 [1728–1729] place before you this petition in the name of all the holy Kaal.

We earnestly request you all as well as your Haham to communicate it to members of your holy Kaal, so that they may contribute all they can to the building of a holy synagogue which we have decided with the help of God to erect. We have already purchased an appropriate site for the edifice and another for the cemetery, but for want of sufficient means, the Yehudim here being but few, we have not been able to carry out our intention, and until our hopes are realized, we must continue for the present to congregate in a Synagogue rented from a Goy.

May the Almighty grant our wish, and May He move your hearts that you may to the best of your ability assist us in the matter, and also help us build a fence around the cemetery. And we will ever pray that you may prosper and increase in your holy service. Amen.

From your servants and the assistants above mentioned

Luis Gomez, Parnas

Daniel Gomez

NY 16 Shebat 5489 [January 16, 1729][76]

The particular appeal of the New Yorkers to the Jamaicans — that they needed their own synagogue because they were presently forced to pray in a house owned by a non-Jew — would have elicited sympathy from their Jamaican brethren because it both underscored their own fragility in being indebted to a Christian and affirmed the fraternal bonds between Jewish communities.

The Jamaican community was not the only synagogue outside of America to give money. The Jews of Barbados gave £22.13 [$1,704], and a contribution of 300 florins came from Dutch Guinea. Some of the overseas gifts, though, came with strings attached. The Jews of Curaçao gave pieces of eight and silver that would ultimately net Shearith Israel £136 [$10,472]. But the generous donation to the new building came with a stipulation. The Jews of Curaçao wrote to Shearith Israel that all the members of the congregation should sign a compact where the Ashkenazim would agree not to take authority of the congregation despite their being the numerical majority over Sephardim.[77] Shearith Israel accepted the donation but apparently did not sign such a compact.

This was not the last time the Curaçao community would try to impose a Sephardic hegemony with a donation. In 1764, the Curaçao community received a donation request from the Jews of Newport, Rhode Island. The Curaçao congregation made a donation to the Newport building on the condition that the Sephardic rite be preserved in the synagogue and that the Curaçao congregation, Mikve Israel, be blessed every year on Yom Kippur.[78] The Curaçao Jewish community, unlike North American communities or even its sister community in Surinam, was almost devoid of Ashkenazim. That they saw themselves as a center of a pure Sephardic Jewry may help explain their continued demands of Sephardi power.[79]

Another example of the Sephardi-Ashkenazi tension in capital campaigns is the case of Kahal Kadosh Beth Elohim (KKBE) in Charleston in 1794. Like other colonial congregations, KKBE asked Sephardi congregations from all over the world for donations. The congregation received contributions of £20 [$1,420] from the Bevis Marks Congregation in London and £25 [$1,775] from Congregation Nidhei Israel in Barbados.[80] Although this represented just a small portion of the total cost of more than £4000 [$284,000], Daniel Ackerman suggests in his essay on the synagogue's architecture that the congregation felt themselves caught between its Sephardi and Ashkenazi donors:

> The building committee faced a problem: how to remain part of the Sephardic Judeo-Atlantic world with its valuable religious, mercantile, and social connections, while meeting the desires of a growing Ashkenazic community and a clearly important local Ashkenazic donor base. . . . The Judeo-Atlantic world represented important international webs of trade and commerce. Sephardic congregations in London, Barbados, and New York gave money towards the building effort. Moreover, Jewish merchants from London, New York, and the Caribbean expected to find a Sephardic minyan when they visited Charleston. Meanwhile, the Ashkenazic Jews who funded much of the building clearly wanted a spatial experience that met their expectations.[81]

The solution to this dilemma was to create a physical structure that was a compromise between Sephardi and Ashkenazi expectations. The bimah (pedestal where the Torah is read) was placed between the typical Sephardi position of being at the back wall and the Ashkenazi position of being in the center. The financial and political requirements of satisfying donors embedded itself in the architectural and ritual question of where to place the bimah.

For Shearith Israel, having exhausted outside sources, the rest of the financing for the building had to come from their own members. In 1729–1730, there were at least four different appeals for funding. Wealthier members of the congregation like the patriarch Mordecay Gomez gave roughly £25 [$1,925] toward the new building, while a more typical gift came from Nathan Levy, who gave £9 [$707]. There were contributions from women who, unlike their male counterparts, are always identified in the records with some title: Rachel Levy, for example, is "ye wido [sic] Rachel Levy," and Bilah Levy is referred to as "Bilah Levy daughter of Saml Levy decd." The gifts from women ranged from 10 shillings [$38.50] to £5 [$385]. Some contributions were targeted toward specific aspects of the new building; for example, 10 shillings were given "for work done to ye ten commandmts [sic]."[82]

A year after the initial call for funds for a new home, the congregation was ready to move forward and lay the cornerstones for the building. The parnas, Moses Gomez, spoke to the congregation on Shabbat, saying, "Almighty God having permitted us to reach this so anxiously awaited moment, when we begin to carry out our intention, so long the object of our desire, let us now fulfill our duty . . . let us now prepare for the foundations . . . It is hereby made known to you all that the foundation stones are now for sale."[83]

The congregation auctioned off the foundations stones, which were bought, not surprisingly, by some of the most prominent members of the community — Jacob Franks, the Gomez family, and Binjamin Pacheco — who paid between £5 and £7 for each stone [$385 and $539]. The congregation was apparently wary that some might buy the foundation stones on credit, because they stipulated that "it should be borne in mind that the gentlemen who buy said stones should pay their contribution so as to enable us to advance to the builders the amounts agreed upon."[84] Ultimately, the building would cost over £600 [$46,200] to construct, with the congregation raising all of the money without carrying over any debt.[85]

The cost of the building was relatively small compared to the budget of contemporaneous synagogues like Bevis Marks in London. Much of that was a reflection of the relatively poorer American context, but the congregation was also purposeful in their modesty. The Dutch, Lutheran, and Presbyterian churches, built at the same time, were, according to Sarna in *American Judaism*, "opulently designed buildings, with large spires and towers, [which] transformed and sacralized the city's skyline, displaying for all to see the colonists' burgeoning wealth . . . but the new synagogue building as finally constructed favored tradition over external display." Shearith Israel's building was meant to fit in with its surrounding buildings, "to visually distinguish themselves from established churches and avoid offending the majority faith."[86] By the end of the century, though, some congregations were willing to be bolder in their architecture and in their finances.

Whereas Shearith Israel was built specifically not to emulate the large local churches, KKBE of Charleston, finished in 1794, was specifically designed to emulate St. Michael's Episcopal Church. St. Michael's was built in 1762 and was, according to Daniel Ackerman, "where Charleston's richest and most prominent families worshipped. The church set the standard for elegant and genteel worship in Charleston." Ackerman continues, "The architectural dialogue between [KKBE and St. Michael's] is striking . . . the most pronounced similarities between the two structures are found in their spires."[87] Where Shearith Israel, in the colonial era, sought to blend in humbly, KKBE, built after the Revolution, announced its presence to the community.

Financially, KKBE would spend £4000 [$284,000] to complete the building. St. Michael's cost £60,000 to build in 1762 but because of the lower value of the pound in South Carolina before the Revolution, this translates to only $190,285 in current dollars. KKBE effectively spent more for its building than the leading church in Charleston had.

The financial records for the building are not extant. We only know that, like Shearith Israel, KKBE sold foundation stones for its first building. They honored two of their most generous benefactors — Israel Joseph and Philip Hart — with the first two stones and auctioned off another six stones, fetching an average of £11 [$781] apiece.[88]

KKBE raised in today's dollars roughly ten times more from its membership than what Shearith Israel had. Some of this can be attributed to KKBE being a larger congregation. Estimates are that there were 225 to 250 Jews in Charleston in 1790.[89] This was probably twice the size of Shearith Israel in 1730. Charleston was also a rapidly growing economy at that time. Cotton exports from Charleston rose from 12,150 pounds in 1790 to 17,789,803 pounds ten years later. But this does not fully explain the tenfold increase either. The Jews of Charleston were not particularly well-to-do. With the exception of one wealthy merchant, most Jews were of humble means — 50 percent of the Jewish community was apparently local shopkeepers.[90] Given this, we might say that this moment represents a new economic era for American synagogues, where financing an impressive building would become part of synagogue culture. The congregation made a financial, as well as an architectural, decision to aim higher than Jewish communities had previously done in America. This was signaled early on in the process with the hiring of one of Charleston's most prominent (non-Jewish) architects to build the synagogue.[91]

The decision to spend significantly on a building is an ongoing trope in American Jewish history. It might be only a slight exaggeration to say that capital campaigns have been as central to American synagogues as what happens inside the synagogues once they are built. As we will see, there have been periods when building extravagant buildings has proven to be a disastrous mistake when the economy changes. Charleston represented the first major capital campaign to fund a grand vision for a synagogue. There is, however, some limited evidence that the significant expense for the building was not without its problems.

The December 6, 1794, *Charleston City Gazette and Daily Advertiser* reported that the state legislature received a petition from the "elders and vestry of the Hebrew Synagogue, in Charleston, called 'Beth Elohim,' a house of God, praying for a law to pass, empowering them to raise a sum of £800 by lottery, in order to discharge the balance of the expense incurred for building the said synagogue."[92] The petition was referred to the committee on religion, and we do not know whether it was agreed to or how the congregation ultimately disposed of their debt, but it seems clear the congregation did not emerge financially unscathed from their new building.

KKBE was not the only colonial synagogue to try their hand at a lottery and not the only synagogue to experience debt in the wake of a new building. In the summer of 1788, Mikveh Israel, the first synagogue in Philadelphia, was facing financial ruin. Just six years earlier the congregation had erected its first building, and subsequently added a mikvah (ritual bath) and a schoolhouse. The congregation initially raised £897 [$39,468] from sixty-four men for the new building, but one-third of the total came from just one source — Haym Solomon. All of these projects together necessitated taking out £2200 [$44,000] in loans, however. If they did not come up with funds that summer they would have to sell their building. Jonas Philips, who was one of the signers on the bond for the money to purchase the land (the congregation was not incorporated, so the bond was held by individual members on behalf of the congregation), found himself in real trouble because of the congregation's inability to pay back its loan. One day he found a sheriff at his door who gave him until 5:00 to pay the note on the synagogue's bond.

One significant demographic problem existed for the congregation, which hampered its fund-raising effort. During the Revolutionary War, Philadelphia was the gathering place for Jews who had fled New York, Charleston, and other cities under British control. The Jewish population went from roughly 300 in 1775 to 1,000 in 1781.[93] The influx of these displaced Jews pushed the community to create a formal congregation where none existed before, and almost immediately the congregation sought to build a synagogue. With the war over, some had moved back home, leaving the

Philadelphian Jews to pay the bills. Out of desperation and following the common practice among Philadelphia churches, the congregation searched for funds from outside their own community.[94]

The synagogue approached many of Philadelphia's leading figures with a letter asking for help. After explaining the reasons for their financial distress, they wrote: "[We] are therefore under the necessity of earnestly soliciting from their worthy fellow Citizens of every religious Denomination, their benevolent Aid & Help flattering themselves that their worshipping Almighty God in a way & manner different from other religious Societies, will never deter the enlightened Citizens of Philadelphia, from generously subscribing towards the preservation of a religious house of worship."[95]

The most famous respondent to this plea was Benjamin Franklin, who gave £5 [$220] to retire the debt. Franklin seemingly referenced this gift in his autobiography, writing, "As our province [Philadelphia] increased in people, and new places of worship were continually wanted and generally erected by voluntary contribution, my mite[96] for such purpose, whatever might be the sect, was never refused."[97] Other contributions came in from noted citizens and the building was temporarily saved. They needed to raise an additional £800 [$35,200], however, to permanently retire the debt hanging over them. Having exhausted their own membership and wealthy non-Jewish Philadelphians, they then turned to a relatively new innovation in nonprofit fund-raising — the lottery.

Starting in 1747, the Pennsylvania legislature had granted special permission to nonprofit institutions, including a number of churches, to hold public lotteries to raise funds.[98] The state itself used them for all manner of infrastructure projects so as to avoid raising taxes. In the 1750s, the city began giving licenses to nonprofits that were trying to raise money for projects deemed in the public good. Churches used lotteries in this period to pay for new buildings or to retire debt. In 1765, St. Peter's church in Philadelphia, for example, built a beautiful but too expensive new building, leaving themselves with a debt of £1500 [$87,000].

With financial ruin possible, the church petitioned the legislature, writing, "It being considered that public buildings may be rendered among the chief ornaments of every city and that the Church would [be] of lasting use to the public, it was determined to erect it in a commodious manner with as much elegance as might be consistent with plainness and simplicity."[99] The

Philadelphia assembly passed a bill enabling the church to hold a lottery to raise £3000 [$174,000] to retire their debt. Between 1752, when Christ Church in Philadelphia was given permission to hold a lottery to finish its steeple, and Mikveh Israel's lottery in 1790, roughly thirty-five churches in Pennsylvania held lotteries. Most of the lotteries promised winnings of a few thousand pounds, but a few major church lotteries promised as much as £7,500 [$330,000] for the winner.[100]

The holding of lotteries was not without its critics. The Quaker church, for one, was an outspoken opponent of lotteries, and not a single Quaker church appears on the list of churches that used the system. The pressure from the English government to curtail lotteries along with pressure from those who opposed the lottery on moral grounds caused a diminishment in lotteries from the 1770s forward. The Pennsylvania assembly turned down the majority of requests to hold lotteries — Mikveh Israel was the only institution allowed a lottery in 1790.[101] And by 1808, Rodeph Shalom's petition to the Philadelphia assembly to build their first synagogue was turned down by a legislative committee with the following response: "All places of worship should be built at the expense of a more moral system than that proposed by lottery or some other gambling system or institution."[102]

But in 1790, Mikveh Israel applied and was granted a license to hold a lottery to retire their debt. The synagogue's advertisements for the lottery noted that "besides the satisfaction of having contributed to an object so pious and meritorious," a ticket of $2.50 [$110] could bring $1,400 [$61,600] to the winner. With the lottery, the congregation successfully raised the £800 [$3,200] necessary to cancel their debt.[103]

The brief experimentation with lotteries as synagogue moneymakers was a precursor to the emergence of bingo in the 1950s, which was also initially taken up by churches and also met with severe moral critique. The economic impetus for lotteries and for bingo is easily understood. Synagogues in 1790 or 1950 sought ways to raise revenue from beyond their membership, and lotteries/bingo held a tremendous potential to reach people who had no other interest in the work of a congregation. The allure of finding ways to raise money outside of their own membership was so powerful that it allowed some synagogues to ignore the moral issues involved and embrace games of chance.

The turn of the eighteenth century marked the end of the first phase of synagogue finance. The building of KKBE's large sanctuary in 1794 signaled a new period of significantly expanded synagogue economies. Larger congregations in the nineteenth century felt no need for humble structures that quietly blended into the landscape; rather, they built to announce themselves as a religious presence, and their budgets necessarily followed to support this new vision.

The Shearith Israel constitution of 1805 also marked a turning point. It declared that the congregation would forever use the selling of seats and voluntary contributions as its funding mechanism. Almost all American synagogues used this same system. Synagogue finance thus became uniform in the nineteenth century. Congregations rarely held lotteries or utilized an income tax. All synagogues funded themselves in basically the same way for the next century. Ancillary revenue-generating activity like fines, membership fees, and selling mitzvot remained, but the selling of seats would occupy most of the ink on the ledger books. Together, the growth of synagogue budgets and the broad commitment to selling seats marked this new phase of congregational finances.

TWO

"So Paltry a Way of Support"
[1805–1865]

In 1853, the building committee of Kehilat Kodesh Bene Israel (KKBI) in Cincinnati received the following letter from a longtime member:

> The undersigned most respectfully asks you to reconsider and locate her seat in a more comfortable situation than the one allotted to her . . . It is the most uncomfortable and disagreeable location in the synagogue. She thinks that a lifetime spent in the support of your society and being the first Jewess resident in this city entitles her to a little more courtesy than to be stuck off in a corner, exposed to the draft in winter season and in summer to the heat of the sun. . . . She therefore protests against your allotment and hopes you will endeavor to give her a more desirable place. — Eliza Marks[1]

Eliza Marks may have been treated unfairly by the building committee, but her letter is representative of nineteenth-century synagogue finance, which for most congregations revolved around the selling and/or renting of seats. While there were other revenue sources that continued from the colonial period — annual dues, selling honors, public offerings, and initiation fees — the majority of nineteenth-century synagogues sold seats as their primary revenue source. Shearith Israel's 1805 constitution makes this clear: "The support of the congregation shall forever be from the sale or taxation of seats and from free-will offerings and no poll or income tax shall ever be assessed on the members."[2] The 1823 constitution of Mikveh Israel similarly decrees that revenue in the congregation would be derived solely "from free will offerings, donations and the sale and assessment of seats."[3] The selling of seats also became the central way for congregations to run capital campaigns because members would purchase seats in the future synagogue as a way of raising money to pay for a new building.

But as Eliza Marks can attest, the selling of seats was not without its share of problems. Her letter is far from the only unhappy note related to the quality or pricing of seats that one finds in nineteenth-century synagogue board minutes. The selling of seats also had significant critics in rabbis like Max Lilienthal, who believed that the obligation of poorer members of the congregation to buy seats represented an unfair burden. But congregations chose to deal with such problems in return for the surety and consistency of revenue that the selling of seats promised.

As synagogues proliferated in this era, and the first rabbis came to America, the issue of clergy pay very quickly became a central issue of congregational life. Although there were disputes in the colonial period between congregations and spiritual leaders, needing to pay clergy with rabbinic ordination meant a more significant portion of the congregational budget would be devoted to salaries. Previous historians have believed the many tales of woe that rabbis of the era told about their paltry support, but a close look at salaries suggests that rabbis in antebellum America were compensated on par with, if not better than, most ministers and were firmly part of the growing American middle class.

This era also saw the emergence of synagogue competition. In 1825, in both Charleston and New York City, new synagogues opened up to challenge the traditional synagogue. Since this moment, American Jewish history has been profoundly influenced by the idea that a free market would obtain in the religious realm as well as the commercial one. In contrast to much of Europe, where communities had one established synagogue, American synagogues would compete against each other for membership. This meant congregations had to be more responsive to the needs of their members or those members could simply join another synagogue. The result was a more democratic synagogue. This religious "market" also pushed synagogues to remain vibrant because there was no surety of membership based simply on being the one synagogue in an area.

The introduction of synagogue competition came against the backdrop of two significant national events. The year 1825 was a high-water mark for the religious revival known as the Second Great Awakening. The fervent religiosity, as well as the democratic impulses of the revival, influenced the Jewish community and the creation of new synagogues throughout the country. Growing industrialization was also crucial in this period. Jewish manufacturers and traders would become some of the more successful economic stories of the mid-nineteenth century, and many synagogues benefited from the largesse of wealthy merchants.

The burgeoning industrial American economy of the period also had profound implications for how clergy understood the acquisition of wealth. As we will explore, ministers of the period tried to temper the impulse toward "mammonism" — the acquisition of wealth — while Jewish clergy for the most part steered clear of addressing the topic. The few rabbis who took stands against commercialism by denying honors to those who would work on the Sabbath found that either they or their rules did not last long.

Selling Seats

KKBI, the synagogue where Eliza Marks felt she was unfairly shunted into the corner, is a good example of the centrality of selling seats in the financial life of the congregation. The congregation, known as the oldest congregation in the west, was established in 1824 and built its first building in 1836.[4] In 1845, the congregation had income of $1,820.52 [$44,887]. Slightly more than half of that income was derived from assessments on seats. The rest of the income came from an assortment of revenue streams: member offerings, admissions fees (it cost $5 to join the synagogue), donations from strangers, burial of strangers, and other smaller items. The congregation received $32 [$822] for "seats during the Holy days," indicating that the selling of High Holiday seats, which is done by so many synagogues today, has an old pedigree.[5]

The budget of B'nai Jeshurun in New York City tells a very similar story. In 1854, the congregation had recently built a new synagogue, hired the well-regarded Morris Raphal as the rabbi, and began the B'nai Jeshurun Educational Institute, all of which had significantly increased the membership from 150 to 250 members in five years. The total budget of the congregation was roughly $10,000 [$246,420]. The sale of seats accounted for 60 percent of that budget, with offerings and other activities making up the rest.[6]

In New York City, Temple Emanu-El's budget from the same period shows a congregation almost entirely reliant on selling seats. Emanu-El was the first congregation in New York City to sell seats on a permanent basis when it was built (as opposed to leasing seats annually, which was the practice at Shearith Israel). They also eliminated the practice of making offerings, so they were truly reliant on seat sales. In 1855, for example, their annual budget was $5,804 [$143,022], with over 95 percent coming from income related to the sale and rental of seats. The congregation had just moved into a new building, so they also recorded as an asset the sale of seventy-eight seats, netting them a total of $31,188 [$766,809].[7]

The system of selling or renting seats differed somewhat among congregations, but the basic model was that each seat in the congregation was placed into one of three or more categories, usually labeled simply "A," "B," "C," or "first class," "second class," or "third class." Each category of seats had a set price. The best seats were of course rated the most expensive. Some congregations rented all the seats annually or biannually, while other congregations sold permanent seats. Buying a seat in perpetuity meant the member would pay an upfront cost of the seat plus an annual assessment determined by the board to be paid yearly. The seat would then be the property of the owner as long as the yearly payments were made. Larger and wealthier congregations sold seats in perpetuity while poorer congregations sold or rented annually because of the difficulty in asking members for a large upfront payment. The yearly assessments on permanent seats were typically 10 to 15 percent of the value of the seat, so, for example, at Mikveh Israel in 1845, a first-class seat, which cost $100 [$2,465] to buy, had a yearly assessment of $14 [$360].[8] A few congregations like Temple Emanu-El declared an annual taxation percentage on seat owners — in 1855, the seat tax was set at 12.5 percent, which netted the congregation $3,898.50 [$96,067] in income from the seventy-eight seats that had been sold.[9]

The distribution of seats happened in two different ways. In some cases, like at KKBI, a member would buy a seat in a category but the congregation would determine the specific seat the person in each category received, hence Eliza Mark's frustration at having paid for a seat but being placed in a dreadful corner. But in other synagogues, specific seats were auctioned to the highest bidder provided that the bid was at least equal to the price of the seat in that category.

In small congregations, each seat had the same price and they were distributed by lottery. Congregation Beth El in Buffalo, for example, converted a schoolhouse into a synagogue in 1849. Each seat cost $50 [$1,380] and was assigned to members randomly. Selig Adler and Thomas Connolly, in their history of the Buffalo Jewish community, write that the board of the congregation repeatedly had to urge people to sit in the front rows. "In America a new attitude toward synagogue seats arose. Unlike European Jews who highly prized the front seats, American Jews . . . had to be urged to occupy these seats. Apparently they seemed to prefer the seats at the rear of the synagogue. Perhaps there they found it easier to slip out unobtrusively before the conclusion of services."[10] Although this is an interesting insight into American Jewish piety (or lack thereof), one cannot find similar cases in the nineteenth century of Jews unwilling to sit up front.

Congregations that did not have their own building, typically smaller and less established ones, usually rented seats annually. In 1851, Keneseth Israel in Elkins Park, Pennsylvania, leased a building for use as a synagogue. The congregation rented seats to their members, charging the same price of $7.50 [$207] for every seat and the seat location was by lottery. The congregation was also renting seats to nonmembers for both the High Holidays and Passover at $7.[11] At Ahavath Achim in Bangor, Maine, in 1849, the congregation charged a monthly fee of 50 cents [$14] for "seat donation."[12] As both of these congregations became more established and bought their own buildings, they both switched to selling seats in perpetuity.

The purchasing of a seat became a prerequisite for membership at some synagogues. In its 1861 constitution, Chicago Sinai declared that members of the congregation who did not buy seats would have a seat of the lowest class assigned to them, which they would need to pay for. Failure to pay would mean loss of membership.[13] Similarly, Keneseth Israel in 1859 held that anyone who did not purchase at least the lowest category of seat would not be considered a member, except unmarried men and temporary visitors, who could rent seats.[14] Most synagogues, though, would allow members to rent a seat to retain their membership if purchasing one was not fiscally possible.

The price of renting a seat would typically be set higher than the yearly assessment on that seat. In 1845, for example, at Mikveh Israel, a first-class seat in the men's section cost $100 [$2,465] with a yearly assessment of $14 [$345], but if someone were to rent that seat it would cost $20 [$514] per year.[15] Slightly higher rental prices were meant to encourage seat ownership, which would provide greater revenue for the congregation in the upfront purchase cost. The encouragement of ownership of seats as opposed to renting may also reflect long-held American values around property ownership.

Seats in the women's section at Mikveh Israel cost $60 [$1541] with a yearly assessment of $8 [$205], or 40 percent less than the best men's seats.[16] Women's seats were less expensive because they were typically in the balcony or obscured in some way, so they were not as desirable. The cheaper prices also undoubtedly reflected the status of women in the synagogue at this time. The home was the sphere of authority for women, while their presence in the synagogue was considered less significant.

The cost of purchasing a seat at large synagogues represented a significant expense. In 1846, KKBI had five categories of seats; the price for the first-class seat was $120 [$3,069], with seats in descending categories costing $90, $70, $60, and $50.[17] Seats were often bought on credit with interest paid to the congregation. This meant it was possible that years after the buying of a seat, a member might still be paying off the seat, plus interest, plus the yearly seat assessment. KKBI decreed that at the time of purchase one had to put down at least one-fourth the cost of the seat. Mikveh Israel in Philadelphia was even more demanding in this regard. At a special meeting of the congregation in 1833, it was decreed that unsold seats would go on sale September 1, and the entire price of the seat plus the first year assessment would need to be paid within ten days of the sale or the purchase of the seat was null and void.[18] The timing of the sale was clearly done with Rosh Hashanah in mind, which started that year on September 13. This tactic is no different from what many congregations do today in forcing congregants to be up-to-date in their dues payments to receive High Holiday tickets.

At KKBI, the relative cost of buying a seat in the synagogue mid-century can be seen in the context of statistics we have about net worth. The median net worth of Cincinnati Jews at this time was around $4,000 [$98,624], with a few wealthy merchants having substantially more assets.[19] Given the average seat price was $70 [$1,726], buying a seat would have amounted to 1.75 percent of a typical member's net worth. This is a relatively low figure compared to later periods. Just after the Civil War, KKBI charged roughly fifteen times more for seats than in the 1840s, and buying a seat would cost closer to 5 percent of net worth.

Because the sale of seats was so central to the synagogue economy, determining when the synagogue needed to repossess a seat due to nonpayment was a significant issue for congregations. A nineteenth-century constitution of KKBI is quite explicit in this regard. If a member failed to pay his or her assessment on the seat, or failed to pay any special assessments that arose because of special circumstances for a twelve-month period, "then the Board of Trustees, without any notice or legal form whatsoever to the member in default, shall proceed to sell, either at public or private sale . . . the pew or seat belonging to said member, and after payment of the amount due, the surplus, if any, shall be paid to the member in default."[20]

The board minutes of Keneseth Israel in the 1850s spell out the myriad issues involved in repossessing seats. Keneseth Israel was a growing congregation at this time. It had embraced Reform Judaism, including the decision in 1858 to introduce family pews, making them one of the first synagogues to adopt the practice of mixed seating.[21] The annual revenue of the congregation in that same year was $2,582 [$68,511], with $1,412 (55 percent) of the revenue coming from seat assessments.[22] First-class seats cost $125 [$3,316] to buy with an annual assessment of $32 [$902]. The success of the congregation is seen in a board note from 1856 stating that those who wanted to join the synagogue would not be able to purchase a first-class seat, as none were presently available and there was a waiting list to obtain one.[23]

But in 1853, the congregation was not yet thriving. They had just purchased their first building and were in a fiscal crunch when they promulgated the following rules regarding the repossession of seats: "Should the member come in arrears, the congregation has the right to buy back the seat. Should the member wish to keep the seat, he has to pay the appropriate price for it and pay interest of 6 percent on the rest of the money. Should a member resign, he has no right to demand his money before 5 years and will collect no interest."[24] This last clause in particular is quite important when considering the finances of the congregation.

Buying a seat was akin to buying a type of property — different, of course, than buying a house, but it was property nonetheless, and when members resigned, they could, with the approval of the board, sell their seat and recoup some of their money. Sometimes the member would sell the seat to another person and the congregation would be given a percentage of the sale, but more often the congregation would buy back the seat at the existing price. The clause that delays any expectation of repayment for five years was a reflection of the congregation's fiscal concern that they could not buy back seats because of the debt they took on to construct a new building. The congregation did carve out an exception for widows and those who were moving out of the country; they would receive their money immediately when the seat was resold.

In some cases, members who resigned gave the seat back to the congregation as a gift. A note like the one from a Joseph Laferty to the Keneseth Israel board was common: "Gentlemen! Please accept my seat No. 24 as a present and likewise my resignation as a member of your honorable society."[25] But more common were negotiations with members over their seats. Moses Levy wrote the board in 1856 to say that he had paid off half of his seat, which he had purchased for $125 [$3,329], but he could no longer afford to make payments. He did not wish to resign his membership, however. He asked the congregation if they would be willing to rent his seat out for three years, which the congregation agreed to do.[26]

Max Hertz wrote to the congregation in 1858 asking for his seat to be sold and for him to receive the money after his debts to the congregation were paid off without waiting for the five-year period, writing, "In my present unhappy situation I see myself forced to offer my bought seat to you. I will not be able now or ever to belong to any congregation to take on obligations and so I hope you will except [sic] my resignation." The congregation responded to this plea and gave him the money for the seat.

Matters did not always end peacefully, though. Moses Levy, for example, appears in the synagogue board minutes two years after his first notice. The congregation informed him that they could not rent his seat that year. They then gave him four weeks to pay up on the amount he still owed for the seat or be taken to court. Threats of lawsuits were common from synagogue boards. The board of Baltimore Hebrew Congregation threatened to sue a member who had accrued a total of just $4.50 in fines.[27] Nineteenth-century America was a litigious place and synagogues were no stranger to the system.

Six months after the congregation initially threatened a suit against Moses Levy, the congregation received a note from Memphis, where Levy now resided, saying that he no longer lived in Philadelphia. He wrote, "I beg you therefore to take the seat back or sell it." Levy went on to say that if the congregation sold the seat and it did not cover the debt, he would make good on the rest when he came to the city. The congregation responded testily by saying they would not take him to court and they would take the seat back, but he still had to pay $10, which he had committed for the organ, and he had to pledge before a Pennsylvania commissioner in Memphis that he would give up all his rights and privileges in the congregation.[28]

Further complications of seat ownership arose when a seat holder passed away. Because the seat was a kind of property, when a seat holder died, the seat was part of the estate and would be passed along with other assets to the beneficiary. Problems arose when the heir to the seat was unable to pay the yearly assessments, or even in the more unusual circumstance when the inheritor of the seat was not even Jewish. The odd situation of a non-Jewish person owning a seat in a synagogue was dealt with in Keneseth Israel's bylaws in 1856: "Should a seat through inheritance go to a non-Israelite the congregation has to pay back the original price for it."[29]

If the seat holder died owing money on the seat, this debt would be passed on to his heirs, and board minutes suggest that synagogues would actively pursue this debt. It may be surprising from a contemporary perspective to read of synagogues going after potentially bereaved relatives to make good on seat debt. A brief note from Keneseth Israel's board minutes in 1852 is almost shocking in its apparent callousness. The minutes read that the synagogue secretary was to send a note to a Mr. Oppenhemer, reminding him "that he still owed a money offering for his dead child."[30] The board seemingly had no qualms about pushing a father who had lost a child to make good on his financial commitments. The board of Keneseth Israel was not without compassion, however, as seen from the various times they acquiesced to people in need, but it is also clear from their willingness to threaten lawsuits, and the time they expended going after debt, that they saw themselves as defenders of fiscal discipline. Pastoral and spiritual concerns were left to the purview of the rabbi; money was the concern of the board.[31]

A Note of Dissent on Selling Seats

While the selling and renting of seats became the primary way that synagogues raised money over the course of the nineteenth century, there was the occasional note of dissent. The most interesting and public one came from Max Lilienthal. In 1855, in the pages of *The Israelite*, Lilienthal wrote an editorial called "The Taxes in Our Congregation." The essay began: "Nothing is more unfair and more unjust than the repartition of taxes in our congregations in America. The poor has to pay annually as much as of regular taxes as the wealthiest members of the congregation; and being in arrear with his dues, though in proportion he has contributed by far more than any of his regular wealthy fellow members, he is exposed to the danger of being expelled from the Synagogue to which for a number of years he has punctually contributed his share."[32]

Lilienthal's piece was published after he had taken over as rabbi of KKBI, where the lowest price to buy a seat was $50 [$1,232], no small investment for poorer members of the community. Lilienthal's inspiration for the editorial, beyond the concern for the poor, might have been the financial distress of KKBI when he first arrived. The congregation was going through a period of significant financial trouble, having lost many members to B'nai Jeshurun and taken on building debt.[33] Lilienthal hoped that a revised financial system would not only be more equitable but would also provide more revenue for the synagogue in general.

As a solution to the problem of the poor paying nearly as much as the rich, Lilienthal called for the imposition of an income tax similar to what some Jewish communities had in Europe called the *Erekh*. In this system, synagogues empowered a group of individuals to assess each member a tax based on their wealth, so as Lilienthal said, "the poor one was contributing six guilders of regular taxes, the wealthy had to pay 100 guilders and over." Lilienthal already anticipated that an argument against the proposal was that the wealthy might have an undue share of influence, as they would be funding more of the synagogue. He wrote that in Europe the wealthy did have outsize influence on the congregation, "but the poor did not feel displeased, willingly acknowledging the principle, that those most contributing to the common treasury shall also have a larger share in its government."[34] Lilienthal's proposal was precisely the system that Shearith Israel had banned in its 1806 constitution.

Lilienthal said that it was the "fundamentally misunderstood and misapplied principles of American equality [so that] the contribution of the members is most unproportional." Further, he wrote that the selling of seats was adequate for when synagogues rented rooms and paid a hazan a "trifling recompensation," but the new growth of synagogues demanded a new method of financing. He ended the call to arms by saying that in every American city, municipal governments were raising taxes to pay for some municipal improvement, and "will the same not be the case in our congregations?"[35]

Lilienthal's editorial provoked a vehement and fascinating response from someone using the pseudonym Justitia. Justitia agreed that there was a problem of synagogue finance but the solution proposed by Lilienthal was "obnoxious." He wrote that the idea that the poor would willingly acquiesce to the wealthy having power might work in Germany, where the poor were accustomed to such things, "but in this country the air breathed is too pure to admit the fact that any man's wealth should entitle him to any greater influence than his poverty's stricken and perhaps more deserving brother. The principle is totally at variance with all ideas of right, repugnant to self-government, and would engender a spirit of everything but friendly feeling and peace."[36]

Justitia continued by saying that the *Erekh* would just sow discord among the membership with complaints about how much each person was assessed, and new members would be fought over based on their financial worth. The author noted that many synagogues effectively used the practice of renting seats by category, as it allowed people to choose their own assessment. He discredited the sale of seats in perpetuity for not bringing in enough yearly income. Justitia suggested the solution to the problem of synagogue finance was that membership fees should be set to a level reachable by all, and the wealthy should be encouraged to make up any deficit through voluntary contribution and not by imposing taxes. "Convince [wealthy] men, reason with them," he wrote, "but don't attempt to drive them; they may be mules, but you cannot stir a mule but by coaxing."[37]

The next issue of *The Israelite* contained a rejoinder to Justitia from Lilienthal. Lilienthal emphasized again the sorry state of synagogue finance as both "unjust and inefficient." He then cited an example from his time as rabbi at Anshe Chesed, when the congregation was in a fiscal dilemma and the solution was to ask members to commit themselves to a contribution over and above what the yearly costs were. This saved the synagogue, and despite the wealthy contributing far more than the poor, synagogue leadership was chosen out of the most able men and not necessarily the wealthiest. But he did emphasize that not all people can be synagogue leaders. Just as in American democracy all have the right to vote, but only some individuals have the capacity to be elected president or to Congress because they have the "mental, moral, military and other kinds of superiority" over the large masses, so too in synagogue leadership some will always have the natural advantage.

He concluded by saying that Justitia's solution of a voluntary commitment from the wealthy might be a fine idea, but there was no one to inspire and encourage the wealthy to do this. Lilienthal suggested that if the rabbi were to do this he would be told, "Your province is the spiritual not the financial; yours is the pulpit not the trusteeroom; please mind your own business and do not meddle with our finances."[38]

This was not the only time that an income tax plan had been proposed to fund synagogues in the mid-nineteenth century. At Temple Emanu-El in 1853 there was a proposal to fund the synagogue by income tax, which was rejected by the board with the following statement, "*Fur de Direction Mitglieder nach ansicht verschieden zu taxiren findet sich mit unserem republikanischen system durchaus nich uberein, noch fur die Direction ausfuhrbar.*"[39] ("In the committee's opinion, taxing members at varying rates does not conform with our Republican system nor would it be feasible for the committee.") Isaac Leeser offered a similar opinion when commenting on a congregation in St. Thomas that utilized an income tax. St. Thomas was a Danish colony, and under Danish law the congregation had the authority to enforce a tax on everyone in the Jewish community. Leeser wrote that such a tax would be enviable in making sure that everyone contributed their fair share to the synagogue, but "in America . . . the various contributors would hardly submit to be so taxed."[40]

What is noteworthy in all of the comments regarding the income tax plan is the repeated turn to American ideals as the arbiter of its appropriateness. Lilienthal suggested that synagogue governance and American democracy were in complete harmony, and just as taxes worked for government so they could work for synagogues. Justitia countered the "pure air" of democracy was incompatible with a system that forced some to pay more than others. It was a reflection of Jewish life in antebellum America that the idea of taxing membership was measured by its compatibility with American democracy rather than any recourse to Jewish ideals.

Fundamentally, the exchange between Lilienthal and Justitia centered on a tension in synagogue finance between equality and fairness. Lilienthal wanted a system premised on fairness, where each gave according to his resources, knowing that this meant some would give significantly more and have more influence. Justitia argued for equality — that everyone should be compelled to give on a relatively equal basis so that there was a commonly shared commitment. The argument was also about a voluntary gift versus compelling people to give. Justitia argued that a system where people can choose what to give was preferable to being forced to give. Lilienthal would not have argued against voluntary giving, but he argued it would be impossible to inspire the necessary gifts. These two different arguments recurred throughout American synagogue history. As we shall see, the decision to abandon the selling of seats and move to free seating in the early twentieth century was a result of a very similar argument over fairness, equality, and American ideals.[41]

Paying for Torah Honors: Schism, Democratization, and Competition

One source of congregational income that would be phased out in many synagogues over the nineteenth century was the paying for honors. The very first group dedicated to Reform Judaism in America, The Reformed Society of Israelites for Promoting True Principles of Judaism According to Its Purity and Spirit, in Charleston in 1825 made the elimination of paying for honors a central plank in their push for reform.

For the Charleston Reformers, the paying for honors raised two primary concerns. First, the part of the service in which bids were solicited was conducted in Spanish. The practice therefore conflicted with the goal of developing a modern English service. Spanish was also seen as problematic because it was the language of the Inquisition. More important for the Reformers than the language, the selling of Torah honors led to a diminishment in the sanctity of services.

Prior to their objections, selling honors was a ubiquitous practice throughout early American synagogues and synagogues all over the world. The Reformers' objections reflected a new set of values around the role of money in synagogues. Their distaste for mixing money and liturgy would ultimately become the standard American view, and continues to have implications today for how synagogues relate to money.

Despite its ubiquity, the practice of selling honors has almost no mention in rabbinic literature. One of the earliest and most fascinating mentions of the custom comes from a responsum by the Maharik, Rabbi Joseph Colon (fifteenth century, Italy). A question came to him regarding the practice of buying the first aliyah on Simchat Torah, the proceeds of which would go to paying for the synagogue lights. The potential problem with this was that the first aliyah of a Torah reading customarily goes to a Cohen.[42] The Maharik writes:

> [Concerning] the custom of Ashkenazi and French synagogues in all of
> their communities that on *Shabbat Bereshit*[43] one of the community pays
> for the lights of the synagogue in order to be called up first to the Torah.
> The custom is for a Cohen to pay for this mitzvah or he can release his
> honor and leave the shul. It once happened though that a Cohen did not
> want to buy this mitzvah and also did not want to leave the synagogue,
> even to go to another synagogue that did not have this practice [of
> paying for the honor, thus the Cohen could be given his aliyah].... The
> congregation agreed to bar him [the Cohen] from the synagogue so that
> he will not enter the synagogue and they can follow the custom [of paying
> for the first aliyah]; by this the congregation will not diminish the honor
> of the Torah, nor the custom of our fathers. And so they did, and they
> compelled him by the city police to be out of the synagogue.[44]

The responsum is interesting in many respects, not the least of which is the use of the gentile police force to remove the obstructionist Cohen from the shul. It should also be noted in light of the congregational schisms to be discussed that paying for Torah honors was historically associated with trouble and dissension.

The Maharik defended the paying for Torah honors with two arguments. First, paying for Torah honors paid homage to the Torah, and second, paying for Torah honors was *minhag avoteinu*, a custom handed down by the generations. The Maharik repeatedly returned to the idea of paying for Torah honors being an old custom. It is unclear, though, when this custom exactly started, and how it spread from Ashkenazi communities in Germany and France to the rest of the Jewish world.

Ismar Elbogen, in his history of Jewish liturgy, gave only cursory attention to the custom of paying for honors. He claimed the practice originated in the late Middle Ages and noted derisively, "Certainly, this paying for ritual functions was bound to lead to undesirable consequences, especially since for a time, they were even sold at public auction to the highest bidder."[45] He alluded to the problem of aliyot potentially going to the wealthiest individuals and not necessarily to the most respectable or pious. In his footnote to this section he was even more condemnatory, saying flatly and without expansion that the practice of auctioning Torah honors "has nothing to do with Judaism."[46] Presumably he meant that the practice was picked up from gentiles and does not comport with anything in Jewish tradition.

Despite Elbogen's contention that the practice was not Jewish, there was some form of paying for honors in all American synagogues in the first half of the nineteenth century. At Mikveh Israel in Philadelphia, Leeser wrote in 1842 of his desire to remove the practice, as it "interfere[s] with the solemnity of the service" and burdens regular worshippers over those who do not attend. He noted, "I would leave it to the good sense of the congregation to determine whether a mode of annual subscriptions could not be devised, which would effect a more equitable assessment."[47] The congregation heeded Leeser's plea and ended the practice a year later.

For the Charleston Reformers, the issue of paying for Torah honors was bound up with the larger agenda of synagogue reforms. The Reformers were primarily young, and some were politically active.[48] Many were also native born and influenced by their Christian surroundings. As Sarna notes in *American Judaism*, "Like many Protestants of the day, the Charleston Reformers argued for changes that would, simultaneously, improve their faith and restore it to what they understood to be its original pristine form."[49] The Reformers' agenda was laid out in a memorial sent to the board. It began with dismay over the state of Jewish life: "[We] have witnessed with deep regret, the apathy and neglect which has been manifested towards our holy religion." The reasons for this apathy and neglect according to the memorialists were "certain defects which are apparent in the system of worship, [which] are the sole causes of the evils complained of."[50] The petition then elucidated the evils and the proposed solutions. The first part of the proposed solutions all relate to adding English to the service. The second part of the memorial focused extensively on paying for honors.

The memorialists started this section by saying they would "set forth the entire uselessness and impropriety of this custom." The custom of KKBE in Charleston was to announce the person bidding and the amount pledged in Spanish, a practice that extended back to the initial founders of the synagogue who hewed to Sephardic traditions. By 1824, few members of the congregation spoke Spanish. The memorialists were outraged by the whole practice, but the use of Spanish just infuriated them more. They wrote: "Besides the free scope which the practice of offering in a language understood by few affords to mischievous and designing men to pollute the holy altars by gratifying their evil intentions — we certainly think it highly inconsistent to select for this very purpose, the language of a people from whom we have suffered, and continue to suffer so much persecution."[51]

It is noteworthy that the Reformers had such an antipathy toward Spanish. The Inquisition still loomed large for the Jewish community. Members of the Charleston community had fled Savannah in the eighteenth century when it was threatened by Spanish forces.

The Reformers observed an even bigger problem than Spanish. They wrote that paying for honors was "idle and absurd indulgence" because according to the bylaws of the congregation, the amount that one paid for Torah honors was subtracted from the yearly subscription (the assessments on seats). Therefore, paying for honors raised little additional money; it was just carried on for the sake of the custom. The Reformers then described how some individuals who had previously paid for Torah honors equal to their annual subscription left the synagogue and went into the courtyard at the time the honors were sold, lest they be pushed into buying honors and thus spending over and above their yearly assessment. While conceding that the practice did raise some money, they called upon the board to devise some other means by which to get this additional money. Finally, they suggest that getting rid of Torah honors would ultimately be a boon to the synagogue's bottom line because it would induce more people to join the synagogue.

In analyzing the Reformers' attitude toward paying for honors, the central question is how they came to be so vigorously opposed to the practice when members of their own synagogue, as well as most other synagogues in America, were comfortable mixing money and religion in this way. There is no clear answer as to when and how this change in worldview came about, but we may speculate based on certain statements in the petition.

The Reformers seemed particularly upset over the fact that people were leaving services to avoid paying for Torah honors and congregating in the courtyard. They described this custom as "a practice irregular, indecorous, and highly to be censured — because it sets an ill example to our children, *and draws upon us the eyes of strangers* [italics mine]."[52] The Reformers seemed more concerned with non-Jews seeing Jews in the courtyard during services than they were concerned about the disruption to the service itself.

The concern about, and influence of, their Christian neighbors were quite central to the push for reform. Lou Silberman argued in a significant essay on the Charleston Reformers that they were deeply influenced ideologically by the Charleston Protestant community. Silberman noted that the Charleston Reformers had read the journals of the German Reform movement and even quoted from the *Frankfort Journal* in their petition, but the bulk of their arguments seem native born. He traced the origins of their ideas to the Congregational church in Charleston, which itself had experienced a schism over religious reform a few years earlier and had split into Congregationalist and Unitarian churches.[53]

Central to Silberman's argument was an 1826 essay by the reverend of the Unitarian church[54] on the "Constitution of the Reformed Society of Israelites." The essay appeared in *The North American Review,* and it was full of praise for the Reformers. Reverend Samuel Gilman wrote of the Reform Jews "imbibing the liberal spirit of the age, as to admit the possibility of improvement from within their pale." He also wrote of having visited the synagogue. He noted approvingly of the Reformers' great desire to eliminate the practice of paying for Torah honors, writing, "These Spanish portions of the liturgy are employed only for a particular purpose, namely, to express the amount of *monies offered* for the benefit of the synagogue and its institutions . . . thus interrupting the prayers and worship with the fiscal concerns of the establishment, and that, too, in a language unknown to almost all present."[55] It is important to bear in mind that Gilman's church did not raise money during services to support the church. Most Protestant churches of the time utilized pew rentals for their income and would "pass the plate" only for special missions or specific causes.[56]

It was also possible that the Reformers were particularly anxious not to draw attention to the fact that Jews were haggling over money during services. For nineteenth-century Jews, money and Judaism was of course not a neutral topic. The caricature of Jews as Shylocks obsessed with money was part of American culture at the time.[57] Isaac Harby, the most prominent of the Charleston Reformers, was particularly unsettled by Shakespeare's portrayal of Shylock. A playwright himself, Harby idolized Shakespeare's literary genius, but, "unfortunately, Harby concluded, Shakespeare's attack on Shylock branded every Jew as a 'heartless userer.'"[58] Perhaps it was out of this fear of being labeled as Shylock Jews who cared too much about money that they so vehemently wanted to get rid of this practice.

It can be concluded that the Charleston Reformers came to see the paying for honors as a crass practice within their Christian milieu. Their own fear of connecting worship with money struck too close to the antisemitic notions they sought to distance themselves from. The use of Spanish only made the practice more threatening and obscure. The Reformers were not immune to caring about synagogue finances, but they made clear in devoting so much of their attention to this issue that removing money from worship would be significant in the Reform cause.

Ultimately, when the petition of the Reformers was rejected by the adjunta, the Reformers started their own group and created the first Reform liturgy in America. Not surprisingly, paying for Torah honors was not utilized by the society to raise money. They funded themselves with a yearly dues assessment of $10 [$202] for an individual and $12 [$242] for a family, but were unable to raise the necessary funds to build their own building.[59]

The schism in the Charleston community was significant for its place as the beginning of Reform Judaism in America, but it was also significant for the creation of an alternative synagogue in Charleston, becoming the first city in America with two functioning synagogues.[60] This introduction of synagogue competition had profound effects on the development of American synagogues, and Charleston was not the only city where synagogue competition emerged in this period. In the same year that Charleston had a schism, Shearith Israel in New York had a dispute that would ultimately lead to the creation of Congregation B'nai Jeshurun, the second synagogue in New York City's history. Like Charleston, the dispute at Shearith Israel pitted the religious ideology of younger members of the congregation against its older members. And also like Charleston, at the center of the dispute was paying for Torah honors.

In 1825, Shearith Israel relied primarily on selling seats to raise money, but they still maintained voluntary offerings as a supplemental source of income despite occasional attempts throughout the nineteenth century to remove the practice.[61] The problems with voluntary offerings were twofold. Those who came regularly to services ended up paying more than those who did not come. Some argued that it was fair that those who used the synagogue more should pay more. But the arguments from those who opposed the offerings believed the upkeep of the synagogue to be a communal responsibility regardless of how often one came to services. The other issue with voluntary offerings was budgetary. The congregation could not budget ahead of time for what someone might feel moved to give. To alleviate the latter issue, in 1805 the adjunta regulated that the payment for an aliyah would be two shillings and the money raised by this practice was to go toward its budget for communal tzedakah.[62]

The two shilling regulation turned out to be a flashpoint for a religious dispute. The skirmish began on the eighth day of Passover in 1825. Barrow Cohen was called for a Torah honor on that day but refused to pay the two shillings. Cohen was called to stand trial before the adjunta for this infraction of the rules. He claimed he was ignorant of the custom, as he had seen others not make an offering. The board held that Cohen would not be reprimanded, but must follow synagogue policy in the future. Cohen was irate over being called before the board and rejected the adjunta's authority. The adjunta fired back, barring Cohen from ever receiving an honor in the synagogue. Cohen and his supporters rallied against the adjunta's treatment, and the board ultimately backed down and eliminated the two shilling requirement for honors.[63] But the damage was done. This seemingly inconsequential skirmish over a few shillings on the last day of Passover would have major repercussions as Cohen and his associates would ultimately form an alternative synagogue, Congregation B'nai Jeshurun.

The dispute over Torah honors was not entirely about Cohen's ignorance of the two shilling rule. The Torah paying dispute was symbolic of the underlying tensions that had been plaguing the synagogue. Cohen was part of a younger, Ashkenazi, group that clashed with what it perceived as the less observant and elitist Sephardi leadership. For Cohen and his cadre, the two shilling price for an aliyah reaffirmed the elitism of the synagogue by effectively reserving the honors only for the wealthy.

The Charleston Reformers formed a group and published their "Memorial," much like them the young Ashkenazim also formed a society and published their religious program, which spelled out their aims. The name of the document is the Constitution and Bye-laws of the *Hebra Hinuch Nearim* (Society for the Education of Young People).[64] A number of the articles in the *Hebra* constitution reflect directly on the Torah honors dispute. The constitution was explicit regarding the democratization of the synagogue, saying that in worship there would be no distinction made among its members, and it called for all synagogue honors to be "distributed in such a manner that every member shall have an equal portion." Another article reduced the minimum offering to be given for the honor of Torah reading from two shillings to six and a quarter cents (a drop of 75 percent).

When compared one to the other, the two schisms can shed light on differing approaches to synagogues and money at this important moment in American Jewish history. Although both disputes had paying for Torah honors as a crucial aspect, the New York group did not have a hesitancy about making such offerings — they in fact included making Torah offerings in their constitution. The problem with paying for Torah honors for the members of the *Hebra Hinuch Nearim* was that the high price of honors at Shearith Israel created distinctions within the synagogue. Against the backdrop of the Second Great Awakening, an age of increasing democratization, a system that privileged the wealthy was problematic.

In Charleston, the argument to eliminate the practice arose out of a desire to assimilate into a Christian milieu. The Reformers did not argue the practice was problematic on the grounds of inequity and disenfranchisement. Rather, the introduction of money sullied the holiness of services. Selling off honors, they thought, was a relic from a previous era, and should be removed to create a modern Judaism in both religion and finance.

Most American synagogues would eventually follow in the Reformers' footsteps and not retain the practice of selling honors. The discomfort with money in services became the American norm. Isaac Leeser attacked the practice of public declarations of money offerings during services quite vociferously in 1847, writing, "Show us a single good feature which results from mentioning money in our places of worship, and we will be silent; show us whereby piety is elevated by watching and noting down, on the holy days of the Lord, a long list of complimentary offerings, in which no one is interested except the offerer and the exchequer of the Synagogue: and we will acknowledge that we are wrong in urging a change."[65]

The idea of money as incompatible with elevating piety during services may seem natural to us as inheritors of this line of thought, but the elimination of paying for honors and making public donations was a significant ritual change for Jewish practice. That change was born out of Jews living in a Christian and American context.[66]

The disputes over paying for Torah honors also correlates with another well-known schema of American Jewish historiography. Jonathan Sarna argues that the two congregational schisms initiated a fundamental change in the structure of the American Jewish community as it moved from "a synagogue-community" to a "community of synagogues." Prior to the 1820s, each American city had one synagogue, whereas the congregational schisms of the 1820s saw the establishment of competing synagogues. The creation of alternative synagogues would quickly replicate itself as some of the breakaway synagogues in turn spawned other synagogues. "The result," writes Sarna, "was nothing less than a new American Judaism — a Judaism that was diverse and pluralistic, whereas before it had been designedly monolithic." Because there was now competition among congregations, "[synagogues] had a new interest in minimizing dissent and keeping members satisfied.... This led to the rapid demise of the system of disciplining congregants with fines and sanctions. Congregations became much more concerned with attracting congregants than keeping them in line."[67] The Dutch governance model of heavy-handed authority gave way to a more democratic institution, responsive to the needs of its members.

Competition among synagogues became a defining aspect of the American Jewish milieu and had a fundamental impact on the economics of synagogues. Synagogues could not raise the cost of seats at their whim for fear that people would leave the synagogue and join elsewhere. Competition among synagogues, like competition in all other aspects of the economy, would be a restraint on prices and revenue. Competition would also impact expenses. Each synagogue would need to replicate all of the expected functions of a synagogue — that is, have their own rabbis, buildings, and schools — or they might lose membership. This meant there would be limited sharing of resources, creating larger individual synagogue budgets.

It may be no surprise that the advent of synagogue competition arose at the same time when American industrialization began to take hold, and the market would come to so define the American way of life. The embrace of the market as a fundamental American value meant that synagogues too needed to operate in a competitive environment.

Anti-mammonism and the Contrast between Churches and Synagogues in Raising and Speaking about Money

While selling/renting seats became the standard way for synagogues to fund themselves, some Protestant churches moved in the opposite direction. During the first half of the nineteenth century, a number of Protestant churches abandoned pew renting and by the Civil War many had adopted a voluntary contribution model known as "systematic benevolence." Charles Grandison Finney, the most well-known evangelist of the period, was a central figure in this transition. Finney preached the need for a free church, which eliminated the buying of seats on the grounds that everyone should be able to hear the gospel regardless of wealth. In place of seat rentals, Finney argued that Christians "should not be left to think that anything is their own, their time, property, influence, faculties, bodies or souls." Rather, God was the ultimate owner and as such it was their responsibility to give back to God's earthly institution — the church.[68]

Protestant leaders of the nineteenth century believed that "becoming Christian ought to make a difference in one's use of money."[69] Ministers promoted giving to the church as a fundamental principle of what it meant to be a Christian, on par with any other responsibility of a believer. They also understood, though, that support of the church should not be subject to the vagaries of the believer's religious fervor, and so they stressed plans that specified how much members should be giving to the church — the "systematic" part of systematic benevolence. Many of these plans based themselves on biblical verses and precedents like the system of tithes. The end result for the church was that "throughout the nineteenth century, the ways in which religious groups, and especially Protestants, raised the funds to pay for their activities became more and more steeped in religious rationale, biblical precedent, and the language of sacred obligation."[70]

Jews, however, diverged sharply from their Christian neighbors on this point. Jewish clergy and synagogue leaders in this era did not promote ideas of sacred obligation, benevolence, or stewardship. When Max Lilienthal suggested a change in funding structure, he presented not a single biblical or rabbinic reference in his opinion, nor did he use any theological language. Synagogues understood giving as a matter of community, not theology — a sensibility that remains very much alive today. It is noteworthy that there has never been a serious Jewish attempt to institute tithing despite its biblical foundations.

The explanation for the dichotomy between church and synagogue in the religious call for funding may be ascribed to the general notion that Jews are less theologically oriented and more hesitant to speak about God's will than Christians are. There was also no tradition in Judaism to understand giving to the synagogue as a divine imperative. It may also simply be the case that synagogues found willing ears when they stressed communal responsibility, and thus found no need to buttress the call to give with divine proclamation.

Synagogues and churches not only differed around fund-raising, but they also differed when it came to the broader questions of money and the growing American economy. There has been significant scholarly attention given to the role of the Protestant church and the expanding American economy in the antebellum period. Historian Richard Pointer noted, "The Christian's duty to prosper, self-help as a way to wealth, Christian piety as an asset to temporal success, the ordering and disciplining effects of Christian morality, the material and moral benefits of the machine . . . all of these themes were common fare for Protestant ministers in the second quarter of the nineteenth century."[71]

Other historians suggest that there was a synthesis between Protestant values and the emergence of industrial capitalism. The rise of evangelicalism in this period was in part a result of the evangelical message accommodating itself to the transformations happening to the American economic system. The growth of the economy was in turn fed by Christian values around industry and prosperity.[72]

Mark Noll, in an important volume of essays on Protestants and money in post-colonial and antebellum America, claims that evangelicals may have acclimated to a market economy but most ministers were wary of the acquisition of wealth and spent considerable time preaching on this theme. He writes, "The basic Protestant stance throughout the Antebellum period remained an uncomplicated acceptance of commercial society, alongside an extraordinary elaboration of scruples concerning how the wealth engendered by commerce should be used."[73] Noll cites a sermon published in 1857 that expresses the same idea in simple religious terms: "Our object is to baptize the riches of men with the spirit of the gospel."[74]

Some Protestant thinkers moved in even more radical directions, offering a full-scale critique of American capitalism and its inherent inequalities. An 1845 religious tract urged preachers to proclaim not charity to the poor but a just distribution of wealth to the laborers who produced it.[75] In the wake of the Panic of 1857, the *Episcopal Church Review* wrote, "The pursuit of wealth, if not essentially and universally a selfish pursuit, is, nevertheless, so nearly related to selfishness, and places one in such a dangerous proximity to the polluting gangrene of the moral nature of man, that but few if any escape the effects of its poisoning virus."[76]

For southern clergy in particular, the critique of avarice was a basic trope in their preaching; "few themes — excluding the general call to repentance and salvation — rivaled, in force or in quantity, the ministers' antimammon message."[77] The southern economy saw a dramatic expansion in the nineteenth century: the cotton trade became international, credit was cheap, and the possibility existed for making money in an unprecedented manner. "[The clergy] detected, that despite popular, external religious affectations, the economic enthusiasm of the day was leading to a deadly indifference toward higher, spiritual things. The ministers suspected that the men and women sitting before them in the pews each Sunday were more interested in commerce and cotton than salvation and saintliness."[78] Ministers preached that the growth of "mammonism" would lead to God's vengeance on the South for their obsession with wealth.

Southern preachers were not "levelers," believers that wealth needed to be dramatically redistributed and class eliminated; they accepted the benefits of the market and capitalism as well as the traditional southern distinctions of class. What they disdained was the market's gross excesses and the damage it was doing to traditional southern unity by pitting classes against each other.

This brief survey of antebellum Protestants and money should be contrasted with Jewish leadership at the time. In the writings of Isaac Mayer Wise, the most prominent rabbi of the period and the founder of organized Reform Judaism, we see a significant concern for the economy and the clear influence of Protestant preaching. In 1857 in *The Israelite*, Wise wrote an extended essay about the degradation of current times, the second part of which was called "The Age and Its Corruptions II: Mammon and Science." In the essay, Wise wrote vehemently that he was living in an age of corruption as a result of mammonism:

> When a singer, player or rope dancer makers more with his art than ten generals, senators or professors; when all services rendered to man are valued by the standard of their material profit or amusement, the age must be called corrupt in its vital principle. This is an age of materialism, mercantile speculations, swindle, cheat, singing, playing, gambling and rope dancing; because Mammonism has subjected science and art to be his tools . . . and cheats religion and conscience no less than his neighbor.[79]

Another example from Wise occurred on the eve of the Civil War, when in a manner very similar to Christian preachers he blamed the crisis on "speculators in property, stockjobbers, and usurers whose God is Mammon."[80]

Jacob Rader Marcus, in his essay "The Americanization of Isaac Mayer Wise," noted Wise's bitter critique of the American obsession with wealth. Marcus suggested that Wise's opposition to the market economy was a result of having grown up in a relatively stable Germany economy before the industrial revolution. "[Wise] wanted a return to a more primitive economic system, where, he imagined, huge fortunes and dire poverty were both unknown, where tradition and custom and law protected the economic status of the lower middle classes."[81] It is ironic perhaps in an essay about the *Americanization* of Wise, that Marcus ascribed Wise's critique of the market to his childhood in the German economy, when a more likely explanation for Wise's insistent critique of the market is the influence of American Protestantism. Wise's approach to the market was identical to contemporaneous anti-mammonist writing. Wise, like his southern Protestant counterparts, was not a leveler looking to fundamentally change capitalism; rather, it was the excesses of the market that he resented, noting, "We have already an alarmingly large number of millionaires, much too large for a sound republic, and much too influential for the public welfare."[82]

Abraham Rice, the first rabbi in America, also spoke out against the desire for wealth as a corrupting influence on American society:

When one acquires much gold and silver, the results are the same as in the
practice of idolatry. . . . How [the Jews] put all their faith in their wealth
and neglect God's commandments! How they neglect to observe the
Sabbaths and holidays as commanded by God! . . . How they are never
satisfied with their gold and silver and mislead others to ceaselessly seek
its acquisition! . . . In our day and age, hypocrites and flatterers swarm
around every rich man, praising all his acts. . . . Our moral standards
are low; jealousy and envy, passion and hatred, are no longer accidental
among us.[83]

After a few years spent decrying the lack of observance of Baltimore Jews,
he resigned from his congregation and left the rabbinate.[84]

While Wise and Rice were critics of the new material culture they saw
around them, other Jewish leaders seemed less concerned. "Mammonism"
was simply not the preoccupation that it was for Protestant clergy. Leeser's
newspaper *The Occident*, for example, was completely silent on any topics
regarding wealth — he did editorialize on rabbinic salaries — but in general
he did not seem interested in the acquisition of wealth as a religious problem. Leeser was not alone in this regard; we see very little from other Jewish
leaders on this topic. One might have thought that the anti-mammonist
writings would be an appealing trope for Jews to counter accusations of
Jews being obsessed with money. Or perhaps it was precisely this concern
that led rabbis and synagogue leaders to stay away from the topic.

Another possibility for why rabbis were relatively silent on the topic of
wealth emerges when considering who the leaders of synagogues in this
period were. There was significant overlap between economic elites and
synagogue elites prior to the Civil War. In the period around 1860, there
were six Jews with a net worth of over $100,000 [$2,556,270] in Cincinnati,
and of those six, five of them served at one time as president of either KKBI
or B'nai Jeshurun.[85] Baltimore had a similar dynamic, where "the roster of
big businessmen of Baltimore reads like the roster of directors of the charity organizations and the synagogues."[86] Moses Wiesenfeld, for example,
invested $5,085.91 [$115,073] in 1841 to start a wholesale clothing business
that by 1860 was worth over half a million dollars [$12,781,354]. Wiesenfeld
also served as president of the Lloyd Street Synagogue. Business leaders

also headed the synagogues in Milwaukee. As Gartner and Swichkow note in *The History of the Jews of Milwaukee*, "Most of the early congregational leaders were already substantial businessmen, who had established a fair reputation in the general community."[87] The Buffalo Jewish community was yet another example. Joseph Lessler was a successful clothing merchant and land speculator who served as president of Congregation Beth El in Buffalo in 1849 and then president of the rival Congregation Beth Zion in 1853 after a synagogue secession.[88] Having the wealthiest Jewish men serve in synagogue leadership served congregations well, as evidenced by the large budget expansions in synagogues prior to the Civil War. And it may explain in some part why we don't find anti-mammon preaching. Simply put, this newly acquired wealth was serving the Jewish community well, and it may not have behooved anyone to suggest that the new acquisition of wealth was a religious problem.

An additional essential question here is not just whether rabbis were anti-mammonist, but whether they spoke and wrote in ways that would promote Jewish participation in the economy. Do we find a Jewish corollary to the Protestant virtues of work and prosperity? Did the synagogue promote accommodation and industriousness in the growing market?

These questions have recently taken on renewed interest among scholars. Just as scholarly attention has been paid to the relationship between nineteenth-century Protestantism and the growth of the industrial economy, so too has attention turned to the question of the Jewish relationship with American capitalism. Rebecca Kobrin's volume, *Chosen Capital: The Jewish Encounter with American Capitalism*, is a prime example of this new effort. Kobrin uses Werner Sombart's famous essay on the success of Jews in the economy as a jumping-off point for this investigation. Sombart contends that "Jews' intrinsic proclivities made them central provocateurs in the creation of modern capitalism."[89] While much has been written about both Sombart's essay and the success of German Jewish immigrants in antebellum America, the specific question is whether one can link the world of the synagogue to the success of Jews in the economy.[90]

We see very little explicitly said from clergy and synagogue leaders on the virtue of work. Unlike Protestant ministers of the time, we find no exhortations that piety will lead to material reward, or that there is a Jewish value in industriousness, but we do see clear cases where Judaism accommodated itself to the demands of the economy. The most obvious example was the clash between Shabbat observance and the need to work on Saturday. As noted above, Abraham Rice was a vocal opponent of his members working on Shabbat and putting the needs of money over observance. But of course Rabbi Rice lost this struggle. Initially, he called for those found working on Shabbat to be barred from receiving Torah honors, but there were so much disagreement with this order, in part because the synagogue needed the money that people would pay for Torah honors, that he backed down. He ultimately allowed Sabbath breakers to have an honor, but no one should say "amen" to their blessings.[91] Rice ultimately retired from the rabbinate, frustrated that his members were not listening to his pleas.

In Congregation Beth El in Buffalo in the same time period we see a similar dynamic. The congregation had as part of its bylaws instituted a fine of 50 cents for those who missed Shabbat services. But the congregation abandoned this fine because most of the members had to work on Shabbat. They reinstituted the fine a few years later but in a compromised form, fining only those members who had specifically been asked to come to Shabbat services.[92] Although the evidence is minimal, one may extrapolate to say that while Jewish religious leaders did not promote industry, neither did they prevent it. Rabbi Rice was the exception that proves the rule. When religion attempted to get in the way of industry, it was religion that lost.

Clergy Salaries

In an editorial for the *Occident* regarding clerical pay in 1847, Isaac Leeser wrote of the financial indignity of serving as a clergyperson:

> We all know how miserably most of the Jewish ministers are supported; and for how small a pittance they perform duties which require not rarely talents and natural powers of no mean order; and let any one point out to us that servant of the Synagogue who was ever able to leave the smallest patrimony to his family from his salary. The usual cry is, that the funds will not permit a more liberal endowment, and that in addition the minister receives *Mattanoth* [gifts] and fees. But this much is certain, the small salary is all he can depend upon, the presents and fees may come or not, as the donors may seem disposed to give; . . . It is absurd to expect an

independent and high-souled ministry; while so paltry a way of support is only open to the incumbents; but render the office respectable by attaching to it a respectable salary and no dependence upon the caprice of the wealthy, and you will have rendered a great service to the cause of religion, by inducing many good men to devote themselves to a calling which will, in the case we are speaking of, be free from one of the greatest drawbacks to which it has been subjected.[93]

Leeser's was certainly not the only voice complaining of poor clerical pay while wishing for an independent and high-souled ministry. It was a common trope in the nineteenth century to claim Jewish clergy were not supported. Even at his own synagogue, Leeser was just following a line of unhappy clerics.

At the beginning of the nineteenth century, the hazan Jacob Cohen repeatedly had to berate the congregation for their failure to pay him in a timely manner. "I had expected from the repeated promises made me on the part of the Congregation with respect to the Settlement of these arrears so long due, that there would draw no necessity of another application, but I am sorry to find that this [is not true]."[94] Cohen was at the time being paid by the congregation $250 [$3,822]; additionally, he was allowed to live in a house the congregation owned free of charge and was also given $10 [$153] for wood and $10 for matzah. Clergy salaries typically also included gifts members would give to clergy as well as marriage fees, but such additions could not be counted on and ranged widely from one year to the next. Cohen's duties at the time included leading all prayer services for Shabbat and every holiday, leading every funeral, attending to the sick, and conducting shivah (house of mourning) services. He was also to act as a shamas — cleaning the synagogue, stoking the fire, and making sure the alcohol cabinet was locked.[95]

When Isaac Leeser came to Mikveh Israel in 1829, the congregation had not had a hazan for seven years. The congregation had offered the position to Eleazar Lazarus, grandfather of Emma Lazarus, who had turned the position down when the congregation refused to grant him a lifetime contract. The congregation turned to Leeser as the next candidate, although he was not universally desired by the congregation. They elected him with a salary of $800 [$17,227] on a two-year contract.[96]

Did the salaries of Cohen and Leeser reflect a paltry way of support, or was it possible on these salaries to be an "independent and high-souled minister"? Previous historians have agreed with Leeser's judgment that Jewish clergy were treated shabbily and paid poorly. Isaac Fein, in his history of the Baltimore Jewish community of this period, stated unequivocally, "As a rule, rabbis, cantors, and teachers were underpaid."[97] But this is a questionable assessment.

As we saw in the colonial era, clergy salaries when translated into today's dollars appear quite insubstantial, but this is misleading and points to the difficulties in translating income. When compared against other salaries of the day, another picture emerges. In 1829, when Leeser signed his contract, the average artisan's salary in Philadelphia was $1.80/day; the average laborer made $1.05/day.[98] If we presume a six-day workweek, salaries would roughly be $563.40 [$12,132] per year for a skilled worker and $328.65 [$7,077] for a laborer. A captain for ships leaving Philadelphia in this period was earning $600 [$13,127] a year, while a ship's mate was earning $300 [$6,564].[99] At $800 [$17,502] a year, Leeser was obviously making significantly more than any of these figures. Despite his complaints of a paltry salary, he was a firmly middle-class figure.

By contrast, Jacob Cohen's salary in 1804 stood him decidedly less well off. The average skilled worker in 1804 was making $500.80 [$7,780], while the average laborer was making $313 [$4,863]. Cohen's salary of $250 [$3,884], even including the free rent and money for wood and matzah, put it below the average unskilled laborer. But it should be noted that at the time the congregation was in financial difficulty, suffering from internal divisions and only six years earlier had almost closed its doors.[100] By 1825 its fortunes had substantially reversed, and it was able to build a new synagogue at a cost of $13,000 [$263,664] without any debt, allowing it to offer Leeser a middle-class contract.

At Shearith Israel in New York, one finds a similar story of congregational inconsistency with regard to clerical pay. After the death of Gershom Seixas, his good friend and merchant Moses Peixotto took over the position of hazan, but on the condition that the salary and gifts he received go to Seixas's widow. Five years later, Peixotto could no longer afford such generosity and asked to be paid a salary or he would be forced to go back to being a merchant. The congregation was seemingly quite fond of Peixotto and kept him on happily. By the end of his tenure in 1828, the congregation was paying him $1,200 [$25,065] per year, a figure substantially higher than Leeser and firmly grounding Peixotto in the middle class.[101]

After Peixotto passed away, the congregation turned to Isaac Seixas, the nephew of Gershom Seixas, who was offered just $600 [$12,033] to be hazan, plus free use of a home the congregation owned.[102] Months after taking the position, Seixas wrote to the congregation, "The winter is now approaching and I am without food, my children without clothing, and myself without the means of procuring either, besides being largely indebted for the common necessaries of life." Seixas then reminded the congregation that his predecessor was making double his present salary.[103] His entire income, $600 [$12,033] in salary plus another $300 [$6,017] in gifts, would not have been a robust salary, but it is not clear why Seixas's children were without clothing when this salary still represented far more than the average laborer would have made. Perhaps there was some hyperbole in this sentiment to draw on the compassion of the congregation, or the real issue might have been social prestige. He finished the letter to the board asking the congregation for money "to support that standing in society which the character I bear ought to."

The reason for the drop in salary between hazanim was the financial difficulties for Shearith Israel when Seixas took the position. Shearith Israel now faced competing synagogues and many of its members had moved uptown. In 1834, the congregation moved buildings to follow its membership and immediately their finances improved. Seixas's salary was increased to $1,080 [$21,906] in 1837 and eventually $1,500 [$32,332] in 1839.[104] The Panic of 1837 does not seem to have affected the congregation's finances. The move to a new synagogue proved a more important factor than general economic trends.

Not surprisingly for both Mikveh Israel and Shearith Israel, the salary of the clergy was very much tied to the fortunes of the congregation at a given moment. As more congregations were formed in the middle part of the nineteenth century and the first ordained rabbis arrived in America, this general pattern would not change. Congregations that reached a numerical tipping point and were not experiencing particular financial trouble (most often due to building debt) paid their clergy on par or better than most Christian clergy and established their rabbis firmly in the middle class. Smaller and less secure congregations paid salaries so that their clergy were not penurious, but not at the same level as the more successful clergy. Rare was the Jewish clergy paid as poorly as Methodist preachers, who generally made only $100 [$2,464] a year if they were single but twice that if they were married.[105]

In looking at the decade before the Civil War, salaries for the more successful rabbis ranged from $1,000 to $2,500 [$24,642 to $68,995]. Isaac Mayer Wise, for example, came to Albany's Congregation Beth El in 1846 at a salary of $250 per year plus an additional $9 for every child enrolled in the school, which brought his salary to less than $800 [$20,461]. When it came time to renew his contract, there was significant tension and multiple scenes of Wise ripping up his contract and threatening to leave the synagogue and never come back. Ultimately, he agreed to stay and be paid $800 per year with the addition of school fees. In 1853, when Wise had established himself and moved to Cincinnati's B'nai Yeshurun, he was paid $1,500 [$41,397].[106] Max Lilienthal's career followed a similar trajectory. When he arrived in New York City in 1845, the second ordained rabbi to settle there, he served three German congregations simultaneously at a salary of $1,000 [$25,051].[107] When he moved to KKBI a few years later he, like Wise, was paid $1,500.[108]

Morris Raphall was reputed to be the most well-paid rabbi of the period. In 1849, B'nai Jeshurun in New York paid him $2,000 [$55,196] yearly, thought to be the largest salary of any preacher in the country. B'nai Jeshurun succeeded so well under Raphall's leadership that it was able to also employ a hazan at $1,000 [$26,959] a year in 1858.[109] Moses Nathan was paid an even higher salary of $2,500 [$70,099] in 1850 as the rabbi of Nefutzot Yehudah. The congregation was unusual in that it was primarily funded by Judah Touro. Touro paid approximately two-thirds of Nathan's salary for two years. When this period was done, Nathan was frustrated that the rest of the congregation did not step forward to continue paying him at that rate. Nathan resigned, feeling too dependent on Touro's generosity for his salary, and left the congregation and moved back to England.[110] Nathan and Touro must have remained on good terms, though, because he was left $3,000 [$77,888] in Touro's will.[111]

Rabbi George Jacobs at Beth Shalome in Richmond, Virginia, was paid $1,200 [$30,053] in 1857, a figure that placed him as a solidly middle-class figure who also owned slaves. However, three years after the Civil War, in

1868, he was still being paid $1,200. He wrote to the board recalling all the sacrifices and hardships he had suffered and asked for an immediate salary increase or else he would leave.[112]

At Keneseth Israel, Solomon Deutsch was the rabbi of the congregation beginning in 1857. In 1860 he was making $1,200 [$30,675] a year, while the hazan was making $800 [$20,777] a year. The total congregational budget was $3,560 [$92,459], so the congregation was spending 34 percent of the budget on their rabbi. Including salaries for the hazan, the choir, and teachers, salaries took up roughly 85 percent of the congregational budget.[113] At Beth Shalome, Jacobs's salary represented 75 percent of the congregational budget. These percentages are slightly higher but not entirely out of place from what one finds in contemporary synagogues, where rabbinic salaries range from 20 to 35 percent of an annual budget and total salaries in the congregation can be as high as 60 to 70 percent.[114]

Deutsch's career at Keneseth Israel ended with some acrimony. Deutsch claimed the hazan acted in an abusive and insulting manner toward him and demanded the congregation force the hazan to apologize. The congregation reprimanded the hazan but did not force an apology. Deutsch then told the congregation that he could no longer work with the hazan and he would leave if the congregation would pay him one year's salary. Recognizing the rather large payout, he wrote, "If the congregation considers that my contract with them runs by law still another 5¾ years, that I [will be] unemployed with my family in a strange part of the world, that I lost $800 by coming here, I would have been much better off money wise and in a better position in Europe, but I followed your call to come here, you will recognize, that my demand is a reasonable one."[115] The congregation took out a bank loan to pay the rabbi's demands and somewhat surprisingly, given the acrimony, published tributes to the rabbi in the German Jewish newspapers; the rabbi responded with a heartfelt letter wishing the congregation well. The board noted that the congregation emerged from the dissension very successfully. In this case, money was quite a salve to a difficult situation.

Many rabbis were not remunerated quite so well. Rabbi Henry Hochheimer at Baltimore Hebrew Congregation earned $400 [$10,385] in 1854. But a number of congregants applied to the board to remedy this low salary, saying it was an injustice that he was not paid more. Isaac Fein noted that the real reason for their insistence on a pay raise may not necessarily have been concern for Rabbi Hochheimer; rather, they stated, "It must appear to our non-coreligionists that the Israelites do not appreciate the services of their religious leader."[116]

Rabbi Henry Lowenthal moved to the small Jewish community of Macon, Georgia, from New Haven, Connecticut, to serve Congregation Beth Israel. During his very brief and difficult tenure at the congregation, his wife passed away. He sent a letter to Isaac Leeser detailing his travails with the congregation, writing that the congregation was impious, unobservant, and unfeeling and he had to leave his post because "my salary is never paid punctually nor in a becoming manner." After serving for just a year, he moved back to England.[117]

The Beth Hamedrash Hagodol was established in 1852 on the Lower East Side of New York City. The congregation has the distinction of being the first Russian-American congregation in America. The first rabbi of the synagogue was Joseph Ash, an immigrant from Semyavitch in Russo-Poland. Ash was one of several traditional rabbis who had emigrated from Russia during this period. Ash received just $2 a week to serve as rabbi, plus presumably an additional small sum for gifts. The salary was not sufficient; during the Civil War, Ash became involved in the manufacture of hoop skirts, gave up the rabbinate, and became parnas of the congregation.[118]

Rabbi Ash's poor salary portends the salary gap between traditional rabbis and more Americanized rabbis, which in some ways continues today. Rabbis serving *haredi*, or traditional, communities earned less historically than rabbis serving Reform and what would become Conservative and Modern Orthodox congregations. Nontraditional communities tended to be larger and wealthier. Rabbi Ash's community was small and had a number of congregational disputes, which led to rival congregations being formed and members leaving. His members were primarily Russian immigrants new to the country. Rabbi Ash was probably the first in a long line of Lower East Side rabbis whose salaries paled in comparison to the salaries of uptown rabbis in New York City.

Another historical trend that developed in the period before the Civil War was the cleavage in salaries between ordained rabbis and hazanim. After rabbis began coming to America in the 1840s, hazans, financially speaking, were relegated to second-class clergy.[119] In *The Rise of the Jewish*

Community of New York, Grinstein notes, "With the arrival in New York of many Germans and Polish Jews, opposition to the important role assumed by the hazan soon arose. . . . German Jews maintained the tradition that a rabbi was superior to a mere hazan. . . . The Polish Jews, moreover, came with their old traditions intact. Both groups united in objection to making the hazan a spiritual leader; they sought, instead, to place in the ministerial position men who were either rabbis or maggidim [preachers]."[120]

A congregational dispute at Congregation Emanuel in San Francisco amply makes the point that Americanized rabbis were more expensive than hazanim. In 1854, the congregation called to their pulpit Rabbi Julius Eckman with the promise of a tremendous salary of $3,500 [$86,247]. This salary made Eckman the best-paid rabbi in America and presumably on par with any minister in the country. The only problem was that the congregation did not actually have the money. The salary was immediately reduced to $2,000 [$51,925] in the congregational vote, which confirmed his hire. This would still have been a significant salary but even this was hard for the congregation to achieve.

It seems that the congregation was driven by two rival factions. One faction was looking for a learned minister like Eckman who could lead modern services, while the other faction wanted a traditional (and cheaper) hazan. In the wake of the gold rush, Emanuel built a synagogue worth $18,000 [$426,327], on which they owed $1,500 [$38,944] in annual interest. The congregation did not sell seats; they relied on dues, and collected $2 a month per member. With 120 members, they had a yearly revenue of roughly $2,900 [$75,292]. Given the interest payments and other expenses of the building, the congregation did not have enough revenue to meet either the original or the reduced salary of Rabbi Eckman. When the congregation proposed doubling the dues to pay for Eckman, the faction opposed to a rabbi demurred. At a congregational meeting the following year, the group that wanted a cheaper hazan pushed forward their own candidate, who would receive a salary of $600 [$15,577] a year, and Emanuel would go another five years without an ordained rabbi.[121]

The salary for hazanim in this period generally ranged from $250 to $1,000 [$6,388 to $25,554]. Some congregations continued to desire hazanim who could also preach, effectively combining rabbinic and cantorial functions. Congregation B'nai Israel in Memphis, for example, advertised for a hazan who could lecture in German and English, lead prayer services, lead a choir, and teach in the Hebrew school for $1,000 [$25,554] a year.[122] Mishkan Israel in New Haven, Connecticut, advertised for a hazan for $600 to $800 [$15,578- to $20,770], stating, "Applicants must be competent to deliver lectures in German, and one conversant with the English language will be preferred, although this is not essential."[123]

The hazan at a smaller community was often expected to serve as prayer leader, preacher, mohel (circumciser), and shochet (kosher butcher). Congregation Tememe Derech in New Orleans advertised for a hazan and shochet who would be paid $300 [$8,088] a year but with the possibility of making an additional $600 to $800 [$16,175 to $21,567] a year depending on gifts and the amount of meat butchered.[124] At Ahavath Achim in Bangor, Maine, the hazan of the congregation was paid $250 [$6,491] in 1854 to act as cantor, mohel, and shochet. He also received 5 percent of bills that he collected on behalf of the congregation, which amounted to just a few dollars. This salary was, of course, quite small given the other figures seen above, but it should be noted that the congregation at this point was quite small, and with annual revenue of just $319 [$8,282], it meant that the hazan's salary represented 78 percent of the congregational budget. It should also be noted that the hazan at Ahavath Achim had a few unusual duties added to his list. Besides slaughtering, leading services, and circumcising, the hazan was "obliged to take the first watch" by the bedside of any members who were dangerously ill. In light of this responsibility, the congregational rules also stipulated that "on no condition may he [the hazan] leave the city over night."[125]

B'nai Yeshurun in Cincinnati hired a hazan who was also called assistant minister (perhaps the first time this appellation was used) for $400 [$10,385]. The congregation advertised that "only Hebrew grammarians and those acquainted with vocal music need apply."[126] Its amicable rival, KKBI, hired a hazan for $300 [$7,511]. They also made a deal with a "backup" hazan, who agreed to lead services in case the regular hazan was indisposed; in lieu of payment, he would be allowed to live in the basement of the synagogue. The finance committee noted both men were "fine Hebrew scholars."[127]

In looking at the general trends of Jewish clerical salaries in this period, E. Brooks Holifield, in his article on the history of clerical salaries, claims that there was a significant regional difference in clerical pay for all denominations and faiths. He uses census data from 1860 to show that the wealth of southern clergy far exceeded northern clergy. Although his focus is on Protestant clergy, included in his findings is a claim that southern Jewish clergy were five times as wealthy as northern Jewish clergy. Southern Jewish clergy had an average wealth of $3,100 [$79,244], while northern Jewish clergy had just $578 [$14,775] — note this is total wealth, not income. He ascribes most of the wealth difference to the fact that a good percentage of southern clergy owned slaves at the time, and slaves were included as assets in the census data. Northern clergy were also far more likely to be immigrants, making it less likely they would own any real estate.

In terms of Jewish clergy, a close look at his data shows that there were only twelve Jewish clergy in the data set, and only three were in the south, so the numbers are quite small.[128] I would suggest if we had a full data set, we would not see a regional difference despite the fact that the southern economy in this period was rapidly expanding. In looking at the totality of available evidence on clergy salaries, one is hard-pressed to see any significant difference between the north and south in terms of Jewish clerical pay. If anything, New York in 1860 was home to the most well-paid clergy in Morris Raphall and Samuel Adler. It is possible that southern Jewish clergy owned land, and northern Jewish clergy did not, but as in the example of Henry Lowenthal in Macon, Georgia, cited above, Jewish clergy in the south were as likely to be immigrants as in the north.

Holifield also found that nationally Jewish clergy were the least wealthy clergy of any religious denomination with the sole exception of Seventh-day Adventist ministers (Catholic priests were not included in this study, as their wealth was difficult to calculate because it was bound up in parish property).[129] Given everything we have noted regarding the pay of Jewish clergy, this finding is also dubious. It is possible that because most rabbis and hazanim were immigrants, Jewish clergy lagged behind ministers in total wealth, but a comparison of annual salaries reveals that Jewish clergy were on par with their Christian counterparts.

Successful urban Baptist clergy made between $1,000 and $1,500 [$25,972 and $38,958] per year and urban Presbyterian ministers made between $1,200 and $2,000 [$31,116 and $51,944].[130] The top New England clergy received between $1,200 and $2,000, while the majority of New England pastors made between $400 and $500 [$10,389 and $12,986].[131] These numbers suggest that there was a similar range of salaries for ministers as there was for rabbis and cantors. The successful Jewish clergy were making $1,500 [$38,958] or more, less successful clergy made $250 to $300 [$6,493 to $7792], while the majority of Jewish clergy earned between these figures. In a period when Christian clergy who made these salaries were considered middle-class professionals on par with physicians and lawyers, the Jewish clergy were doing well.

An 1854 statement by the Society for the Relief of Aged and Destitute Clergymen estimated that an annual salary of at least $800 [$20,770] was needed in the cities and $450 [$11,683] in small towns and county parishes to have a decent standard of living.[132] Most Jewish clergy met this standard. Despite the complaints that clergy were underpaid, the evidence in the antebellum period suggests otherwise.

The reason for the relative success of Jewish clergy was a result of a few factors. The era before the Civil War saw a growth in the number of successful Jewish merchants who accumulated real wealth. These businessmen were quite often the same individuals who were leading synagogues. The increase in Jewish wealth led to a large jump in synagogue budgets during this period. As wealth increased, the demand increased for modern Americanized clergy — rabbis who were both learned Jewishly and could represent the Jewish community in broader circles. There were, however, not that many rabbis in America who could function as modern rabbis. So while demand was increasing, supply was limited. Thus, rabbis with the requisite skills were able to command middle- to upper-middle-class salaries. One may also surmise that the higher wages given to the most well-known rabbis — Wise, Raphall, Morais, and others — brought up the wage scale for those who were at smaller synagogues, because these figures "set the bar," as it were, for what rabbinic pay should be. Of course not every rabbi or hazan was compensated lavishly, but most of them would have been firmly ensconced in the middle class. Perhaps it was not enough for Leeser's dream of an independent and high-souled ministry, but it was surely more than paltry support.

Capital Campaigns

Just as the sale and/or rental of seats was the primary revenue source for congregations, so too did the selling of seats often form the core of the nineteenth-century capital campaign. When KKBI set out to build their first building, revenue came from a variety of sources. Joseph Jonas, an early member of the congregation, reported that "fifty-two gentlemen of the Christian faith, our fellow-citizens, gave us towards the building *twenty-five dollars each* [italics mine]."[133] This represents no small donation, as $25 in 1835 equates to roughly $556 in today's money. The congregation was clearly seen as an accepted and even welcome part of the community as non-Jewish neighbors put forth a total of $1,300 [$28,925] toward the construction of a new synagogue. The synagogue received donations from Jews in New York, Philadelphia, and Baltimore totaling roughly $850 [$19,215], and received five large brass chandeliers from Congregation Shearith Israel that had been used in their first building but were no longer being utilized.[134] The synagogue also took out small loans from local banks, but it was the selling of seats for the new synagogue that provided the largest revenue source. The synagogue sold seats in the future building amounting to $4,500 [$100,125], which "enabled us to finish the interior of the building in a much superior style than we originally intended."[135] The raising of over $100,000 in today's money suggests the efficacy of selling seats as a revenue source.

In 1841 the synagogue needed to increase the seating capacity of the congregation. The westward migration was pushing larger number of Jews into the area. The congregation increased the size of the building so that it could accommodate 250 men in the men's section and 100 women in the women's gallery (separate seating still being the norm). The congregation paid for the enlargement through the selling of seats, and "when completed, a number of the seats were sold for a sum much more considerable than the expense of the alterations."[136]

Just as some congregations required people to buy a seat in order to be considered a member, so some congregations used this requirement to ensure they would receive the necessary money for the new building. Temple Adath Israel in Louisville, Kentucky, for example, built its first building in the late 1840s by auctioning off seats, with each member of the shul being required to purchase ahead of time at least one $50 [$1,349] seat.[137]

When Mikveh Israel opened its second building in 1825 at a cost of $12,875 [$261,129], the capital campaign consisted primarily of the advance selling of seats. The congregation did raise $1,000 [$20,606] from five wealthy donors, including a $300 [$6,182] donation from Judah Touro, in an early example of what today might be termed a major gifts campaign.[138] But it raised roughly $7,500 [$154,548], representing 58 percent of the total cost of the building, through advance seat sales.[139] As they had done some forty years earlier, the congregation again turned to the public lottery to raise the additional moneys needed to pay off the building. Despite the general winding down of the use of lotteries in Pennsylvania, the congregation was able to get a legislative permit to conduct one, perhaps through the political influence of one of their members. The congregation had grown more sophisticated, though, and did not run the lottery on their own. They sold the permit to a professional lottery operator, who ran the lottery on behalf of the congregation.[140]

When the synagogue built its third building before the Civil War, they were again going to rely on advance seat sales to provide cash, but an unspecified issue arose that required a more expedient method of raising capital, so they secured a large mortgage to pay for the new building. Taking out a mortgage to cover the cost of a new building was not an unusual step for wealthy synagogues. Nonetheless, congregations were typically averse to carrying loans without a specific plan for repaying them. It is unusual to see significant debt on a nineteenth-century synagogue balance sheet. The board thus sent out a letter to the congregation assuring the membership that the synagogue would run with "strict economy and good management."

The same letter explained to members that the seat prices in the new synagogue would be significantly more than in the old synagogue to cover the mortgage payments. When a synagogue was constructing a new building to replace an old one, members who owned seats in the old synagogue would not need to pay the entire purchase price for a new seat. Usually seat prices were higher in the new synagogue, and so they would pay the difference between the seat they wished to purchase in the new synagogue and the assessed value of the old seat. The unexpected costs of the new synagogue, said the board, came about because it was "anxious to build the new Synagogue in a style of unsurpassed beauty and convenience, and that this has been carried out, is apparent to all who have seen it."[141]

Not every synagogue relied on selling seats to finance a new building. In 1851, at Keneseth Shalom in Syracuse, New York, each member of the synagogue paid $23 [$635] to buy land for the new synagogue at a total cost of $1,400 [$38,637]. The synagogue itself would cost $10,000 [$280,397] to build, financed primarily out of $10 [$280] bonds that members of the congregation purchased. The synagogue had acquired a building just five years earlier, but had seen such rapid growth that a new building was needed. Leeser was present at the dedication ceremony for the new synagogue and extolled the financial grit of the community:

> It must be taken into consideration that the far larger portion of the members, who now number eighty-six, mostly married men, are persons of very limited means; and but few among them, perhaps not above ten, can be styled comparatively rich. Still did this fact not deter them from devoting their money and their time — this capital of the poor — to the service of their God, and they resolved, as with one voice, in the spirit of *concord* and brotherly fellowship, to erect a more permanent and a much more spacious building than had hitherto served them.[142]

After a description of all the pomp and circumstance of the opening of the new building, Leeser finished his account by noting that the congregation gathered for Sabbath services the next day, where they raised $400 through public offerings and blessings. Because of all the public offerings, services did not end until past 2:00 p.m. Leeser, who, as noted previously, reviled public offerings, agreed that on this particular occasion the public raising of money was well worth the time and interruption.

Syracuse was not the only synagogue to issue bonds to raise capital for a new building. In 1852, KKBI sold $25 bonds at 6 percent annual interest. The bonds were clear that the repayment would be paid "from surplus funds on hand after all debts and encumbrances of the erection of said building are liquidated and fully paid."[143] By specifying that the bonds would be paid off only out of surplus funds, the congregation was of course protecting itself from potential financial peril.

At Keneseth Israel in Elkins Park, Pennsylvania, the congregation had taken out a $12,000 [$336,475] mortgage in 1853 to finance their new building and found itself in significant trouble in repaying the loan. They owed $1,800 [$50,471] as a second payment installment and had seemingly none of it. The plan had been for the synagogue to divide up the seats in the new congregation into separate categories — $100 [$2,804], $75 [$2,102], and $40 [$1,122] — and repay the mortgage through these sales. But something went amiss, because they held three separate special meetings to hash out new plans. They ultimately decided to take the $12,000 and divide it into "shares" and offer it to the congregation. Each shareholder would then be responsible for paying $65 [$1,823] in installments, and those who did not make good on the latter installment payments would lose their "investment." It is not clear from the board minutes how much, if any, interest was to be paid on these shares. Ultimately, the shares were sold and, although they had trouble collecting the money — they threatened to fine every member of the congregation who did not come to a special meeting to work out the plan — they did eventually manage to raise the $1,800 and straighten out their finances.[144]

Using the language of "shareholders" and "investments" with regard to paying off the mortgage not only reflects the penetration of market ideas and language into the realm of the synagogue but also says something regarding the wealth of the board. Presumably the board utilized these terms because they were shareholders and investors themselves in various enterprises and were accustomed to using this language.[145] The increasing wealth of Jews at this time was reflected in the financial language and financial instruments that the congregation was using. It is also the case that between the sale of seats, the issuing of bonds, and the discussion of the rabbi's contracts, synagogues were quite comfortable in thinking of the operation of the synagogue in business terms.

Another funding source for capital campaigns was asking other synagogues for donations. This was a primary mode of fund-raising in the eighteenth century and remained prevalent in the nineteenth. Whereas synagogues may have been businesslike when raising money from their own members, when they asked other synagogues for money they practically gushed theology. To just give a few examples among many, Congregation Mogen David in Nashville in 1860 sent a note to congregations across America asking for help in "fulfilling the high and important duty which we owe the Almighty of building a House of Worship."[146] Beth Elohim in Charleston in 1838 sent a circular to congregations after the synagogue had burned down in a terrible fire. Referring to the conflagration as a "calamitous visitation of Heaven, . . . We but invoke your aid, in raising from its ruins, a pure and consecrated altar, before which your own posterity, may yet bend in grateful devotion."[147]

In a related practice, some congregations reached out not just to other synagogues but also to their non-Jewish neighbors. Tifereth Israel Congregation in Cleveland published a letter seeking money to help complete the building of their synagogue. The letter is testimony to a radically inclusive religious vision:

> We have the intention to erect here in Cleveland, a house to God, not with the narrow feeling [of] professional distinctions, but for the advancement of the purest morality. . . . We beseech, therefore, all of those to whom God has dispensed prosperity and blessings, to apply a part of these for the furtherance of our pious cause. . . . We therefore beseech you, generous and honorable fellow-citizens, to grant us your aid that we may complete the most lofty and noble of all human works! A House of Worship to the Author of all our blessings, the common Father of Mankind.[148]

Tifereth Israel would become a leading Reform congregation, and one can certainly see here a strong theological vision of a universal Judaism that would become characteristic of Classical Reform. Part of the impetus for Tifereth Israel's building was a bequest from Judah Touro. Touro, both in life and through his will, helped finance more synagogue buildings than probably any other American Jew.

The story of Touro's philanthropy — his buying and supporting a church, his "return" to Judaism, the financial magnitude of his will — has been well recounted by historians.[149] In his lifetime, an entire congregation, Nefutzot Yehudah (The Dispersed of Judah), was created seemingly to allow Touro to fund a Jewish community. In one of the more unusual acquisitions of a synagogue, Touro gave land he owned to a church for them to build a new building, while he gave Nefutzot Yehudah the church building to retrofit as a synagogue. Touro was also involved in the capital campaign for New Orleans's oldest congregation. Shangarai-Chasset built a new building in 1851, with 100 members of the congregation buying bonds of $50 with an interest rate of 6 percent. Touro also gave the congregation $5,000 [$140,198] and loaned the congregation an additional $6,528 [$183,403].

Touro's will was perhaps the most impressive act of Jewish philanthropy in the nineteenth century. Touro left $387,000 [$9,889,298] to Jewish causes. Hospitals, alms houses, caring for the Jews in Palestine, benevolent societies, Hebrew schools, and many synagogues all benefited from his will. Touro gave to synagogues throughout the country. Besides the two congregations in New Orleans, he gave $5,000 [$127,769] to the Hebrew Congregation of Hartford and the Hebrew Congregation of New Haven, both of which used the bequest to build their first synagogues. Touro also gave $10,000 [$255,538] to the Newport synagogue and between $3,000 and $5,000 to congregations in Boston, Richmond, Baltimore, Memphis, Savannah, Charleston, Louisville, Cleveland, St. Louis, Buffalo, and Mobile, Alabama.[150]

Even in a small survey of capital campaigns it is important to note the variety of ways that synagogues in the nineteenth century tried to raise money to construct buildings. They sold seats, took mortgages, issued bonds, sought "leadership gifts," held lotteries, asked other congregations, asked non-Jewish neighbors, and simply requested members to give more. The variety of approaches reflects the lack of established methods. So many new synagogues were being built in this period — often the first synagogue of a city — that there was no standard manual on how to raise money for a building. Later periods would see less variation in capital campaigns, but in this early era all methods to raise capital were on the table.

Synagogue Finances During the Civil War

An extraordinary correspondence between the two synagogues of Richmond is found in the records of Congregation Beth Shalome. On October 21, 1863, amid the ravages of the Civil War, the congregation held a special meeting to debate the proposal put forward by Congregation Beth Ahaba: "That all Israelites of this City hold a mass meeting to take in consideration the condition of the poor, and to find means for alleviating their suffering. Also, to consider such other matters as may be brought before the meeting to indicate our character as Jews and good Citizens which have been repeatedly and grossly assailed in public prints."[151]

Beth Shalome's response offers a fascinating insight into southern Jewry at this heightened moment in history:

Resolved I: That as citizens of Richmond we will join cheerfully in any endeavor to ameliorate the condition of the poor of the city, but think it unadvisable to take any distinct action as a religious body, unless an appeal is made to Congregations of all denominations.

Resolved II: That whenever such appeal is made on behalf of the poor, this Congregation will co-operate cheerfully with the other Jewish Congregations of Richmond, in raising contributions from the Israelites of this city for the purpose of carrying out such charitable designs.

Resolved III: That while this meeting denounces the unfounded aspersions made against the Israelites of this City, and feel satisfied that this acts of our co-religionists can well bear the test of comparison with those of any other denomination in this community for Patriotism, Charity or freedom from selfishness; yet think the best and most dignified course to be adopted will be to treat them with silent contempt, confident that the unenlightened and unprejudiced do not join in this unjust crusade against our people.[152]

As this exchange indicates, the Civil War saw a heightened period of antisemitism in the South, particularly as economic conditions worsened. Jews were depicted as Shylocks, profiting from the economic turmoil.[153] The *Richmond Examiner* in 1863 wrote that Jews "flocked as vultures to every point of gain."[154] *Southern Punch* was a weekly humor magazine published in Richmond at the time. It editorialized: "The dirty greasy Jew who might be seen with a pack on his back, a year or two since, bowing and cringing even to negro servants, now struts by with the air of a millionaire.... [Jews] bought up everything that was to be sold and at once ran up the prices upon every necessary article from 500 to 3000 percent on the consumer."[155] It is within this context that these synagogues exchanged plans about their responsibilities for helping the poor of Richmond.

The argument between the synagogues regarding the public nature of Jews raising money specifically as Jews was happening simultaneously in the North. On January 8, 1864, the Ladies Hospital Association in Rochester, New York, asked the women of Congregation Brith Kodesh to take part in a benefit bazaar. The president of the sisterhood objected, saying, "The only national character in which they wish to appear would be under the Star Spangled Banner, the glorious flag of the Union — the banner of civil and religious liberty." The president did enclose a check, though, for $400 in the name of the Jewish women of Rochester, presumably to allay any concerns that the Jews were not patriotic. Bertram Korn noted this issue repeated itself yet again in New York City with regard to raising money at a Sanitary Fair.[156]

At Congregation Beth Shalome, the issue was resolved in a similar manner to the Rochester case. Although the congregation decided not to raise money as a specifically Jewish cause, two months later the congregation donated $2,003 [$37,976] on behalf of sick and wounded soldiers, and a notice that the congregation had done this was published in the city paper, "and has doubtless been seen by most."[157] The congregation no doubt felt itself caught in a bind between wanting to ignore the issue for fear it would segregate Jews but also wanting to prove Jewish patriotism, and so the muddled solution of raising the money and having it noted in a newspaper.

The financial picture of Beth Shalome was surprisingly rosy during the Civil War. The total congregational budget was roughly double what it had been seven years earlier.[158] The commitment of the congregation to the southern cause was clearly seen in their finances. In 1863, the congregation invested $1,800 [$34,126] in Confederate bonds at 8 percent yield, $300 [$5,689] in Confederate notes, and $600 [$11,375] in Virginia state stock. The congregation also listed an investment of $5,000 [$94,797] in South Side Rail Road Stock.[159] But in looking at synagogue records from the period, what is just as noteworthy as the unusual nature of these synagogue investments is the many usual and quotidian aspects to the minutes. At such a heightened moment in American history, one might have expected the synagogue to concern itself only with matters of sick soldiers and the war, and the congregation did devote itself certainly to these causes, but it is also true that even in Richmond in 1863, regular congregational life proceeded.

On September 6, 1863, the congregational balance sheet showed that it paid out $3,109.04 [$58,945] in expenses that year and took in $4,215.49 [$79,923], leaving a healthy balance of $1,106.45 [$20,977]. It expected to receive additional money from its investments. The board minutes noted, "[The congregation] will make an actual excess of receipts over expenditures of $2,906 [$55,096], a result which cannot be otherwise than gratifying to the congregation."[160] These same board minutes discussed the rabbi's salary, a bequest from a will, committee reports — all the things congregations typically discuss. Congregations carried on and continued to finance themselves as best they could.

In much of the North, though, congregations did more than simply carry on. Reading congregational budgets from the North during the Civil War, with a few exceptions, one might not even realize a war was taking place. In fact, many congregations in the North prospered during this time.

At Keneseth Israel in Philadelphia in December 1863, with the war very much still raging and just a few weeks after the Gettysburg Address, the congregation voted to establish a new synagogue with a cost of $60,000 [$1,119,647], five times the amount spent on the building just ten years earlier.[161] First-class seats in the new synagogue would cost $250 [$4,665]. Part of the capital campaign would be a ball at the Academy of Music — the congregation expected 500 people to pay $5 [$95] a ticket. Balls were not unusual at that time, even during the war. Purim balls in particular were popular in congregations, so no one seemingly raised any issue with the propriety of holding an opulent ball during wartime. The building campaign reflected the sensibility that regular life was going to continue. The congregation was, of course, not immune to the war effort. In July of 1863, it created a fund to aid needy and wounded soldiers, but the board minutes did not reflect how much was raised.

In the beginning of 1865, with the war winding down, KKBI began a capital campaign for a building that would eventually be completed in 1869. Seat prices in Cincinnati at the new synagogue were roughly fifteen times more expensive than they had been in the 1840s. The congregation valued sixteen first-class seats at $1,800 [$31,050] each; thirty-four second-class seats at $1,400 [$21,348] each; forty third-class seats at $1,000 [$15,249] each; thirty-two fourth-class seats at $600 [$9,149] each; and fifty-six fifth-class at $400 [$6,100] each. This represented a total of $158,000 [$2,725,512] in potential revenue for the congregation.[162] The congregation also aggressively courted donations for the building. One hundred and twenty-two members gave an average donation of $256 [$3,903] for a total of $37,415 [$570,536]. Between donations and seat sales, the congregation raised $160,284.88 [$2,444,160] toward the new building.[163]

KKBI's building was a response to the synagogue being built by its competitor, B'nai Yeshurun. B'nai Yeshurun raised funds during the Civil War for what would become known as the Plum Street Temple, which opened in 1866 and cost the congregation an astounding $250,000 [$6,390,557].[164]

Historian Allan Tarshish, in an article on Jewish economic life during

the Civil War, explains the general economic trends that allowed for the expansion of Jewish wealth — and thus synagogue budgets — in this period:

> When the country was expanding slowly, between 1840 and 1860, Jewish
> economic development was gradual. With the outbreak of the Civil War
> in 1861, the whole country suffered a temporary depression due to the
> sudden loss of Southern accounts, the cancellation of many Southern
> debts, and the uncertainty of events. . . . The depression was, however, of
> short duration, lasting only about a year, and ended when the government
> began to place orders for various goods. Then Civil War business boomed,
> especially in the North, and many Jews prospered with the rest of the
> business community.[165]

Cincinnati Jewry in particular was well positioned economically, as the
clothing industry would see tremendous opportunities and growth during
the Civil War and sixty-five of the city's seventy clothing wholesale retail
businesses were owned by Jews. Henry Mack was perhaps the most successful of these owners. Mack's journey from peddler to store owner to
manufacturer of ready-to-wear clothes was typical of the Jewish route to
commercial prosperity. Mack's company was awarded the state's contract
to produce army clothing. His business, which was prospering before the
war and valued at $100,000 [$2,597,171] in 1860, was valued at the end of the
war at $500,000 [$7,644,424]. Mack, like so many other successful Jewish
businessmen, was also dedicated to his synagogue. He led the building drive
for the Plum Street Temple.[166]

These two Cincinnati congregations represented a new phase in synagogue history that began during the Civil War and came to fruition in the
Reconstruction era. As Jonathan Sarna notes in *American Judaism*, "The late
1860s and early 1870s were a period of confident optimism in American Jewish life . . . numerous congregations from New York to San Francisco built
massive new synagogues in the immediate post–Civil War era. The seating
capacity of America's synagogues more than doubled between 1860–1870
. . . and the total dollar value of the community's synagogues increased an
astonishing 354 percent."[167]

This substantial increase in synagogue budgets and the construction of
large new synagogues was a direct result of the greater prosperity of the
Jewish community. Reconstruction in the South provided its own economic

opportunities as the foundations of the southern economy were reconstituted after the war, and Jewish merchants filled these opportunities.[168]

But Jewish economic expansion is only half of this equation. Wealth was created in the Jewish community, but that did not mean it necessarily was going to be put into synagogues. With the creation of Benevolent Societies, Jewish hospitals, and B'nai B'rith lodges, there was within the Jewish community a new competition for philanthropic dollars. The synagogue nevertheless remained at the communal center. The vast expansion of synagogues during this era testifies to the continuing endurance of the institution in a rapidly changing America.

THREE

Mushroom Synagogues, Free Synagogues, and the Hazan Craze [1865–1919]

In 1887, Moses Weinberger, a critic of Jewish religious life in America, noted that the most prominent New York City Orthodox synagogues were leading the Jewish people backward. These synagogues were full of "wealthy, God-fearing Jews who everywhere proudly profess their devotion to Orthodox Judaism." But instead of building houses of Torah study, rabbinical seminaries, or schools, the synagogues chose to build lavish congregations, "reaching up even into the heavens." Weinberger claimed that the annual expenses of the three major synagogues of the Lower East Side together had a combined budget of $50,000 [$1,227,042]. He wrote, "Fifty thousand dollars! All from three congregations that all together don't have more than 300 members. And don't forget . . . that no . . . student, teacher, widow or orphan has yet benefited from this sum; indeed the sum is lost to charity."[1]

The late nineteenth-century period is marked by two countervailing trends in synagogue financial history. On the one hand, synagogue finances continued to function as they had in the previous era. Many synagogues' budgets continued to grow and expand as Jews gained wealth and numerical strength. Selling seats remained the primary way to raise money, and well-to-do businessmen anchored and expanded synagogue budgets. But this same period is also marked by new questions precisely around the growing wealth of synagogues and the way they spent their money. Moses Weinberger was not alone in his critique of synagogue finances. His skepticism was echoed by many, including Rabbi Clifton Levy, one of the first rabbis ordained by Hebrew Union College, who lamented that "the synagogues are built for the rich," and only the wealthy have a say in how they are run.[2]

These concerns about the price of religion would lead to some fascinating challenges to the prevailing synagogue structure, including free synagogues (no paying for seats and no dues); mushroom synagogues (for-profit High Holiday synagogues), *landsmanshaftn* synagogues (small community synagogues with Eastern European roots), and institutional synagogues (large synagogues that expanded the notion of what synagogues should offer). All of these models represented alternatives to the established synagogue financial systems. Continuity and experimentation thus defined this era of synagogue finance.

The tension around synagogue budgets was also reflected in clerical pay. The 1880s saw a unique moment in synagogue financial history called "the hazan craze." For a brief period, synagogues began competing with each other for the services of the most well known hazanim. Salaries for some of these hazanim reached extraordinary levels that were essentially untethered to the economic realities of the synagogues that were hiring them. Although synagogues and economic bubbles are generally not thought of together, the best explanation for the hazan craze, as we will explore, is to understand it precisely as an economic bubble that roiled the Lower East Side.

This period also saw a crucial stage in the evolution of rabbinic salaries. As synagogues and synagogue budgets grew, rabbinic salaries grew. But not all rabbinic salaries. Reform congregations, typically made up of more well-to-do German Jews who had established themselves in America, paid significantly larger salaries than most Orthodox congregations, which were typically filled with newer and poorer immigrants from Eastern Europe. Part of this was straightforward supply and demand. There was a limited supply of Reform rabbis, as Reform congregations wanted to hire graduates of the newly established Hebrew Union College, so these rabbis could command higher salaries. For Orthodox rabbis, it was the opposite case. There were many recently immigrated Orthodox rabbis who could serve traditional communities, which meant excess supply and lower salaries. Ultimately, the creation of rabbinic seminaries and rabbinic bodies in all of the denominations created a check on rabbinic supply and set a professional standard, which would allow rabbinic salaries to rise throughout the twentieth century.

Clerical Salaries

Moses Weinberger had one other significant critique of synagogues besides their building large new edifices: their "lust" for great hazanim. Weinberger wrote: "Let me faithfully describe for you, dear reader, the enormous commotion surrounding the hazan question during these past two years. It has brought tumult to every Jewish home, turned sons against fathers, brides against grooms, men against brothers. There is fighting over the hazan question all day long."[3]

In the mid 1880s, the Orthodox synagogues of New York City had a "hazan craze." Huge salaries were paid to bring well-known hazanim from Eastern Europe to America. Synagogues battled with each other to bring the best ones, and members within synagogues battled with each other as to whether hazanim were really worth the money.

In the post–Civil War period, there were few hazanim from Eastern Europe working in America, and with rare exceptions, those who were in America were making a marginal living in small communities scattered around the country. But in the late 1870s, the desire for more aesthetically pleasing music pushed some congregations to begin to spend more on their hazan, as well as their choirs. In 1879, Simcha Samuelson was given $700 [$17,525] by one of New York City's Orthodox congregations. This figure was raised to $800 [$20,760] in 1884, and finally $1,000 [$25,950] in 1885. The salary of $1,000 for a hazan was nothing less than a sensation. A retrospective on the hazan craze that appeared in the Hebrew American newspaper *Ha-doar*, noted, "Hazanim from all over Russia and Poland heard the news about the hazan in New York being paid $1,000, and began to come to America. Each one of them left their home filled with the hope that they would gather handfuls of gold and become rich."[4] In 1885–1886, hazanim came to New York and began publicizing themselves with names like "the king of cantors" or "the lion's roar." Synagogues began to compete and "steal" each other's cantors.

Some of the major congregations then took the competition for great hazanim to another level by specifically importing well-known cantors from Eastern Europe as opposed to just hiring one of the newly arrived hazanim. There are differing accounts of which synagogue was the first to utilize this practice. According to a *Yizkor* book of the Jews of Suvalk, the first synagogue to bring over a famous cantor from Eastern Europe was Mishkan Israel Ansche Suvalk.[5] Ansche Suvalk was founded in 1870 by immigrants from Suvalk. According to the *Yizkor* book, the number of immigrants from Suvalk increased substantially as a result of pogroms in Warsaw in 1881, when twelve Jews were killed. With the influx of new immigrants, Ansche Suvalk set out to build a new synagogue to accommodate all the worshippers. The synagogue went into debt to cover the cost of the new building. To raise revenue, the synagogue brought the well-known hazan from Suvalk, Chaim Vinshell, to America, at a cost of $1,000 [$25,950] per year. *Ha-doar* wrote, "The first time he prayed at the synagogue, the streets around the shul were filled with crowds of people pushing to get inside."[6] The synagogue sold High Holiday tickets and the increased attendance allowed them to pay off their debts.

The success of Vinshell made other synagogues envious and fearful that people would leave to join Ansche Suvalk. The Kalvarie Synagogue (also known as the Pike Street Shul) responded by bringing its own famous cantor, Israel Kuper from Vilna, at a salary of $2,000 [$51,899] while also paying $1,000 [$29,950] to a choir.[7]

But according to an 1886 news report in the *Jewish Messenger* on the hiring of Israel Kuper, it was the Kalvarie Synagogue that had "paved the way for high-salaried hazanim," and was the first synagogue to import a famous cantor. The Reform-leaning *Messenger* approvingly wrote of the Kalvarie being the first Eastern European Orthodox synagogue to build a handsome edifice, engage learned rabbis, and "they even seem to have an ear for singing, and are willing to pay for it."[8] Regardless of which synagogue and which hazan was first, the "craze" was on, and other large Orthodox shuls followed suit.

Beit Midrash Hagadol hired Israel Michalovsky, initially for $2,000 [$51,899], but quickly raised it to $2500 [$64,874] — nearly ten times what the rabbi of the synagogue made.[9] Khal Adas Jeshurun (the Eldridge Street Synagogue) made the biggest splash by hiring Pinchos Minkowsky of Odessa for the enormous sum of $5,000 [$129,747], plus $1,000 [$25,949] to release him from his contract in Odessa, plus $300 [$7,785] as a moving expense.[10] Minkowsky arrived just before Rosh Hashanah of 1887 to great acclaim with the promise that his prayers would bring peace and comfort to all who heard them and healing to the sick. He was proclaimed "the first hazan of New York."[11] The congregation sold $950 [$24,652] worth of High Holiday tickets on the first day after his arrival.[12]

To put these contracts for hazanim in perspective, the average annual wage for a male unskilled worker in the clothing business in 1890 in New York City was $635 [$16,478], and $740 [$19,202] for a skilled worker in the clothing business.[13] The highest paid hazanim were thus making five to seven times what a typical salary for a Jewish worker was. Another point of comparison is to view these salaries in relation to the synagogue budget. The monthly expenditures for Beit Midrash Hagadol in 1884 averaged around $400 [$10,380], for a total yearly budget of roughly $5,000 [$129,748].[14] Israel Michalovsky's salary alone increased the annual budget by 50 percent.

A few rationales have been put forward to explain the hazan craze. Abraham Karp, in his study of the synagogue minutes of Congregation Beth Israel in Rochester, New York, noted the centrality of hazanim to synagogues at this time. The hazan was the central clergyperson; he led all services and interacted regularly with members, while the rabbi's primary function was to provide legal decisions on questions of practice. Significantly, the congregation believed that the rabbi was a public figure whose duties went beyond one particular congregation, and thus his salary should be paid collectively by all the congregations in the city. As the president of Beth Israel said, "A rabbi is not a minister. He does not belong to one congregation, but to the city."[15] Unfortunately for the rabbi of Beth Israel, the other congregations did not share this vision. In the 1880s, the hazan at Beth Israel was consistently paid between $400 [$9,848] and $600 [$14,772] while the rabbi was paid between $100 [$2,462] and $200 [$4,924].[16]

Mark Slobin, in his history of the cantorate, suggests that the hazan craze reflected the desire for a "comforting transitional figure" as immigrant communities oriented themselves to America. Beautifully singing hazanim from Eastern Europe would allow communities to be connected to their old homes through the power of music, while at the same time they could feel ethnic pride in their hazan's vocal talents, believing their hazan was as talented as any American singer.[17] Kimmy Caplan, in his extensive study of rabbinic salaries in this period, argues, however, that the hazan craze should not be seen as an immigrant phenomenon. Caplan argues that the importance and higher pay of hazanim compared to rabbis was not new but was already part of Eastern European Jewish life, which immigrants brought to America. "It seems as though in many *mitnagdic* East European communities [hazanim] earned more than rabbis. . . . Therefore, the desire by American Orthodox immigrant congregations . . . to employ good cantors, often described as a craving, should be seen as a continuum rather than an independent immigrant phenomenon."[18]

These explanations provide a piece of the story, but a significant rationale for explaining the hazan craze may be found by viewing the craze through an economic lens. The hazan craze follows the classic pattern of economic bubbles — historical moments when prices seem to explode beyond economic rationality. Charles Kindleberger, in his seminal work on economic bubbles, *Maniacs, Panics, and Crashes: A History of Financial Crises*, claims that bubbles do not occur in isolation. A bubble for one particular good is typically accompanied or preceded by speculative booms in other areas of the economy. Dutch tulip mania in the 1630s is often cited as the paradigmatic historical bubble. Kindleberger notes that the Dutch economy was booming when tulip mania broke out, and the mania for tulips may have even been eclipsed by the Dutch "fever" to build canals and clock towers, and their speculation in shares of the Dutch East India Company. Kindleberger describes the tulip bubble in terms of an economic contagion, which moved from one realm of the economy to another. Most typically for historical bubbles, real estate speculation and building booms directly precede other kinds of speculative bubbles.[19] The hazan craze may be a small reflection of this general pattern. The craze in hazanim was preceded by a large synagogue building boom.

As already noted, Ansche Suvalk, the congregation that started the hazan craze, brought over a famous cantor as a response to having taken out a large debt to pay for its new building. The Eldridge Street Synagogue opened its grand new synagogue just before the High Holidays of 1887, coinciding precisely with their hiring of an acclaimed new hazan. Beit Midrash Hagadol purchased their large new sanctuary, originally built as a church, in 1885. They paid $45,000 [$1,167,727] for the building, taking out a $30,000 [$778,485] loan to cover their costs.[20] They would soon after join the hazan craze and bring Israel Michalovsky to their shul. The Pike Street Synagogue, also one of the first to bring over a hazan, had renovated their shul just a few years earlier. All of these synagogues were responding to the massive influx of immigrants, but it was precisely this building "craze" to establish large new edifices that led to the hazan craze. The debt taken out to build and/ or renovate laid the groundwork for further risk and speculation. Paying hazanim unsustainably exorbitant salaries was a result.

The hazan craze ultimately lasted only a few years. By 1891, Pinchos Minkowsky's $500 [$12,975] annual bonus was eliminated. The congregation could no longer afford the bonus because its "treasury was in arrears."[21] Minkowsky decided to go back to Odessa, where he spent the rest of his cantorial career. The Eldridge Street shul decided to hire a cantor just for the High Holidays for $500, with the cantor needing to pay his own choir. For the rest of the year, the congregation hired short-term hazanim at $30 per month. The congregation thus effectively cut their cantorial budget by 500 percent. It seems that the public's appetite to hear famous hazanim weakened, and synagogue attendees were satisfied with one of the many hazanim with skill and talent who had come to New York after hearing of the exorbitant salaries being paid. "The expense of star cantors proved something immigrant congregations found hard to sustain," writes Jeffrey Shandler in "Sanctification of the Brand Name." "What had been a seller's market quickly became a buyer's market. Rather than seeking out major cantorial talents in Europe, immigrant congregations could take their pick of newly arrived talent."[22]

For at least one famous hazan there were still great financial rewards for coming to America well into the twentieth century. Joseph Rosenblatt, regarded as the greatest hazan of his time, was paid $10,000 [$250,300] in 1911 by the Hungarian congregation Ohab Zedek in Harlem, and was not even obliged to be at the congregation every Shabbat.[23] His contract was more than paid for by the desire of people to hear him sing. Bernard Drachman, who served as one of the rabbis of the congregation during Rosenblatt's tenure, wrote in his memoir: "The congregation fairly idolized him. Whenever he officiated, the synagogue was filled to the doors, and on the High Holidays not a seat remained unsold. The income of the congregation from this one source, which was mainly attributable to the popularity of the hazan, was very large, indeed, approximately twenty-five thousand dollars a year."[24]

While Rosenblatt's salary was an outlier, the salaries of hazanim in Orthodox congregations were typically higher than those of the rabbi even after the hazan craze ended. This pattern would last until the 1930s. Caplan contends that one factor for the higher pay of cantors at the turn of the century was the severe personalities of many Orthodox rabbis, who continually chastised their congregations and thus were paid less because they were quite simply disliked.[25] Presumably, not all Orthodox rabbis were chastisers, but perhaps the general reputation of dour rabbinic personalities depressed rabbinic wages relative to those of cantors.

A typical Orthodox rabbi in the late 1800s made between $6 and $10 per week, or $300 [$7,785] to $500 [$12,975] a year.[26] Yehuda Lazarov, a rabbi who immigrated to America in the 1890s, published a collection of Yiddish sermons where he wrote of the difficulties for congregational American rabbis: "When I came to America . . . I saw the situation of the Rabbis of shuls, that a Rabbi earned between $8 and $10 a week, and the life of the rabbi was constantly up in the air, dependent upon the will of a majority of members voting for him . . . and he sadly lives under the thumb of the President and even under each member, and he cannot say what he wants to say."[27]

Rabbis at the large Eastern European shuls earned $8 [$208] a week in the late 1880s. Rabbi Abraham Ash at Beth Hamedrash Hagodol, for example, was paid $400 [$10,380] in 1887, as was Rabbi Isaac Margolis of the Pike Street Synagogue.[28] But rabbis at many of the small immigrant synagogues that dotted the Lower East Side in New York as well as other cities might earn less than $200 [$5,190]. Journalist Hutchins Hapgood found that, "[The rabbis] are mainly very poor, live in the barest of tenement houses and pursue a calling which no longer involves much honor or standing. . . . The congregations are for the most part small, poor and unimportant. Few can pay the rabbi more than $3 [$78] or $4 [$104] a week."[29] An 1892 report in an American Jewish newspaper, *Hapisgah*, reported that rabbinic salaries in Orthodox congregations were paid for by door-to-door begging: "Every Friday or Sunday two people go about the doorways of all the congregants with their kerchief in hand to beg small coin to small coin."[30]

Because of their relatively small salaries, Orthodox rabbis often made additional income from other sources. They made extra money giving eulogies,[31] serving as judges on a rabbinic court,[32] performing weddings,[33] or working as kosher food supervisors.[34] Incomes from these sources varied significantly, but some rabbis were able to match if not exceed their congregational salaries based on outside income.[35]

Not all Orthodox rabbis were relegated to earning money as a kosher supervisor. A few were able to make a significant income from congregations. A 1907 contract between Rabbi Joseph Levin and Congregation Ahavath Achim in Atlanta stipulated that he was to receive $1,200 [$30,026] annually. The contract then spelled out the duties Rabbi Levin should uphold as rabbi of the congregation: "The members of said congregation agree to obey the said Rabbi J. Levin in all things concerning the Hebrew or Jewish faith. . . . Rabbi Levin agrees . . . to answer and explain all questions concerning the Hebrew or Jewish religion in regard to purity, chastity and cleanliness, etc. . . . Rabbi Levin agrees to teach and study, every evening with the members of the said Congregation the Hebrew of Jews, Laws and ethics and all such studies as the said Rabbi shall deem necessary and advisable."[36] The contract also noted that Rabbi Levin had to give a sermon every Shabbat afternoon and Jewish holiday, and he had to oversee the kosher butcher to make sure he was acting in accord with the Jewish faith.

Rabbi Bernard Cohen, the leader of Congregation Beth El in Buffalo, was also paid relatively well. Rabbi Cohen's tenure was marked by frequent disputes over his liberalizing approach to ritual, including the confirmation of girls in 1881. Cohen was paid $1,100 [$27,538] annually beginning in 1879 but left his shul in 1882 when it refused his wishes to introduce mixed seating.[37] Mordecai Kaplan, later to become one of the most influential rabbis of the twentieth century, began his career at the Orthodox synagogue Kehilat Jeshurun in New York City at a salary of $1,500 [$38,921] in 1904.[38] Perhaps the most well-known rabbinic contract of the time was given to Rabbi Jacob Joseph, who was brought to New York City by a group of synagogues to serve as Chief Rabbi of the city. Although the position was an abject failure — after a few years the congregations could no longer afford him — he was initially contracted for six years at $2,500 [$64,874] a year plus an apartment valued at $1,350 [$35,032].[39] The large variation among Orthodox rabbinic salaries is explainable by straightforward factors like the size of the congregation and the socioeconomic status of its members — rabbis of small immigrant synagogues were paid less than rabbis at large urban established ones.

In viewing Orthodox rabbinic compensation as a whole, though, one striking feature is how significantly Orthodox rabbis' salaries lagged behind Reform rabbinic salaries. Orthodox rabbis themselves were well aware of this phenomenon. Rabbi Gedalya Silverstone, who served at Ohev Sholom in Washington, D.C., decried that Reform rabbis were paid ten times more than Orthodox rabbis. He sarcastically observed in a Hebrew sermon that Reform rabbis needed to be paid more because they led people in such a convoluted and torturous path, while Orthodox rabbis held to the simple straightforward path to God. Just like a taxi is paid more than it should be when it goes around and around to get to its destination, so Reform rabbis were unjustly paid more by taking people around and around instead of going on the "straight" path.[40]

Evidence of the substantially higher wages for Reform rabbis can be seen in an 1893 letter from Isaac Mayer Wise. In the letter, Wise responded to a request from Congregation Beth Emeth in Albany (his former synagogue) for help in hiring an assistant rabbi from Hebrew Union College. Wise wrote that five students were due to graduate that year from Hebrew Union College:

> Every one of them — although their talents are not alike — is fully prepared to fill the office of Rabbi; . . . as pulpit orator, minister and teacher of Sabbath school classes. Some of them can preach in English only, all of them are conversant with the German language, as well as with the Hebrew, Latin, Greek and kindred languages. Three of them are Americans and two foreigners, which however, is not perceptible in their English style and pronunciation. . . . The salary which is expected is something which I could not tell. I only know that those who went out from the college [last year] had the salary of $1,500 to $2,000 [$38,924 to $51,899] per annum.[41]

Brand-new Reform rabbis were thus earning more than all but a handful of Orthodox rabbis.

The salaries of Reform rabbis at large synagogues could range even higher. Rabbi Israel Aaron, a member of the first class of Hebrew Union College, was given a five-year contract of $3,000 [$77,849] annually at Temple Beth Zion in Buffalo in 1887.[42] The previous year Alexander Kohut had signed a ten-year contract with an annual salary of $6,000 [$155,697] from Congregation Ahavat Chesed in New York City.[43] Gustav Gottheil was paid the extraordinary sum of $10,000 [$259,495] in 1888 by Temple Emanu-El of New York, and his assistant rabbi was paid $5,000 [$129,748].[44] But this was not even the highest rabbinic salary of the period. That distinction goes to Emil G. Hirsch of Chicago Sinai Congregation, perhaps the most prominent congregational leader of his day, who was given a salary of $12,000 [$336,131]. Hirsch was offered even more — $14,000 [$392,153] — by Temple Emanu-El in New York City, which he initially accepted but subsequently backed out of after Sinai asked him to stay and gave him a fifteen-year contract.

Despite his stature and the financial largesse of the congregation, the financial dealings between the rabbi and the congregation were at times far from serene. The board minutes of Sinai reflect a dramatic showdown at the turn of the twentieth century over money and rabbinic authority. The tension seems to have begun with Hirsch's frequent absences from the Sinai pulpit as he was in demand as a speaker all over the country. There were other issues that certain members were unhappy about, including the belief that the rabbi was alienating the wealthiest members of the congregation.[45] At an annual meeting Hirsch was challenged over his absences, and the notes record his response: "Dr. Hirsch responded that he had a right to absent himself whenever he chose; that he was not to be regarded as an employee of the congregation . . . he said that he occupied a position in the Congregation, co-ordinate with the Executive Board and not subordinate."[46] The executive committee rejected this assertion categorically but tried to make peace with the rabbi by assenting to another absence so he could speak in New York City.

The issue, however, did not go away. At a board meeting later that same month, board members again raised the issue of Hirsch's absences as well as other matters. Hirsch again rejected their assertion of control over his schedule. He reiterated that he was not subordinate to the board, and he melodramatically stated:

I am not like a book-keeper and paid employe [sic]. I am a man who has a national reputation, and you continue to throw up to me that you are paying me $12,000 a year salary. I am tired of hearing about this matter of my salary. . . . I won't tolerate it! I am sorry I did not accept the call to New York, where they offered me $15,000, $3,000 more than you are paying me.[47] I am ready to resign now. I do not have to be a minister to your congregation. I can turn my hand to law, and within one or two years reading I can fit myself to be as good a lawyer as there is, but I should like to see any lawyer of this congregation prepare himself in two years and be able to keep my position.[48]

The board meeting rose to a fevered pitch as members who resented Hirsch brought other issues forward and the meeting culminated with Hirsch slamming his chair to the ground repeatedly and members telling him to stop disgracing himself and acting like a madman.

Hirsch's argument that he was not subsidiary to the board reflected a rising tension over the status and authority of the rabbi. The board ultimately backed down in their criticism of Hirsch and voted to increase the length of his contract rather than lose him to Temple Emanu-El. Hirsch used that offer of Temple Emanu-El to receive all the benefits he wanted, including his desire to be absent from the pulpit. Whereas in previous American eras, the parnas held premier authority in the congregation, the immigration era saw the increase of rabbinic power vis-à-vis the board.[49] Hirsch understood that he had the power to move to another congregation, and thus did not need to be under the thumb of the president or the board, and this fact changed the power relationships of the synagogue. While Hirsch was the most prestigious rabbi of the era, he was not alone in seeing his authority grow in this period. As we will see later in this chapter, Stephen S. Wise would also command a similar place of independence and authority. This power shift was particularly true at Reform synagogues, where rabbis were often commanding significant salaries.

Caplan suggests three factors for the large disparity of wages between Reform and Orthodox synagogues. First, Reform synagogues, particularly those in large cities, attracted German Jews, who were economically better off than the immigrant Eastern European worshippers who typically attended Orthodox synagogues. Second, Reform congregations did not have cantors, so they could spend more money on rabbis. Third, the creation of the Hebrew Union College led to a fixed supply of qualified rabbis who could serve Reform synagogues, while at the same time the influx of immigrant rabbis created an abundant supply for Orthodox congregations. As a simple matter of supply and demand, Reform rabbinical salaries would be higher.[50]

Another reason for the disparity between salaries was exemplified by Congregation B'nai Brith in Los Angeles. In 1883 the congregation was a traditional synagogue that could not draw a minyan even on Shabbat. According to *The American Israelite*, the synagogue had 136 members, but "minyan in the synagogue on Saturdays is out of the question. The President of the Congregation, J. W. Hellman, banker, visits the synagogue but once a year, Yom Kippur, and then only after banking hours."[51] *The American Israelite* noted that most members of the congregation did not give any money to the synagogue, and the rabbi, Abraham Edelman, earned $75 a month, $900 [$22,514] annually. The membership began to agitate for Reform as a way of renewing the congregation. A mixed choir was introduced, as well as family pews and confirmation. When the membership declared their intention to switch to a liberal prayer book, Rabbi Edelman could stand no more and resigned.

The congregation was energized by the changes, though, and transitioned from Orthodox to Reform.[52] Just two years after Rabbi Edelman was paid $850, the congregation advertised in *The American Israelite* for a rabbi who could preach in English and lead a Sunday school for a salary of $2,000 [$51,899] or an increase of almost 150 percent.[53] The salary difference between what the Reform congregation was offering versus what that same Orthodox synagogue had paid was a result of a renewed sense of institutional vigor. The socioeconomic demographics of the congregation had not changed in two years; rather, the membership was simply willing to give more of its resources. The late nineteenth century saw Reform Judaism in its ascendency, and some of the salary differences between Reform and Orthodox rabbis were a result of more robust congregations.

Reform rabbinical salaries compared well not only with their Orthodox counterparts but also with Protestant clergy. In 1893, the same year that Isaac Mayer Wise said newly graduated Hebrew Union College rabbis made between $1,500 and $2,000 a year, the average national Methodist ministerial salary was $894 [$23,199].[54] Reform rabbis were thus making roughly 75 to 120 percent more than their Methodist counterparts while Orthodox rabbis were on average making less than Methodist ministers.

The 1906 census of religious bodies provides more data to compare rabbinic and ministerial salaries.[55] The census data showed that 656 rabbis reported an average income of $1,222 [$31,708].[56] The census did not break down the denominational affiliation of the rabbis, but given the data presented above, one can presume a mix of Reform and Orthodox respondents.

The average salary for rabbis placed them at the high end of the clerical wage scale. Unitarian ministers had the highest average salary of $1,653 [$42,891], followed by Episcopal ministers, who averaged $1,242 [$32,223]. Rabbinic salaries outpaced salaries for Presbyterian and Congregationalist ministers, who earned on average $1,177 [$30,540] and $1,042 [$26,985], respectively. Rabbinic salaries were far ahead of ministers from Methodist, Baptist, and many other smaller Christian denominations. The average salary for all ministers was $663 [$17,203].[57]

The census bureau's report noted that there existed a significant wage disparity not just between denominations but also between locations. Across all denominations, the average salary for a minister in the major cities of over 300,000 people was more than double the average salary for a minister outside of a city. Rabbinic salaries followed this same pattern. In cities of over 300,000, rabbinic salaries averaged $1,491 [$38,688]; salaries in cities between 100,000 and 300,000 averaged $1,201 [$31,163]; in cities between 50,000 and 100,000 rabbis averaged $1,191 [$30,904]; in cities between 25,000 and 50,000 rabbis averaged $1,172 [30,385]; and the average salary for rabbis outside of cities was $841 [$21,822].[58] There was one large geographic difference between ministers and rabbis. The census reported that 149 of the 656, or just 22.7 percent, of all rabbis responding were from outside of a city. This figure compares to the Presbyterian church, which had 78.7 percent of the respondents from outside of cities. The geographic disparity explains in some part the relatively high average salaries of rabbis compared to Protestant ministers. Because Jews settled in urban areas in a much higher proportion than Protestants did, rabbis were more likely to have higher average salaries.

Another point of evaluation is to see rabbinic salaries in comparison to other occupations. As in previous eras, rabbinic salaries ranged well ahead of manufacturing and farming jobs. In 1906, the average worker in the manufacturing industry earned $506 [$13,129], while the average farmworker made just $315 [$8,173], and the average clerical worker made $1,074 [$27,868].[59] Rabbinic salaries, ahead of federal employees and teachers as well, placed rabbis in the professional class. In 1900, the average physician's salary was estimated between $1,000 [$28,011] and $2,000 [$56,022].[60]

In summary, rabbinic salaries in general placed rabbis in the professional class. They were on par with, or ahead of, all but the most well-paid Christian ministers. There was, however, some degree of cleavage between Reform and Orthodox salaries. Central to the expansion of Reform rabbinic salaries was the creation of the Hebrew Union College and the Central Conference of American Rabbis, which created a professional standard and thus limited the supply of Reform rabbis and pushed higher incomes.

Hebrew Union College's success came precisely at a time when the influx of Eastern European immigrant rabbis might have depressed the rabbinic market by expanding the supply. The subsequent creation of the Jewish Theological Seminary and Yeshiva University followed Hebrew Union College in creating a professional standard for the rabbinate in the other denominations. The result was the steady increase of rabbinic salaries throughout the twentieth century. As the Jewish community advanced economically, rabbis for the most part kept pace with their congregations.

Paul Starr, in his classic study of the professionalization of medicine, *The Social Transformation of American Medicine*, writes that in the early nineteenth century, physicians were by no means presumed to be professionals.[61] It was through the creation of the American Medical Association (AMA) that certain doctors were able to gain a monopoly over the credentialing of American medicine. At the same time, the AMA was able to stave off hospitals and insurance companies from wresting medical authority away from doctors. Something very similar was at work in the rabbinate. The creation of HUC set a standard for Reform rabbis and laid the groundwork for the other denominations to follow suit. And as the AMA edged out other forms of medical training like osteopathy, so too the creation of American rabbinical seminaries pushed out any other potential pathways to the rabbinate like private ordination. Just as the AMA defended the authority of the doctor against hospitals and insurance companies, both of which worked to make doctors subservient, so too the rabbinic movements defended the authority of the rabbinate against congregations.

One important factor to bear in mind in considering the professionalization of the rabbinate is that rabbis had a substantial history before the immigration period of being well compensated. As I have demonstrated in previous chapters, the American tradition was to pay rabbis sufficiently to be in the professional class. The influx of immigrant rabbis, and the stories of congregations begging before Shabbat to find money to pay them, threatened this tradition. But through the creation of the American seminaries and their monopolization of rabbinic standards, the rabbinate as a profession emerged from the early twentieth century strengthened in its professional status and financial outlook.

How Much Did Late Nineteenth-Century Jews Give to Their Synagogue?

The publication of the *American Jewish Year Book* in 1899 was an attempt to provide a comprehensive statistical snapshot of the American Jewish community. There had been almanacs before, but the *Year Book* quickly became a standard demographic reference work for the Jewish community. Of particular importance for understanding the history of synagogue finances was the 1899 *Year Book*, which collected membership and annual revenue data for synagogues throughout America.[62] While not every American synagogue is listed in the *Year Book*, and not every listed synagogue gives its revenue, the following analysis is based on 188 synagogues across the country.[63]

The largest synagogue budgets corresponded, not surprisingly, with the large urban Reform synagogues. Temple Emanu-El in New York City reported the largest revenue in the country of $50,000 [$1,400,547]. This was followed by Congregation Keneseth Israel in Philadelphia, which had an income of $35,000 [$980,382]; Chicago Sinai had an income of $30,000 [$840,328]; and Shearith Israel in San Francisco had an income of $25,000 [$700,273].[64] Most synagogues did not enjoy quite such a large bottom line. The majority reported income between $1,000 [$28,011] and $6,000 [$168,066]. One-third of the synagogues reported income less than $1,000. The median synagogue budget across all 188 synagogues was $2,400 [$67,266].

Using this data set, we can roughly determine the average amount synagogue members were giving to their synagogue.[65] Washington Hebrew Congregation in Washington, D.C., for example, reported an income of $12,000 [$336,131] and 220 members, for an average donation of $55 [$1,541] per member; Congregation Beth Jacob Anshe Kurland in Baltimore reported an income of $2,500 and 90 members, for an average donation of $27.77 [$778] per member, etc.[66] The median donation among the 188 synagogues was $33 [$924] per member.

Focusing just on the synagogues in Baltimore may help shed more light on the finances of this period. Twenty-three Baltimore synagogues responded with income and membership information. The largest synagogues in terms of budget and membership were Reform synagogues, Congregation Ohev Sholom and Baltimore Hebrew, which both had budgets of $20,000 [$560,218]. Their income was at least five times larger than almost all the other congregations. The average budget for all of the Baltimore synagogues was $3,500 [$98,038], while the median budget was $2,000 [$56,022]. The donation per member at the large Reform synagogues ranged from $56 [$1,569] at Ohev Sholom to $106 [$2,969] at Har Sinai. Comparing Reform and traditional synagogues according to average giving tells a clear economic story. The four Reform synagogues had a median donation per member of $89 [$2,493] while the nineteen traditional synagogues had a median donation per member of $22 [$616].[67]

From this figure we can (tentatively) estimate an important statistic, namely the percentage of income that members were giving to their synagogues. To estimate this figure for the Orthodox synagogues, we begin with an 1893 study of immigrants in Baltimore. Roughly 300 immigrants were interviewed and their jobs were noted as peddlers, clothing merchants, or merchants of another sort (i.e., typical jobs for Jewish immigrants).[68] Their annual salary was approximately $780 [$20,241]. Of course, not every member of the traditional synagogues in Baltimore was an immigrant peddler or merchant, but just to obtain a rough figure, these jobs are as good a placeholder as we may find. If members of congregations were giving $22 to their synagogue and had an income of $780, they were spending 2.82 percent of their income on their congregation.

Determining the same number for Reform synagogues presents a more difficult challenge because figuring out an average salary for Reform congregants in this period is difficult to do. There were some Baltimore German Jews of tremendous wealth like Henry Sonneborn, a clothing magnate, who employed 5,000 people in his factory.[69] But the majority of synagogue members were not extravagantly wealthy. The professional class of the time — lawyers, doctors, engineers — had an average salary of around $3,000, although there was significant variation. If we take this as a general estimate and divide by the average amount given to the Reform synagogue of $89, it comes to 2.96 percent.[70] The two figures for Orthodox and Reform synagogues taken together suggest that, on average, synagogue members were donating between 2.5 and 3 percent of their income to their synagogue.

With these numbers in mind, we can also compare Jewish and Christian giving based on a unique study of Christian households. In 1875, the Massachusetts Bureau of Statistics of Labor produced a landmark study of family budgets. The study focused on laborers and comprised interviews of 397 families on their spending habits. The average salary among the interviewees was $700 [$14,877]. One-third of the families in the study said they gave to their church and the average donation was $14.60 [$310].[71] The average church donation was thus 2.08 percent of income. Given these numbers, we can say that Jews and Christians in the late nineteenth century were giving at roughly the same rate to their houses of worship. While there were clearly tremendous differences in how much particular families might have given to their synagogue, generally, people who gave to their synagogue did so at a rate of 2 to 3 percent of income.[72]

The Synagogue Budget

In 1867, a small group of Jews in Poultney, Vermont, came together just before the High Holidays to form a congregation called The Israelite Assembly. The very first sentence of their constitution lays out their financial plan: "In order to establish better order during worship for the approaching holidays, . . . every man should contribute equal payment for the costs, should any occur."[73] The expected costs were minimal as the congregation had no building and no staff.

The congregation's first order of business was to acquire a *sefer* Torah for the holidays. It rented a scroll from New York City with the agreement that it would pay the owner whatever money was raised through the auctioning off of aliyot.[74] They returned the Torah the day after Yom Kippur along with $17.69 [$295]. The congregation recorded other expenses associated with holding services: a shofar cost $5.50 [$92]; an ark cost just $0.63 [$10.51]; a reading lectern cost $1.50 [$25]; and a *parochet* (decorative covering hung in front of the Torah) cost $0.98 [$16]. The space to hold services was donated, as were a few other items like the *ner tamid* (a ritual light hung in front of the Torah ark), so the entire cost of High Holiday services came to $24.30 [$405].[75]

Building on their success of the first year of existence, the congregation made plans in their second year to create a more permanent community. They looked into purchasing a *sefer* Torah, which cost $75 [$1,314].[76] This step toward establishing the congregation, however, would lead to congregational strife and play some part in a future congregational schism. Solomon Mineberg, the president of the synagogue, a butcher, and the wealthiest member of the community, offered to pay half of the cost of the scroll with the caveat that he would only pay if every member of the community came to services every Sabbath. This plan seems to have fallen on deaf ears, as at a meeting two weeks later Mineberg offered two new proposals. First, he offered to pay the entire cost of the scroll, but he would retain control of it. He then offered to pay half of the scroll, but with the condition that every member of the congregation contribute something, and if just one person did not, his offer was null and void.

The congregation rejected both his offers, and instead took up a collection of $5 [$88] per willing member. Mineberg was insulted by the rejection, but he was still one of ten members to pay the $5 for the Torah. In 1876, however, Mineberg would take some revenge on the shul, as the board minutes indicated that he eventually did buy his own *sefer* Torah and held a small competing minyan for the High Holidays of that year.[77]

The tension between the wishes of one wealthy financial patron and the interests of the rest of the congregation has been played out many times in synagogue history. What is somewhat unusual in the case of the Poultney synagogue is the commitment the synagogue had to equally shared fiscal responsibility. While most synagogues of the day had significant disparities between how much people gave based on the class of seats they bought, this small community was explicit in their determination to pay for things equally. The remote location, the relative socioeconomic homogeneity, and the congregation's limited budgetary needs were significant factors in its ideological commitment to shared financing.

At the other end of the financial spectrum from Poultney was Temple Adath Israel of Boston (now Temple Israel). The finances of the large Reform congregation attested to the growing sophistication and wealth of some Jewish communities in post–Civil War America. Even to serve as vice president of the congregation, one had to put up an annual bond of $500 [$8,342] to be indemnified against possible financial losses in the congregation.[78] The congregation had expenses in 1870 of $2,180.86 [$40,234].[79] The major expenses were salaries. The congregation was paying a janitor $400 [$7,379] and a hazan/kosher butcher/teacher $1,000 [$15,681]. Salaries thus accounted for at least 65 percent of total congregational expenses.[80] This figure is in line with what we have seen in previous eras and is still true today; usually 50 to 70 percent of contemporary synagogue expenses are tied to salaries.

The congregational building and a schoolhouse occupied the rest of the budget. Paying for coal and gas lamps, removing night soil,[81] building signs, and keeping the furnace working and in good order were all expenses in the 1870s budget. The congregation also owned a building that they renovated and rented out, and this added to the complexity of the congregational budget because they were acting as real estate landlords. They spent $3,299 [$64,268] on rehabilitating the building, which they planned to rent out for $1,200 [$23,377] annually.[82] It appears that the congregation was able to pay for the renovation out of savings from the bank as opposed to taking out a loan, another indication of the wealth of the congregation.

The congregation did not generally give to philanthropic causes. This was not for a lack of charitable concern by congregants. Wealthy members of the congregation, along with other well-to-do Jewish Bostonians, founded the United Hebrew Benevolent Association in 1864, an organization dedicated to giving philanthropy with "a great degree of system and effectiveness."[83] As noted previously, the philanthropic demands associated with helping new immigrants got too complicated for individual synagogues, and so Jewish communities in many cities created community-wide organizations to dispense charity.[84] Synagogues tended to focus their charitable efforts on unique events or people that would not be covered by the help from the communal philanthropies. Chicago Sinai, for example, supported a rabbinical student from Bombay, India, during his studies at the Hebrew Union College.[85] The one area of ongoing charity that Adath Israel was committed to was helping with funeral costs. The board minutes are punctuated frequently with references to the death of a congregant's child, and the board would provide $5 to $15 to pay for funeral expenses in these circumstances.

The growing commitment to Reform also created congregational expenses. The congregation spent $600 [$11,689] on a choir and music director, as was customary in Reform synagogues. The congregation also gave up $625 [$12,176] in expected revenue when it decided to stop having Torah offerings (except for Rosh Hashanah and Yom Kippur), which was also in keeping with Reform practice.

In 1874, Adath Israel faced a similar kind of decision as the congregation in Poultney. The congregation had a number of significant expenses, most prominently the need to raise money to enlarge their building, as well as to pay a higher salary for a new rabbi. The congregation had raised money primarily through renting seats on an annual basis, as well as charging an annual fee for dues. The seats were rented to the highest bidder. The annual dues were the same price for everyone. The congregation raised the question of whether they should change the dues structure, so that those who bought more expensive seats would pay more dues. While some members pushed to retain "equal dues," the board understood that it could raise more money with stratified dues. Adath Israel decreed that there would henceforth be two values of seats. Members who owned seats on the floor would have to pay $50 [$1,032] annually and those in the gallery would have to pay $30 [$619] annually. Although members of the congregation were already giving different amounts to the synagogue depending upon how much they paid for their seats, the decision to create different classes of dues effectively created different classes within the congregation. Whereas the small community of Poultney held to the notion of equal sharing of cost, Temple Adath Israel, with its growing and more complex financial circumstances, bowed to the financial realities.

The enshrinement of financial distinctions within the fabric of the synagogue would lead to discontent among some Jewish leaders. The belief that synagogues catered to the elite became a rallying cry. This frustration would give rise to a new synagogue movement, which sought to undo all economic distinctions within the congregation and promoted a voluntary system of giving. This would be known as the free synagogue movement.

The Free Synagogue Movement

The Free Synagogue was established in New York City in 1905 by Rabbi Stephen Wise. Other synagogues were modeled on Wise's synagogue, but most quickly died out. Although a relatively short-lived phenomenon, the

free synagogue movement left an important imprint on American synagogue history.

The free synagogue movement should be distinguished from the movement for free seating. The move to free seating occurred primarily after
World War I and was a widespread movement of synagogues that abandoned the buying and selling of seats in favor of members paying a dues
fee. After paying a dues fee, members could sit wherever they wanted. This
is the system we have in almost every American synagogue today. This
transition from free seating to dues will be the focus of the next chapter.

The free synagogue movement overlapped with free seating but was also
distinct. The free synagogue movement pushed for the end to buying seats
as well as the end of dues. Synagogues would be financed completely on a
voluntary basis, as in many Protestant churches. For synagogues, this was
a radical suggestion.

In 1895, Rabbi Clifton Levy, an 1890 graduate of the Hebrew Union College, published an opinion piece in Pittsburgh's *Jewish Criterion* regarding
the apathy of Jews toward synagogues. In his scathing critique, Levy maintained that the reason Jews turned away from religion was that synagogues
had become for the wealthy only:

> If there is any complaint more common than all others it is that of the
> general indifference of the masses of Jews to their faith, as embodied in
> the synagogue or temple. Many have been the panacea suggested for the
> disease, but with all little good result. There has been one view which has
> been expressed privately, which has been felt deeply, but for some reason
> has not been publicly discussed, who has not heard the remark, "The syn-
> agogues are built for the rich?" Is it not true? See the new temples with
> their gilded domes to heaven in many of our cities. Is it not unfortunately
> true that a few wealthy men control all of the affairs of most congrega-
> tions? Is it not true they build gorgeous temples, for which the mass of the
> people are expected to pay, even though they have had no part in the con-
> struction, and enjoy no vote in the conducting of these places of worship?
>
> Our synagogues are governed by plutocratic oligarchy which suits itself
> and ignores the mass of the people altogether. The cause of this situation
> lies in the system under which our synagogues are organized. Anyone
> imbued with the spirit of Judaism, or even barely acquainted with its

precepts, knows that the distinction between rich and poor is altogether foreign to its entire tenor. Distinctions between wealth should stop at the synagogue door. A man is not less manly, less Jewish at heart, because he cannot afford to pay as much as his richer neighbor toward the support of the synagogue.

The system at present in vogue in most of our places of worship is in direct contradiction to this idea. Before a man can become a member of a synagogue he must be able and willing to pay at least several hundred dollars for a pew, besides the annual tax as dues. The result is that the young man, no matter how enthusiastic or interested he may be, is barred from membership. How few they are, even in middle age, who can afford the price of a pew from their limited capital. . . . It is also, too true, these religious organizations are conducted as "closed corporations" in which the officers elect themselves perpetually — concerning which the mass of people have no right to say a word.

If Judaism is anything, it is a religion of and for the masses. We recognize no superiority save in devotion to the cause. . . . How then can a synagogue thrive when they throw away the corner stone on which they ought to be founded — the equality of man, as man, for what he is *and not what he has* [italics mine].

Levy's critique marked a new development in American synagogues. While individuals may have grumbled about the price of pews, a wholesale denunciation of the funding structure of synagogues was an entirely different level of criticism. Levy's solution to the problems of money and synagogues was as dramatic as his critique:

Can a cure be suggested? Considering the limitations of human nature, we are sure that a radical reform is not practicable today — yet it is both probable and necessary to take the first step towards the ideal system. That ideal we might find in the system of the "free churches" where each man gives according to his means and the seats are free to all. We are not ready to rush from the extreme of pew owning to the free seats, but the first step may be and should be taken.

There is no reason why each and every synagogue should not bestow the full right of membership, the right to vote and hold office upon every contributor to its funds, whether he or she owns a seat or rents one. Such a step would be a real invitation to all the people to take an active part in the administration of religious affairs. The congregation adopting such a plan would be surprised to find how ready the people are to respond to such an invitation. It seems to be a trifling matter, but it so far from trifling that the synagogues adopting it will suddenly find themselves full of new life and vigor unfelt before — because the weight and support of the people will be behind them.

The reform suggested in not a cure-all, it will not at once change an apathetic, indifferent mass into an enthusiastic, devoted people, but it can do much to remove the barriers which keep those in the middle and the poorer classes out of our synagogues; it will remove the well-founded charge that temple and religion are only for the wealthy. It will re-Judaize our places of worship and make in the best sense a People's Synagogue! The idea is offered for the consideration, the criticism, and, if it may be, the adoption of our people.[86]

Although Levy's call for the synagogue to adopt the system of the free church movement was radical, his was just one of a number of voices calling attention to the inequity of the high price of pews and dues. In 1896, an article in the *American Hebrew*, entitled "A New Thing in Congregations," reported on Rabbi Isaac Moses's attempt in Chicago to create a synagogue where membership would be open to everyone regardless of annual contributions, and "payments are to be such as each individual member feels that he or she is justified in making." The *American Hebrew* then editorialized that the high cost of synagogue buildings, which are "out of all keeping with the financial condition of the congregation or the social position of the bulk of its members," has stifled membership activity and pushed the price of joining a synagogue so high that young people have had their sense of duty to the synagogue "blunted by a desire to avoid its financial responsibilities."[87]

The Jewish call for dismantling the elitism of synagogues and the concern for "the middle and poorer classes" reflects the Christian environment of the time. The call for free seating was influenced by the Protestant Social Gospel movement, where "concern about the 'unchurched' poor, fear of the urban masses, renewed dedication to social justice, and a resulting surge of religious activism" were central. These then became part of the synagogue, "translated into Jewish terms and stripped of their Christological rhetoric."[88]

The free church model that Clifton Levy proposed as a solution to these problems, and that would be the basis for the free synagogue movement, was part of the Social Gospel movement but also had earlier roots. The model goes back to the first half of the nineteenth century and its founding is generally credited to Charles Grandison Finney. While some Christian denominations had supported voluntary contributions rather than pew rents,[89] Finney was the first to give specific expression to this vision in the creation of a Free Church in New York City. As noted previously, Finney was the most well-known evangelical preacher of the Second Great Awakening, and the free church came out of a meeting between Finney and two wealthy Calvinist silk merchants, Louis and Arthur Tappan, who wanted to bring Finney to evangelize in New York City.

In his biography of Charles Finney, Keith Hardman says the Tappans "were convinced that well-to-do Christians were absolutely obliged to give of their wealth to the kingdom of God."[90] They also agreed with Finney on the principle that the gospel should be free for anyone to hear, and they used their wealth to finance a free church in New York and paid Finney to minister there. The Tappans rented the Chatham Street Theater for $2,000 [$5,963] in 1832 after convincing the theater managers of the holiness of their endeavor and the shamefulness of running a theater.[91] The Chatham Street Theater was rechristened the Second Free Presbyterian Church (the First Free church had also been organized by the Tappans in New York City but without Finney as the pastor) and it was an immediate success, with crowds coming for seventy straight nights to hear Finney preach.

The free churches were established on the principle that all seats would be free and the poor and transient would be welcome. According to Charles Cole in an article in *New York History*, the churches "rested on the assumption that religion was universal, open to all, and that the church had a particular obligation to reach those who could not afford salvation in the regular way. In the nineteenth century such an assumption among Presbyterians was novel and required an emancipation from old religious prejudices."[92] Giving up on the established way of church life and paying for pews was no small financial endeavor. For example, at the wealthy Church of the Messiah in New York City in 1841, 196 church pews were valued collectively at $97,373

[$2,319,212]. But with the financial backing of the Tappan brothers and like-minded wealthy merchants, the free church movement initially prospered. The success of the Chatham Street church led to more free Presbyterian churches being built in New York City, Boston, Rochester, and other cities.

But despite its burst of initial success, the movement began to decline after 1835. "Although pecuniary problems, the financial crash of 1837, and the theological contentions which culminated in the great schism within the Protestant Church all contributed to the collapse of the free church movement," Cole explains, "the chief reason for its decline was the identification of the movement with another radical idea of the time: abolitionism."[93] Many of the supporters of the free church movement were abolitionists, including Arthur Tappan, who was president of the American Anti-Slavery Society. The free churches were used to hold abolitionist meetings and to hear abolitionist speakers. The public soon associated the churches with abolitionism, which sparked occasional violence against them, and Lewis Tappan's home was even ransacked. There were soon church disputes over how far the church should be engaged in abolitionist work as well as whether to end interracial seating within the church.[94] By 1838, the Third Free Presbyterian Church was suffering from debt and it instituted pew rentals. A few years later, a number of the free churches dissolved.[95]

The free church was the first American religious movement to marry the finances of the church to a larger theological and political vision. Ending pew sales and encouraging voluntary donations were in service to the broader aim of democratizing the church. And though the free church movement dissipated, some established Protestant churches would embrace the free church idea and eliminate pew sales in favor of voluntary donations.

Although the free church movement ended in the 1840s, its foundational ideas were incorporated into the Social Gospel movement, which influenced Protestant clergy half a century later. The Social Gospel movement, like the free church movement, placed concern for the poor and the desire to democratize the church as central principles of its religious ideology. But unlike the free church movement, the Social Gospel emphasized concrete action to help the poor above theological salvation. In 1883, William Rainsford, rector at St. George's Episcopal Church in New York City, established the first "institutional church," which would become a model Social Gospel church. Rainsford eliminated pew rentals and established a variety of social service activities to help poor immigrants, including soup kitchens, sewing classes, and recreational clubs.

Rainsford wrote colorfully in his autobiography of the founding of the "institutional church." St. George was a wealthy and significant church through much of the nineteenth century, but in the latter part of the century, most of its members had moved away and the area around the church became primarily immigrant and poor. A core group of loyal members, led by J. P. Morgan, reached out to Rainsford, who had a reputation for his work in urban ministry, to come and save the church. Rainsford made three demands before he would accept the offer — that the church be free of pew rents; that he would have control over who was nominated to the vestry; and finally that he be given $10,000 annually to spend on the church as he saw fit. Rainsford describes the scene after making these demands: "Dead silence followed. I saw Mr. Morgan look around that circle of tense faces. Then he looked at me and said one word: Done."[96]

Rainsford's vision proved successful at revitalizing St. George and it provided an array of services to the community. At the center of the institutional church model was the notion that it was free. He writes emphatically in his memoir:

> On the issue of free church, I stand today where I stood then. There should be one place besides the grave — to which all should have a common place: That place is the Church of God. To my mind, as between free church and pew choice, there is no choice at all. The one is right; the other is wrong. You cannot preach one thing from the pulpit and practice another in the pew. I do not care how liberal pew-holders may be, or how hospitable they may show themselves. To own or rent a foot of the floor of the house we claim to be the House of God is to contradict and deny in practice the Gospel of Jesus.[97]

Rainsford was certainly helped in this endeavor by having industrialists like J. P. Morgan as part of the church vestry. But many churches, even those without millionaires on the board, soon followed suit and eliminated the rental of pews. Rainsford noted that the Episcopal bishop of Massachusetts initially laughed at the plan for free churches, only to declare a decade later that he would do everything in his power to make all Massachusetts churches free.[98]

The institutional church would have a significant impact on the Jewish world. It pushed established synagogues toward enlarging their sense of mission. Emil G. Hirsch, perhaps the most noted rabbi of the era, advocated Social Gospel concerns for the poor and the "unsynagogued," and pushed for Chicago Sinai to become an "open Temple."[99] Rabbi Leo Franklin at Beth El in Detroit was another figure influenced by the institutional church movement who also pushed for an "open Temple," which he said he would have called an "Institutional Temple" but Jews would be "affrighted" by the outright adoption of a Protestant term.[100]

Franklin decried the fact that so many Jews were unsynagogued, and proposed that his synagogue vastly expand its activities to appeal to secular Jews. He suggested choirs, lectures, literary meetings, mother's groups, Bible classes, young people's societies, women's auxiliary associations, and more to bring the unsynagogued into the synagogue.[101] Franklin also became a leading voice for eliminating pew rentals and replacing pew sales with dues.[102] But most of the leading Jewish voices that advocated for institutional synagogues did not carry forward Rainsford's message of a free institution based solely on free will donations.

There was one major Jewish figure, though, who did follow through on the call for a free synagogue. Stephen Wise would ultimately create a synagogue in New York City free from pew rentals and dues. His project to create a free synagogue started earlier with Congregation Beth Israel in Portland, Oregon. Wise served as rabbi of the congregation for seven years beginning in 1899. In 1904 Wise convinced the congregation to become a free seating synagogue by eliminating pew rentals, but keeping dues. Wise had been at the synagogue for four years by that point, and had been an extraordinary success, more than doubling the membership of the congregation and further establishing his national reputation.[103]

When Wise first came to Beth Israel in 1899, it was an unlikely synagogue to be bold in its finances. Beth Israel was the first synagogue founded west of the Rockies in 1858. In 1880 it joined the Union of American Hebrew Congregations (UAHC) and was firmly in the German Reform camp. But by the last decade of the century, it was deeply in debt and its finances were a constant source of frustration. The president of the congregation gave a caustic report to the congregation in 1890:

Our Congregation would be one of the most prosperous in this country if our representative members would but take the interest in our congregation that they should, they show so little interest in our welfare that they do not even attend our meetings. . . . From the sale of seats we have realized $800 less this year than last. It appears to me as if our rich members this year had clubbed together not to buy first class seats. . . . The result will be that before the year is past we will be obliged to borrow money.[104]

The president ends the report on a plaintive note: "But I am pained to state I have not succeeded, therefore you will have to elect a president who probably will succeed better than I have." He then proposed the enforcement of a fine of $1 on members who do not come to meetings. In 1894, a new president again complains that the sale of seats produced several hundred dollars less than expected but notes that much of the problem was a result of the economic depression that took hold of the country in 1893.[105] In the following year, the congregation had a budget of just under $5,000 [$137,849] and expected to balance its budget, but there were still complaints that it was not able to afford paid teachers or a choir.[106]

By 1899, as the national economy improved, the congregation gained new strength. It built a new synagogue, and as its rabbi retired, they sought someone who could lead the congregation forward. The congregation settled on Wise, who already had a widespread reputation as a speaker. It was so anxious to hire him that it voted him a salary of $5,000 [$140,055] — a sum almost equal to the entire budget. To pay for Wise, the congregation took up a special subscription called the "Doctor Wise Fund," and thirty-eight members pledged between $25 and $250 [$700 and $7,000] for five years to pay for his salary.[107] Wise's success was instantaneous. One year after his arrival, the congregation had increased 25 percent to 123 members, and the financial success was also immediate, as the congregation ran a budgetary surplus of $3959.70.[108]

The following year, the congregation experienced some turbulence over its finances. The congregation needed to go into debt to finish the building "through the ignorance or dishonesty of the Architect and the Contractor who originally erected our building." The congregation also had members resigning over the issue of seat rentals. The congregational bylaws required that members rent at least two seats at a minimum of $10 (widowers and single members needed to rent only one seat). The congregation also charged $5 monthly in dues. Some members who paid the dues refused to pay for the seats, claiming they did not occupy seats (presumably they meant they did not attend services enough to warrant buying a seat). The congregation had previously remitted people's money under such circumstances in order not to lose a member, but "it was thought unfair to those who regularly paid all their dues to the Congregation," so they insisted on the payment, and some members left the synagogue in dispute.[109]

By 1904, however, the congregation had firmly turned its fortunes around. Membership had doubled since Wise had come, and finances were even more successful. The congregation had taken out loans for $9,500 [$261,913] to pay for the building in 1899. They subsequently had to add $21,000 [$556,598] in loans for reconstruction due to the "ignorance or dishonesty" of the architect. The congregation paid off this entire debt with receipts that year of $37,840 [$966,394], which covered both the annual $10,000 [$259,476] budget and the building debt. Wise led a ritual to burn the mortgage after it was paid off.[110] "Beth Israel today," reported the president, "for the first time in a quarter of a century, is free from burdensome debt, with a handsome sum in the treasury, its membership greatly increased and all of this accomplished during the past eleven months. This splendid result never could have been achieved but for the leadership of our able rabbi, whose ceaseless efforts aroused the enthusiasm of the members of our congregation." As a tangible reward for his efforts, Wise also received a salary increase to $6,000 [$155,686] annually.[111]

With this financial success as a background, Stephen Wise moved forward with a proposal to end paying for seats. Wise had by this point built an impressive reputation. Besides his success at revitalizing the synagogue, he was a political leader outside the congregation. He aligned himself with Social Gospel concerns and was a passionate and effective advocate for progressive policies. He took part in creating the state's first child labor laws, and passionately lobbied against a law aimed at excluding Chinese from immigrating to America. The issue was particularly potent in Portland, which had a significant Chinese community. *The Oregonian* covered one of Wise's fiery speeches in opposition to the proposed bill on its front page.[112]

Wise's call for a free synagogue was not new. He had been speaking about his vision of a free synagogue from his very first sermon as rabbi of the congregation. For Wise, the elements of a free synagogue were twofold. First, he believed the synagogue should be free for the rabbi to speak about moral concerns of the day without oversight from the board. Presaging his showdown with the board of Temple Emanu-El over this issue, Wise declared in his inaugural sermon that he "asked but one condition. I ask it as my right. You will and must allow it . . . this pulpit must be free! This pulpit must be free!"[113]

The other element of the free synagogue was that the congregation should be free from pew rentals. Later at the Free Synagogue in New York City, Wise would eliminate dues as well, but in Portland selling pews was the only target. Wise deemed the selling of pews as particularly problematic. It created distinctions between rich and poor, and it commoditized seats, both of which Wise thought were fundamentally at odds with the values of a synagogue.

Wise's proposal to do away with pew sales was adopted with surprising speed. No doubt in an effort to please Wise, whom they rightly feared might be looking for a larger congregation back east, the congregation eliminated pew sales within months of Wise's proposal. In place of pew rentals, Wise advocated raising money from voluntary contributions. In 1905, one year after its adoption, the president of the congregation reported on its success: "Despite much misgiving, this plan [to eliminate pew sales] was put into operation tentatively in connection with the late holy-days. . . . The members of the congregation rose to this higher ideal of synagogue administration, with the result among other things, the total of voluntary contributions, $7,118 [$181,786] exceeded by nearly $1,000 [$25,948] the sum collected last year. . . . Moreover, it is now to be hoped that considerable addition will be made to the membership of the congregation."[114]

The following year would see very similar success. The synagogue raised $6,883 [$178,597] out of a budget of $13,357 [$346,582] from voluntary contributions, with dues providing $5,534.50 [$143,607] and ancillary income making up the rest.[115] The same year, though, Stephen Wise would leave to start the Free Synagogue in New York City, and Rabbi Jonah Wise (no relation) was hired. In some sense, the next few years would provide the real test for the free synagogue model, as it would have to survive without the charisma of Stephen Wise.

In 1907, the first year after Stephen Wise's departure, the congregation continued to raise money through voluntary donations, but by 1909 problems arose. The board of trustees began to call upon the membership for more generous contributions, and by 1911, the board reported that "receipts are not quite sufficient to meet expenses" and resolved to raise dues.[116] At some point over the next few years — the board minutes do not make clear exactly when it happened — the congregation reinstated paying for pews, such that by 1920 the congregation required members to rent seats. No explanations for the turn of events is given in synagogue documents, but one presumes that Wise was the champion and chief enthusiast for the venture and his departure meant that there was less passion for this cause.

Although Congregation Beth Israel abandoned free seating, Wise would go even further with his vision of a free synagogue when he came to New York City. After the success Wise had at Beth Israel, "it seemed only natural that the most promising young rabbi in America should eventually be called to the pulpit of New York's Emanu-El, the cathedral of Reform Judaism in America," Melvin Urofsky writes in his biography of Wise.[117] But Wise's call to Emanu-El's pulpit would become famous for his rejection of that call. Speaking on behalf of the board of the synagogue, Louis Marshall made clear to Wise that the rabbi of Emanu-El was subservient to the board: "The pulpit of Emanu-El has always been and is subject to and under control of the Board of Trustees."[118] In practical terms, this meant Wise was not at liberty to speak from the pulpit on political issues without the board's approval. Wise rejected the job offer, claiming that freedom of the pulpit was essential. "How can a man be vital and independent and helpful," Wise wrote in his autobiography, "if he be tethered and muzzled? A free pulpit, worthily filled, must command respect and influence; a pulpit that is not free, howsoever filled, is sure to be without potency and honor."[119] Wise's rejection of Emanu-El was significant enough news to be covered extensively by the *New York Times*.[120]

Like William Rainsford's evocative picture of his encounter with J. P. Morgan, Wise colorfully recounted his showdown with Louis Marshall in his autobiography. Like Rainsford, Wise had audacious demands, most notably the demand for a free pulpit where he would be at liberty to speak his mind on political opinions. But where Rainsford's story ends with Morgan's acquiescence, Wise's story ends with Marshall refusing his demands, and Wise striking out on his own.[121]

Rainsford, however, was dealing with a church in desperate need of revitalization, whereas Emanu-El was at the height of its authority. Wise quite clearly understood that his deepest hopes for a free synagogue modeled on the commitments of the Social Gospel movement would have no chance of succeeding at Emanu-El. Wise's decision to reject Emanu-El was nonetheless bold, and his determination to create a new synagogue and to fund it in a way that no synagogue had previously funded itself was equally audacious.

The free synagogue would be funded entirely on the basis of voluntary contributions. This was beyond where he had gone in Portland, where dues were still assessed. In the free synagogue, money was entirely to be given as a free will donation. The constitution of the free synagogue makes this clear: "Desiring of vitalizing and reasserting a fundamental ideal of Israel, the founders of the Free Synagogue resolve that it shall not at any time for any reason impose any fixed pecuniary dues, tax or assessment upon its members, nor shall pews or sittings be owned by members; but it shall be supported fully by voluntary contributions."[122]

Wise, in his autobiography, articulates a powerful critique of pew owning and of dues and lays out the fundamental ideas of the free synagogue: "The synagogue must again become democratically managed and . . . there could be no synagogue democracy as long as the pews and dues system obtained. Both together introduced into what should have been the democratic fellowship of religious communion all the unlovely differentiation of the outer world."[123]

Wise thought selling pews was problematic because the best pews should have been places of honor regardless of wealth; instead, pews became a "purchasable and taxable commodity." Dues were a problem as well because they "exacted sums" from individuals interested in affiliating with a congregation — in today's parlance, dues would be called "a barrier to entry." But the issue of voluntary contributions went beyond a commitment to economic equality. "Not only was the pulpit to be free and unfettered and the pew untaxed and voluntary in its support, but something more important than these," Wise wrote. "The synagogue was to be inwardly free, free in its innermost ideals and aspirations, free to follow the high traditions of its prophetic genius."[124]

For Wise, the paying for synagogues out of a free will donation was emblematic of the inner freedom that would liberate synagogue life. The freedom to choose what to give to support the synagogue was thus linked symbolically with the freedom to preach, democratic freedom, and a transformative spiritual freedom. These freedoms were the practical and ideological underpinnings of the free synagogue movement.

Wise was as immediately successful at the Free Synagogue as he was in Portland. He attracted some of the wealthiest and most influential members of the Jewish community — Jacob Schiff, Henry Morgenthau, and Adolf Lewisohn among them — to be initial subscribers of the congregation, each of them providing between $5,000 [$127,737] and $10,000 [$255,474]. One year after its founding, the synagogue had one thousand members, had raised $40,000 [$1,038,248], and reported expenses of $15,000 [$389,343].[125] Wise refused a salary for the first year.[126] Wise drew such large crowds initially that the synagogue quickly moved to a larger venue. It also started a Lower East Side branch, so Wise could reach the "downtown Jews" as well. This was a kind of urban mission, paid for by those who sought to wean the immigrants away from Old World Orthodoxy. A few years later, the Free Synagogue rented out Carnegie Hall for Sunday morning services, which would regularly attract 1,500 people.

Wise also moved forward on his plans to make social services an intrinsic part of the synagogue. Echoing the institutional church and its Jewish variants, but going beyond these institutions as well, Wise created the first (and perhaps only) social services department within a synagogue. The social services department ran programs to help those in need and included child adoption services, a mental health clinic, a home for at-risk adolescent girls, and clothes for World War I refugees, and they provided a significant cadre of volunteer visitors and helpers at Bellevue and other hospitals in the area. Funding for the social services branch apparently came from collections on Friday night and the High Holidays. Sydney Goldstein, the founder of the Free Synagogue's social services department and himself a rabbi, recounted in his autobiography how the money for the department was raised: "At every service, Friday night and during the Holy Days, we take a collection." Goldstein claimed that the synagogue raised $34,000 annually to fund the social services department at the height of the synagogue's prosperity. The synagogue's financial records do not indicate whether money was actually handed over on Shabbat. If indeed Wise was passing the plate on a Friday night it would have been a remarkable occurrence given that Jewish law and custom strictly forbids handling money on the Sabbath. A more likely explanation was that individuals were utilizing some loophole in Jewish law, such as folding a corner down on a pledge form that had their name pre-printed on it.[127]

The success of the Free Synagogue created interest in other parts of New York City for Free Synagogue branches. There were ultimately five "divisions" of the Free Synagogue in the Bronx, Newark, Washington Heights, Downtown, and Flushing. The extent and success of Wise's institution has perhaps not been fully appreciated by historians. The Free Synagogue occupies just a few pages in David Kaufman's study of synagogues of the era, *Shul with a Pool*, and Sarna devotes less than a paragraph to it in *American Judaism*. But in significant ways, Wise's synagogue was unparalleled. No other American synagogues can lay claim to creating multiple satellite campuses, a social services department, a new financing structure, a teacher's institute, an ongoing ecumenical service with a church, a rabbinic fellowship for new rabbis, and myriad other innovations. Wise's Free Synagogue also inspired the creation of other Free Synagogues across the country, only a few of which were ultimately successful.

In 1909, Mikveh Israel in Philadelphia moved into a new building but created a free synagogue with their old building to be called the Mikveh Israel Free Synagogue. Rabbi Leon Elmaleh had pushed for keeping the old building, "in which so many have felt comfort and delight." Mikveh Israel was not intending to create "an institutional synagogue" like Wise's, but the synagogue was in fact going to go beyond Wise in terms of how "free" financially the synagogue would be. The *Jewish Exponent* explained Mikveh Israel's plan: "This synagogue is to be free in its most literal sense of the word, and in this respect will be the first to be thus set apart in America. The free synagogue conducted by Dr. Stephen S. Wise in New York is not free in the same sense. The New York rabbi speaks of a 'free pulpit.' There will be no membership charges here, nor any offerings. No money will be accepted from those attending services even if proffered."[128]

The funds for the Free Synagogue would come from the general budget of the synagogue. Expenses for the Free Synagogue were limited, as the acting rabbi, Arthur Dembitz, as well as the acting shamas donated their services, and the building itself had no mortgage. The cost to the synagogue was only for upkeep of the structure.

The synagogue had seemingly two aims in providing the funds for this experiment. The first was the desire to preserve a historic space as a symbolic linkage to Mikveh Israel's storied past. Mikveh Israel was also interested in reaching immigrant Jews who might otherwise go for the High Holidays to mushroom synagogues — for-profit synagogues that opened just for the High Holidays. Elmaleh claimed, "If by a free synagogue we could do away with the undignified commerce of the selling of admissions tickets for the High Holidays by individual cantors we should be performing a worthy act."[129]

Two years after the congregation opened, Mikveh Israel proclaimed the experiment a failure and sold the building. The synagogue had been running services every Sabbath during this time but there was a difference of opinion as to its success. In an editorial in the *Jewish Exponent*, Henry Morais, son of Sabato Morais, a beloved rabbi of the congregation, claimed that Jews "eagerly sought" to use the synagogue. He wrote there was always more than a minyan, and quite often the congregation was full on special events. In a rhetorical flourish, Morais pleaded with the congregation to reverse its decision, saying his be-sainted father would never have sanctioned the sale of the historic and beautiful building.[130] But at the final service at the old synagogue, the parnas of the congregation, Louis Levy, told a different story, claiming the synagogue was underutilized. He opined that the synagogue wanted to have a free synagogue to allow new immigrants from Russia a place to pray for free, "but in the two years since the doors of the synagogue were thus thrown open, it has become manifest that a free synagogue . . . was not a need of the Jewish community, not a permanent want of even the poorest."[131]

Other attempts at free synagogues were made around the country. In 1911, Temple Israel of Far Rockaway in Queens, New York, became a free synagogue where there were no pew rentals or dues. Anyone could contribute what they were willing and be considered a member, although the congregation had different membership categories between those who gave at least $25 and those who did not.[132] The synagogue exists today as Temple Israel of Lawrence, but long ago stopped being a free synagogue.

In 1921, a free synagogue was announced for Los Angeles, but "free" meant there would be dues but no seat rentals and the pulpit would be free.[133] In 1930, another attempt to open a free synagogue in Los Angeles was made by Rabbi Meyer Winkler, a prominent leader at Congregation Sinai, one of the largest synagogues in Los Angeles, who had resigned from that pulpit over disagreements with the congregation.[134] Winkler's synagogue was to be entirely based on Wise's vision with no pews, no dues, and freedom of the pulpit. Both Los Angeles free synagogues, however, did not succeed in establishing themselves.

In 1927, the Free Synagogue of Westchester was founded on Wise's principles. After several mergers it exists today as the Sinai Free Temple of Westchester but long ago started charging for dues. The Stephen Wise Free Synagogue itself, ironically, is not even free anymore in the sense that Wise envisioned it. Membership dues were officially instituted in 1984 and annual membership presently costs more than $3,000 a year.[135]

Wise's Free Synagogue would have some significant lasting impact on American synagogues. His call for freedom of the pulpit is enshrined now for many rabbis in their contracts as part of a standard practice for both the Reform and the Conservative movement. His influence in pushing for an end to stratified seating in synagogues also bore fruit. Wise was certainly not alone in this endeavor but his was a significant voice. However, the full fiscal vision of a synagogue based entirely on voluntary donations did not take hold (although the idea has been significantly revived recently — see Conclusion: Today–Tomorrow).[136]

The success of the voluntary contribution plan was in large part dependent upon Wise's charisma. Evidence from the Free Synagogue itself confirms this assessment. In the archives of the Stephen Wise Synagogue is an interview with a former executive secretary who worked under Wise. The secretary described the financial system of the synagogue:

> Under Stephen Wise there were no fixed dues. Everyone was to give whatever he could afford. We called this Fair Share. It cost x number of dollars to maintain a member in the Synagogue. You rated yourself, according to a guide, and paid as much as you could afford. I think that while Stephen Wise was alive, the system worked beautifully, simply because if there

wasn't enough money, he would call Nathan Warshaw and say, "Nathan, I need \$25,000," and he'd get it. Many wealthy Jews adored him. Whatever he wanted he got.[137]

Wise's attempt to create a financing system in keeping with his values of democracy and freedom underscores one of the central tensions of synagogue financing — creating a system that raises sufficient funds while at the same time being in line with the religious values of the synagogue. Wise was one of the few Jewish leaders who took seriously the task of bringing the financing system and religious values together. For Wise, the issue was not simply one of fairness — that people should pay what they could afford; Wise also saw the voluntary nature of giving as a token of religious freedom that was at the heart of his rabbinate.

It is noteworthy that the free synagogue movement failed to catch on given that by this same period churches had almost entirely become free of pew rentals. The voluntary principle, so important for Wise, may have failed to excite the Jewish community for a number of reasons. Theologically, the voluntary principle may not have had the same resonance for the Jewish community as it did for Protestant churches, as Judaism traditionally understood the commanded act as potentially more important than the voluntary one. The free synagogue was also a financial risk. There was greater fiscal surety in charging for seats or dues, as these are fixed figures. One cannot budget for how much someone will be moved to give. So while Wise won the argument over the inequality and elitism of seating, the argument over the voluntary principle was lost.

"Religion at Bargain Prices": The History of Mushroom Synagogues

While Wise was experimenting with a free synagogue, another kind of synagogue financing experiment was taking place in New York City every year at the High Holidays. On August 17, 1930, in *The Jewish Daily Bulletin*, the rabbis of New York City declared war.[138] Their enemy was not antisemites, nor assimilation, nor any of the other typical suspects for rabbinic enmity. The object of their campaign was "the mushroom synagogue."[139] The term *mushroom synagogue* refers to the numerous worship services that sprang up just for the High Holidays and were housed in Yiddish theaters, dance halls, movie picture lofts, sweatshops, and meeting rooms connected to saloons. These services were for-profit enterprises, often advertised as being led by a famous choir or cantor, but usually led by individuals with limited rabbinic or cantorial training. From their inception, mushroom synagogues drew heavy criticism from the religious establishment for luring worshippers away from established synagogues. For the roughly forty years that mushroom synagogues existed, perhaps the only issue on which all Reform, Conservative, and Orthodox synagogues could agree was that mushroom synagogues should be driven out of business. Despite the condemnation, by 1917 mushroom synagogues would grow to serve more than 150,000 Jews for the High Holidays according to one report.[140]

At the beginning of the twentieth century, there were approximately 300 synagogues on the Lower East Side of Manhattan.[141] While some were "great synagogues" that had grand buildings and a large number of congregants — like the Eldridge Street Synagogue — many were small, disconnected, *landsmanshaftn* synagogues, which sought to reproduce the experience of Russian Jewish life in America.[142] While these synagogues may have reflected the feeling of life back in Russia, attendance at them reflected the new American reality. Many Jews worked on Saturday morning and so were unable to come, and many abandoned Jewish practice altogether and did not wish to come. The lack of synagogue attendance was dramatic compared to Jewish life in Russia. *The Yiddish Velt*, commenting on the lack of attendance, reported that no more than 25 percent of Jewish men on the Lower East Side attended synagogue regularly in 1904.[143]

While synagogues may not have been crowded most of the year, the High Holidays were an entirely different story. As Jeffrey Gurock writes in *Orthodox Jews in America*, "They [shuls] were packed to their unsteady rafters on the High Holidays as a palpable sense of religiosity permeated the ghetto. Then a combination of nostalgia, awe over the days of judgment . . . brought all those who had not clearly renounced their Judaism to the shul."[144] Because the great demand for High Holiday services outstripped the seating capacity of the small *landsmanshaftn* synagogues, mushroom synagogues stepped in to satisfy demand and turn a profit.

The presence of mushroom synagogues was reported as early as 1896. In a letter to the *American Hebrew* signed "a Harlemite," the author provides the first description of mushroom synagogues:

> I belong to no congregation at all, though reared religiously, but when the great holy days approach, I feel a desire to attend worship. I cannot, however, afford to pay the sum of money asked for seats by the regular congregations, and have usually attended some temporary place of worship in the neighborhood. Not without a feeling bordering on disgust, I will confess, for the atmosphere of commercialism that dominates these places, together with the surroundings which are usually drinking halls, robs the service of all religious spirit and makes the recital of prayers but a mummery ... [they are] a travesty upon religion.[145]

The next time mushroom synagogues are mentioned in any newspaper is five years later. In 1901, a letter to the editor of the *American Hebrew* reported a placard outside the Grand Central Palace (a hall that stood on the site of what is now Grand Central Station) announcing that services would be held on the High Holidays led by the famous Tomkin brothers.[146] Another letter notes that signs advertising such services with "famous" service leaders were ubiquitous throughout the Lower East Side just prior to the High Holidays. The cumulative effect of these signs was to make it seem "as if a circus has come to town, with its flaming posters ... its dancing dervishes, and its other famous troupes of performers. The Tallith and the sacred Shroud are prominent among the 'costumes' worn by the 'stars' in these performances."[147] The Jewish historian Leon Huhner wrote an editorial also condemning the vulgarity of mushroom synagogues:

> This self-styled "Holy-day rabbi" is generally nothing more than a speculator pure and simple; he rents his hall, sells his tickets of admission, and in most cases nets a profit of several hundred dollars on his investment. . . .
> It is high time, therefore, that such a practice be broken up. The evils resulting there from must be evident upon a moment's reflection. . . . It degrades our religion in the eyes of our Gentile fellow citizens; and in the second place, and what is far more serious, it degrades Judaism in the eyes of those of our brethren who are compelled to attend the temporary places of worship.[148]

While Huhner wanted mushroom synagogues eliminated, he later noted that they were necessary because there were not enough synagogues to satisfy the demand for High Holiday seats and many immigrants could not afford to attend services. He put forward the interesting proposition that rabbinical students from the Jewish Theological Seminary should set up their own mushroom synagogues. Such services would have the benefit of being run by authentic religious leaders, and they would give rabbinical students needed practice in leading services. The money raised by such services would go to the seminary or to a charity. "The dignity of our religion would thus be upheld instead of being dragged in the mire [by mushroom speculators]."[149]

Huhner's plan for seminary students did not come to fruition, and within two decades, for-profit mushroom synagogues proliferated like . . . mushrooms. In 1906, the *Yiddishe Tagblatt* ran an ad for the People's Theater Synagogue, a Yiddish theater transformed into a mushroom synagogue for the holidays. The ad promised that a world-renowned hazan, Reb Israel Fine, would lead services with a choir. The ad read, "Do you want to get pleasure for your money this year? Then comes to the beautiful, airy People's Theater Synagogue. You will hear good singing, beautiful davening, Jewish and sweet. The management guarantees good service."[150] By 1917, there were a reported 343 mushroom synagogues in New York during the period of the High Holidays, with a collective seating capacity of 150,000.[151] In response to this boom in the number of mushroom synagogues, the established Jewish community began a serious call for their eradication. The New York Kehillah would become the central voice in the fight against mushrooms. Founded in 1908, the New York Kehillah was a massive umbrella organization with a mission to centralize the educational, social, economic, and religious life of the immigrant Jewish community.[152] It brought together the philanthropy and the political clout of the uptown German Jews with the downtown Eastern European community and created an array of programs to combat crime, provide social welfare services, increase the quality of Jewish education, arbitrate between Jewish employers and Jewish workers, and more. It also sought to end what it referred to as "the evil" of mushroom synagogues.

Just a few months after the founding of the Kehillah, in 1909, the *New York Times* ran a story entitled, "Warned of Fake Synagogues: Jewish Community Asks Jews to Avoid 'Mushroom Synagogues.'"[153] The article quoted an appeal from the president of the Kehillah to the Jewish community to avoid the temporary synagogues that were set up in "places of cheap amusement. The holding of holy services in unholy places is a desecration, and it is a desire that this public disgrace be avoided." That the Kehillah was focusing on this so soon after its founding reflects the importance of the issue for the organized Jewish community.

But the Kehillah did more than just call for Jews to boycott mushroom synagogues. The Kehillah's appeal to the community put forth an action plan: "To partly alleviate this evil [of mushroom synagogues], the committee has taken steps to organize a number of provisional synagogues in suitable meeting rooms and halls." The Kehillah sought to replace the mushroom synagogues by setting up spaces and providing High Holiday services free of charge. In the following year, 1910, the Kehillah increased these efforts. Their annual report says that they set up six synagogues in diverse places like the Young Women's Hebrew Association (YWHA) of the Bronx, a synagogue library, and the Westfield Day Camp. These efforts were funded by four well-known philanthropists who were backers of the Kehillah: Murry Guggenheim, Adolph Lewisohn, Mortimer Schiff, and Isaac Seligman. However, the leadership of the Kehillah was aware that six synagogues in New York were clearly not going to solve the mushroom problem. "We realize that we have only touched the surface of this vexing question, as to how to secure orderly services in decent places during the holidays," they wrote in their annual report.[154]

The Kehillah's strong objections to mushrooms should be seen within the context of the overall mission of the Kehillah and the influence of the Progressive Era on that mission. The rooting out of corruption and creating order out of chaos were central tenets of the Progressive Era.[155] The Kehillah, with this progressive spirit, sought to centralize the disorganized Jewish community and to end various forms of religious corruption. As part of its organizing mission, the Kehillah established a Vaad Ha'Rabbanim (council of rabbis). Their plan was to divide the city into districts and designate a Vaad rabbi to be in charge of religious affairs for each district. In some sense, the Kehillah was attempting to resurrect a European model of communal structure with an empowered local religious authority. The Kehillah, through the Vaad, also sought to end religious corruption. They went after fraudulent kosher practices, a subject fraught with tension in New

York City.[156] The desire to end mushroom synagogues was similarly a stand against corruption. Mushrooms synagogues sometimes advertised that they would have great cantors and choirs at their services, when in reality they had no trained cantor, no choir, and no trained rabbi.[157] They were run by "charlatans," who in the eyes of the Kehillah were perpetuating religious corruption that needed to be rooted out. Progressive Era values then stood at the center of the Kehillah's ongoing battle against mushrooms.

In subsequent years, the Kehillah changed tactics in its fight against mushroom synagogues. The 1912 Report of the Executive Committee of the Kehillah reported that they set up only two synagogues that year for the High Holidays, but they bought a large number of tickets to give away to the poor at existing synagogues. The Kehillah was clearly frustrated with their efforts to stop mushrooms. They noted that their efforts to buy tickets were "far from meeting the problem of the mushroom synagogues that spring up during the holidays every year in unseemly places. . . . We are eager for suggestions that will point the way to a solution of this difficult problem."[158]

A year later, in 1913, they were still aggressively attacking the problem. They conducted the first survey of mushroom synagogues and discovered 286 such places in New York City. Harlem had the most at 95, a fact the Kehillah attributed to the relatively recent arrival of Jews to that area and, consequently, the lack of established synagogues. The report of the Kehillah to the Executive Committee of the American Jewish Committee noted that having undertaken this research, the organization was now ready to address the problem with yet another plan. The new plan called for renting large halls in conjunction with established synagogues or with local communities in areas most "afflicted" with mushrooms. They claimed that the services held in these halls would be self-supporting, but offered no evidence as to how this was going to function, given the reliance on philanthropic donations for previous efforts.[159]

The Kehillah's plans for a robust effort to eliminate mushroom synagogues faded along with the energy for the entire Kehillah project. The 1915 report to the Executive Committee of the American Jewish Committee noted only that the Kehillah had set up three synagogues that year for the High Holidays.[160] In that same period, the *New York Times* ran a pre–High Holidays article that detailed the Kehillah's efforts to oppose mushroom synagogues. The *Times* claimed that the Kehillah had effectively eliminated mushroom synagogues, writing, "This condition [of mushroom synagogues] has been largely done away with by a vigorous campaign of supervision and reorganization conducted by the Kehillah."[161] Presumably, the Kehillah had oversold its own achievements to the *Times*, because according to their own internal reports, there were still hundreds of mushroom synagogues in existence.[162]

The end of the Kehillah in 1922 marked the end of the first phase in the history of mushroom synagogues. Mushroom synagogues had outlasted their sworn enemy. For most of the 1920s, the established Jewish community tolerated the presence of the temporary synagogues without much comment. The reason for this complacency was the growth of establishment synagogues. Second-generation American Jews sought to expand their institutions to reflect their newfound prosperity, and rabbis of this period articulated a new vision of creating synagogues that served as community centers as well as places of worship. The 1920s was a "golden age" of synagogue construction. "It is the pervasive quality of the building phenomenon that is so striking," Kaufman writes in *Shul with a Pool*. "One can travel to just about any large city in the United States today, and locate the former Jewish neighborhood(s) of the interwar years."[163] Small *landsmanshaftn* synagogues became less common, as new synagogues with large seating capacities were built.

The synagogue building boom came to an abrupt end in 1929. With the Great Depression, synagogues that had only recently built large capacity buildings found it difficult to pay for the expansion. The High Holidays were seen as significant avenues of revenue for synagogues, because Jews would pay for High Holiday seats and would contribute to High Holiday fund-raising appeals. The *Jewish Daily Bulletin* confirmed the increased importance of the High Holidays for synagogue finances in a 1925 article, stating, "The income derived from the sale of [High Holiday] tickets and donations reached high sums, the possibility [existed] of paying off their mortgages, increasing the Hebrew schools, raising the salaries of the officiating rabbis and constructing new buildings."[164]

During the Great Depression, synagogues needed High Holiday attendance more than ever, but mushroom synagogues priced their High Holiday tickets less than established synagogues (usually $2 to $5 [$28 to $70] a ticket) and lured worshippers away. Whereas at the time of the

Kehillah, mushroom synagogues posed a religious threat, now they were a real economic threat. From 1929 to 1934, vigorous attempts were made by organized congregations and rabbinic associations to denounce and eliminate the mushrooms.

In 1932, for example, thirty Orthodox synagogues came together for the creation of an orthodox Vaad Ha'Kehillah (confederation of synagogues) in New York City for the express purpose of stopping mushroom synagogues. Their slogan was, "Don't Substitute the Dance Hall for the Synagogue." The president of the Vaad was quoted in the *Jewish Daily Bulletin* saying, "Every year, about the time of the High Holy Days we are faced with the same evil. In the guise of satisfying public demand, mushroom places of worship spring up, urging the public to come to them, and our regular congregations, whose doors are open all year round and who maintain rabbis, cantors and other budgetary requirements, must suffer. We appeal to the public to attend the permanent edifices."[165]

Another group that sought collective action against mushrooms during the Depression was the United Synagogue, the synagogue arm of the nascent Conservative movement. United Synagogue established a committee to expressly deal with the mushroom problem. Hyman Reit, chairman of the United Synagogue's mushroom synagogue committee said, "Unburdened by the heavy expenses and upkeep which legitimate synagogues and temples must carry, these individuals are enabled to sell seats for the so-called high holy day services at a price below that which regular temples must charge."[166] The Rabbinical Association of Yeshiva College, to cite yet one more example, issued a 1930 pre–High Holiday statement, saying, "The Rabbinical Association urges the Jews not to patronize these synagogues and makes a special plea at this time because the economic crisis makes them a particular menace to the regular congregations."[167]

United Synagogue, the Vaad Ha'Kehillah, and the Yeshiva University Rabbinical Association exemplify the Depression-era fight against mushroom synagogues. Their argument against mushrooms can be distinguished from the earlier arguments of the Kehillah. In the Kehillah period, the arguments against mushrooms were suffused with Progressive Era rhetoric that referred to protecting Jews so that they would not fall under the sway of charlatan rabbis who were running unscrupulous synagogues. During the Depression, the arguments against mushroom synagogues still characterized them as unscrupulous, but added a less pious complaint. Each of the above-cited groups made clear that mushrooms were "evil" because they were taking money away from established synagogues at an economically perilous time. The economic argument may seem obvious, but it was not until the Great Depression that established synagogues stated this explicitly. The difficulties of the Depression clearly evoked a more naked expression of survival.

We have little evidence from the Jews who attended the mushroom synagogues as to what exactly drew them. The *Jewish Daily Bulletin* carried an article in 1934 about a synagogue in Scotland that was going to use the local prison for High Holiday services because their sanctuary was too small and the prison was the largest hall they could afford. The article, in a wisecracking tone, says that it would be impossible for Jews to hold High Holiday services in a prison in America, because before this would happen, "an enterprising group of religious racketeers would have rushed to the rescue with one of their so-called mushroom temples. In a trice they'd have had an empty candy store, or a factory loft, or a decrepit theater rigged up with benches and an altar. 'The world's greatest cantor,' accompanied by an 'imported boys choir from Jerusalem,' would be featured in handbills and the overflow congregation would be handily taken care of, to their ultimate regret and to the profit of the promoters."[168] Despite the parody, the article makes clear that one of the draws of the mushroom synagogues was their promise of talent.

A more significant testimony to the appeal of mushroom synagogues is seen in a letter to the *American Hebrew* in 1931: "Why should not those who cannot afford fancy prices . . . seek religion at bargain prices? . . . Are not mushroom synagogues therefore rendering a real service?"[169] Presumably this was not a unique feeling, and the letter writer likely spoke for most Jews who populated the mushroom synagogues and understood them as a basic matter of competition. New York City Jews regarded mushrooms as a cheaper alternative in the same way a cheaper dry cleaner in the neighborhood might be welcomed. The letter writer also underscored the commonly held belief that synagogues were overpriced and reserved for the elite.

Beyond the bargain prices of mushroom synagogues, there are other cultural factors that explain their growth and popularity. Daniel Soyer, in his study of the *landsmanshaftn* that proliferated in the same time and in the same place as mushrooms, notes, "In striking ways, the Jewish *lands-manshaftn* reflected the influences of the surrounding culture more clearly than they mirrored Jewish communal traditions in Eastern Europe."[170] The influence of New York City's immigrant culture significantly legitimized mushrooms in two ways. In Eastern Europe, the concerted rabbinic outcry against them might have swayed mass Jewish opinion, but in New York a large swath of Jewish immigrant culture was decidedly antiauthoritarian. Jewish culture was famously awash in social and political movements that challenged existing power structures. Even for those Jews who still saw themselves as part of traditional Judaism, the American experience was a democratizing one that shunned coercion and authority. The experience of Rabbi Jacob Joseph and the failed efforts to create a central rabbinic authority and a central system of kashrut regulations speaks powerfully to the desire of Jewish immigrants to be free of central authority.[171] For many Jews of the Lower East Side, rabbinic condemnation of mushrooms was easy to ignore.

Jewish immigrant culture was also famously one of striving. The Jewish immigrant economy promoted individualism and competition, which was a departure for most immigrants who came from an Eastern European culture that emphasized economic interdependence. For some immigrants who were accustomed to looking for economic opportunities, running for-profit religious services may have been yet one more opportunity to make some money. And the mass of Jews who attended these services may have understood the validity of this opportunity as well. Mushrooms were just another spot in the rough and tumble marketplace of the Lower East Side.

As the Depression wore on, the challenge to mushroom synagogues appeared to grow even stronger. A coalition of the major Brooklyn congregations in 1934 hyperbolically declared, "Mushroom synagogues have done so much in recent years to undermine the normal and healthy development of our Jewish religion, thought and learning as [to] constitute a dire threat and sacrilege."[172] Some synagogues sought to build even more seating to fight mushrooms. The Montefiore Congregation announced its intention to spend $10,000 in 1930 to build additional seating for 200 people, "or the equivalent of the number of persons ordinarily attending services at mushroom synagogues."[173] The minutes for Montefiore Congregation are not extant but the announcement reflects a surprising degree of prosperity in the midst of the Great Depression. It also underscores the extent to which traditional synagogues felt themselves under siege by the mushroom synagogues.

We have one report that indicates that not all mushroom synagogues were run by shady and unscrupulous characters. In Newark, in 1933, a mushroom synagogue was going to be set up under the auspices of the Hebrew Orphans Sheltering Home. The orphanage had obtained free use of a theater. The *Jewish Daily Bulletin* writes: "However, when heads of several leading edifices conferred with the orphanage heads, the latter decided to call off their plan and co-operate with the synagogues. Reciprocally, the latter pledged the orphanage precedence in the matter of High Holiday appeals. The action taken by the orphanage has met with favorable response and accordingly created a psychological antipathy to the possible development of mushroom edifices of which in previous years there were a considerable number."[174]

There is no other evidence of mushrooms being run for nonprofits. The attacks against them uniformly characterize them as for-profit enterprises, and certainly had other nonprofits been running mushrooms, it would have been difficult to criticize them with such vehemence. Although Newark managed to control its mushroom problem, across the river in New York, matters were to be settled without compromise.

Unable to defeat mushroom synagogues from within the Jewish community, the established synagogues turned to lobbying the legislature to pass a law to defend their interests. The rabbis and congregational leaders represented an unusually united front against mushroom synagogues and managed to pass a law outlawing mushroom synagogues entirely. In June of 1934, Governor Herbert Lehman signed into law a bill passed by the state legislature, "An Act to Amend the Penal Law in Relation to Frauds on Religious Institutions." The text of the law read:

> A person who in the promotion of his own interests or to receive pecuniary benefit, gain or profit for himself or for any person, firm or corporation other than a religious association or corporation, sells or offers to sell tickets for admittance to or participation in services purporting to be in accordance with the precepts of any recognized religious creed or faith or makes any fraudulent representation as to the nature of the services to be conducted at any place designated or intended to be a house or worship or as to the manner in which such services are to be conducted thereat or as

to the facilities for worship therein or as to the number and qualifications of the persons engaged to conduct such services, is guilty of a misde-meanor.[175]

This law might seem difficult to enforce because it would require the secular authorities to distinguish between accepted and fraudulent practice. But there was a well-established precedent for the state to monitor religious fraud in the Jewish community. In 1915, the legislature passed a law against fraud in kosher food labeling, known in the Yiddish press simply as "the Kosher Bill." The Kosher Bill made it a misdemeanor to sell meat that has been represented as kosher but not "sanctioned by the Orthodox Hebrew religious requirements."[176] Even at the time of its passage, many complained that the law was impossible to enforce because two authorities could, and most certainly would, disagree on what constituted "Orthodox Hebrew religious requirement." This could have led potentially to a secular court choosing between rabbinic opinions.[177]

A test of the Kosher Bill made it to the Supreme Court in 1924, where the court upheld the constitutionality of the law, claiming the term "'ko-sher' has a meaning well enough defined to enable one engaged in the trade to correctly apply it at least as a general thing."[178] Despite the bill being upheld as constitutional, one of the major issues was the lack of an enforcement mechanism. In 1934, the same year the mushroom synagogue law was passed, a bill was passed by the New York State Legislature that set up a Kosher Law Enforcement Bureau with a budget for two inspectors to enforce the Kosher Bill.[179]

Although the kosher fraud law was different than the mushroom syna-gogue law in a number of respects, the general principle could be under-stood as the same: the state had the ability to determine what constituted religious fraud. Presumably, the legislature's experience with the kashrut laws was sufficient for them to enact the mushroom synagogue law. The mushroom synagogue law remains a part of the penal code of New York State but has never been litigated.

Immediately in the aftermath of the passage of the law, there was some internal Jewish debate regarding its wisdom. Max Schneider, the president of the Bronx Federation of Jewish Congregations, made it his mission to push every district attorney in the five boroughs to enforce the law against mushrooms. We have a report that at least one district attorney issued a public warning that he would charge anyone who set up a mushroom synagogue.[180] He also announced plans for the Bronx Federation to set up their own High Holiday services under strict religious auspices to be open to any Jew whether he could pay or not, a strategy that hearkened back to the Kehillah.

On the other hand, the chairman of the Jewish Council of Greater New York, Bernard Richards, showed some ambivalence about the law and castigated the Bronx president for his plans:

> It is bad enough that a state law had to be enacted to remove the evil of the mushroom synagogues and that this could not be done through the moral influence of the community which began to fight the evil through the old Kehillah some twenty years ago. Now, however, that the bill . . . has been enacted into law, Mr. Schneider should not be proposing to have his Federation set up new synagogues to meet the possible lack of accommodation in the regular synagogues for those who wish to attend services.[181]

Richards's comments reflected a fundamental issue for the established synagogues. Their victory in the legislature reflected their political strength but underscored their lack of moral persuasion among Jews themselves.

Despite Richards's ambivalence, the law was effective in essentially eliminating mushroom synagogues. After the law was passed, there were no reports of mushroom synagogues in the Jewish newspapers, no rabbinic organizations rallying against them, and no outcry over what a scourge they were. Although some form of mushroom synagogues continued to exist, Marshall Sklare mentioned mushrooms in a 1960 article as a decreasing phenomenon, one that "is rarely encountered in middle-class areas or prestigious neighborhoods."[182] For the most part, the law succeeded in ending "religion at bargain prices."

The attempt by mushrooms to provide religion at lower prices was initially an issue of supply and demand creating a market opening. Small synagogues at the turn of the twentieth century simply did not have the seats necessary to house everyone who wanted to come just for the High Holidays. When the supply of seats caught up with demand as synagogues got bigger, the driving economic issue became competition and cost. Established synagogues were charging more than some were willing to pay, and mushrooms were a cheap alternative. Rather than adapting an economic model to try and compete with the mushrooms, the religious establishment ultimately found they had the political power to eliminate them.

Mushroom synagogues were a unique phenomenon in American Jewish history and perhaps in American religious history. While American Christianity has had movements that preached a gospel connecting money and prayer, one is hard-pressed to find a case of mushroom churches — that is, churches being set up to make money by holding worship services for a holiday. Having for-profit religious institutions that provided bargain prices for religion is at once entirely in keeping with an American culture that is market oriented and, at the same time, antithetical to an American religious outlook, both Jewish and Christian, which sees the religious experience as priceless and attempts to profit from it unseemly. It was the particular factors of New York immigrant Jewish life — their embrace of competition, their dislike of coercion, and their attachment to Judaism — that allowed so many Jews to embrace mushroom synagogues and ignore the established religious authorities.

Mushroom synagogues and free synagogues were both challenges to the perceived elitism of established synagogues. But their challenges were coming from opposite directions. Mushroom synagogues unabashedly embraced capitalism and the market. They provided competition for established synagogues through low-cost High Holiday tickets. Free synagogues took the exact opposite approach, rejecting market ideology. Stephen Wise abhorred the selling of seats because he objected to the commodification of religion. Free synagogues effectively argued that religion should not have a price; congregants should give as their heart moved them. Perhaps it was the stringency of both approaches that caused them to fail. Wise's hope for completely voluntary funding of synagogues was too radical, as was the mushroom synagogue's "bargain" approach.

Although they both failed to create lasting movements, they did succeed in pressuring congregations to eliminate the elitism inherent in selling seats. As we will discuss in the next chapter, synagogues in the post–World War I era moved away from selling seats as a response to calls for greater democracy in the synagogue. The rejection of differentiation based on wealth that both the free synagogue and the mushroom synagogues embodied has become the norm for American synagogues.

FOUR

"No Aristocracy and No Snobocracy: In God's House All Must Be Equal" [1919–1945]

The president of Congregation Adath Israel, a large Reform Temple in Louisville, Kentucky, used his 1919 annual address to chastise the membership for their apathy, saying, "In this congregation for years there has persisted an undeniable lack of interest, not only in affairs of the Congregation but in Judaism itself."[1] The president blamed the materialism of American culture for leading Jews away from religion, and pleaded for change, stating, "I am convinced that something must be done to resuscitate its religious life. . . . We need more money, we need more interest, we need more activity, and we must have it, and from you." He proposed a number of solutions to revivify the synagogue, but the proposal he was most emphatic about was the need to end the selling of pews as the financial system of the congregation. "It is solely my own recommendation . . . that the time has now come for Adath Israel to take one more step forward in its reform and its democracy by asking that each and every pewholder in the congregation surrender his pew," he said.

Beginning in the early part of the twentieth century with rabbis like Leo Franklin in Detroit, there was a push to end the buying of seats and pews and replace it with the unassigned or free seating system. The unassigned pew system meant that seats would no longer be owned by members; they would be given out on a first-come first-serve basis, and the congregation would be financially supported by members placing themselves into a dues category based on their financial means. These dues categories would be roughly equal to the amount members were paying in seat assessments under the old system.

As we will explore below, the impetus for the change to free seating was a result of both financial and cultural factors. The financial push came from the desire of synagogues to expand their membership rolls. When synagogues sold seats, they were limited in their membership to the number of seats in the sanctuary. With free seating this constraint was removed. The cultural push for free seating was even more significant, though. The buying of seats created visible distinctions in the synagogue based on wealth, which ran counter to Progressive Era values of democracy and equality.

Although there was substantial push toward dues and free seating after World War I, the move to the unassigned pew created tremendous anxiety among congregations contemplating the change. There was a fear that without the status of a prominent seat, the wealthier members of the congregation would simply not support the synagogue. In some synagogues it also meant displacing families that had owned the same seats for generations. There was also a whole range of smaller issues that opponents of the new system put forth, such as the difficulty for families to sit together if they no longer had an assigned pew. The High Holidays, when synagogues would see the most activity, became a particular focus of worry that members would be unhappy without their own seats.

The debate over the unassigned seating system also touched on larger ideological issues. The ownership of seats meant that the wealthy had permanent privileges in the synagogue. For some this was at odds with American notions of democracy and egalitarianism. When the president of Adath Israel claimed that the move to unassigned pews was a move to greater democracy, he was reflecting the American vision of a classless society, where wealth did not confer privilege, particularly in a house of worship.[2]

While synagogues began the process of moving toward dues, this period of synagogue finance was also marked by dramatic boom and dramatic bust. The Gilded Age of the 1920s was a time of dramatic synagogue building. The creation of the synagogue-center provided an ideological foundation for erecting substantially larger and more expansive synagogue buildings. Synagogues with social halls, gyms, school wings, and even pools were built across the country, some approaching a price tag of $20,000,000 in today's dollars. The problem for synagogues was that much of the debt for this building boom came due just in time for the Great Depression.

The Depression decimated synagogue budgets, and many congregations were forced to lay off workers and slash expenses. But most synagogues muddled through. The number of synagogues even increased during the Depression, even as membership in most synagogues decreased. As we will examine in this chapter, the Depression impacted not just the synagogue budgets but also the way in which many rabbis approached money and politics. Like many in the country, Jewish clergy were radicalized by the vast economic devastation, and even the rabbinic associations were articulating basically Socialist positions. This would prove to be a temporary phase for both the country and for rabbis, as the economic expansion after the Second World War would renew the push toward building large congregations and end calls for government taking over industry.

"Democracy Everywhere": The End of Selling Seats and the Creation of the Dues System

The first major experiment of unassigned seating began more by chance than by design. Congregation Beth El in Detroit built a new synagogue in 1903 for the price of $130,000 [$2,672,601]. The congregation paid for the building from a variety of sources: they sold their old building to the Young Woman's Christian Association for $40,000 [$1,037,903]; the Beth El Women's Auxiliary Society raised $13,000 [$337,318] at a "grand fair"; they took out a mortgage for $25,000 [$648,690]; and the rest was raised "easily" through donations.[3] The congregation's move to a new location turned out to be a boon for the synagogue. At the time of the dedication of the new temple the congregation had 200 members; seven years later the congregation had 421 members. Thanks to the automobile industry, Detroit was booming and many Jews and non-Jews were moving there. A problem arose for the congregation, however, precisely because of this growth. There was such a groundswell of interest in being part of the newly built synagogue that they could not figure out how to adequately assign seats. Until they could resolve the issue, the congregation moved into the new building using unassigned pews and created dues categories that each member placed himself into, "his rating of course being subject to the board."[4]

The leadership of the synagogue called a congregational meeting in September 1903 to decide what to do about seating and financing. The notice to all the members laid out the options. The congregation could: (1) sell seats, (2) rent seats, (3) continue with unassigned pews and differentiated dues

categories, or (4) create a uniform dues number and members would give
voluntarily over and above that number. The leadership of the congregation
ended the notice by stating in all capital letters, "NO MORE IMPORTANT
MEETING HAS EVER BEEN HELD BY OUR CONGREGATION. IT IS THERE-
FORE OF THE GREATEST IMPORTANCE THAT YOU BE PRESENT."[5]

Despite their efforts, the congregation could not come to a solution,
as members remained divided on the best plan. More meetings followed
until finally the congregation decided "at a large and enthusiastic meeting"
to continue the unassigned seating system. Even this did not put the issue
to rest, though. Some prominent members threatened resignation — they
complained that they might not be able to sit with their family, that it would
be difficult for older members to search around for a seat, and that if they
came late they might not get a seat at all. No mention was made of a desire
for status that buying the best seats conferred, but presumably this weighed
on the minds of opponents. Ultimately, the congregation compromised
with some of the dissenters. They allowed disgruntled ex-presidents to
choose seats that would be permanently theirs as a special exception to
the unassigned system.[6]

Despite its circumstantial beginnings, Leo Franklin became a true believer in the unassigned pew system and trumpeted the plan nationally. In
an editorial in the *American Israelite*, he opined at length on the virtues of
the system:

> [The unassigned pew] is an innovation of such tremendous significance,
> touching as it does the very fundamental principles of congregational
> organization that it promises to revolutionize ere long, the policy of many
> of our leading congregations. . . . The contention of many that men should
> have material advantage in the synagogue in proportion to the amount
> of money they pay is fundamentally wrong, unjust and un-Jewish. . . . If
> material advantages are to be considered in synagogue at all, they must be
> not in proportion to amount of money one is fortunate enough to be able
> to pay, but rather to the sacrifice he makes in paying anything at all. . . .
> The assignment of seats according to any of the old system leads inevitably
> to the creation in the synagogue of a poor man's corner and a rich man's
> corner. And against this the new policy is a protest. In God's house all
> must be equal. There must be no aristocracy and no snobocracy. Every

man who is worthy of religious fellowship deserves an equal place with every other.[7]

Franklin's editorial then switched from ideological to practical considerations. He noted that the most significant concern over the unassigned pew system was that it would decrease the revenue of the synagogue, but Beth El had not seen their revenue suffer. They instituted membership dues categories ranging from $300 [$778] to $15,000 [$38,920], in which members placed themselves with oversight by the board, and the plan had worked successfully.

Franklin also made clear that the unassigned pew was not to be confused with the free synagogue: "The 'unassigned pew' must not be confused with the so called 'free pew' which is based on an entirely different principle. I do not by any means favor encouraging the congregational bargain-seeker, or more correctly the man who 'uses' the good offices of the minister and congregation when he needs them, but pays not once cent to the support of either."[8]

Franklin understood the unassigned pew system as precisely the right balance between seat owning, which sanctioned privileges for the wealthy, and the voluntary free system, which was open to individuals abusing the system by not contributing a fair share. Franklin claimed, "The system is one that is as nearly ideal as human institution can be."[9]

Despite Franklin's assertion that the system was ideal, he remained one of the lone voices agitating for it for many years. Unlike Wise and the free synagogue, which spawned a number of congregations modeled on the voluntary method, initially there was no embrace by other synagogues of the unassigned pew.

This would change substantially change in 1919 when Pittsburgh's Rodef Shalom moved to the unassigned pew system. Rodef Shalom's success with unassigned pews succeeded where Franklin's had not, it ignited a nationwide debate over the issue, and it inspired a number of imitators. Members of Rodef Shalom pushed the UAHC national biennial convention of 1919 to spend a morning debating the merits of the model. The UAHC ultimately passed a resolution urging congregations to consider changing to the unassigned pew system.[10]

As in the case of Temple Beth El, the initial impetus for the unassigned system in Rodef Shalom was a result of synagogue crowding. The synagogue was forced to close its membership because they had run out of seats to sell to everyone who wanted to join. To be able to admit more members, the congregation proposed a move to the unassigned system on a trial basis. At the end of a two-year trial period, pew owners would vote on whether to continue the unassigned system or revert to pew owning. During the trial, members would give to the congregation "in accordance with their ability (which of course should be at least as much as they have [been] paying heretofore)."[11]

After one year of the trial, the congregation triumphantly reported that the finances of the congregation were booming. The congregation noted that 201 of the 245 pew owners had already agreed to turn over their pew to the congregation. This represented a donation to the congregation of $144,500 [$1,688,740]. The year before the change was made, the congregation had 789 members and seat holders who collectively contributed $40,688.70 [$475,520]. The year after the change, the congregation had 1,038 members who collectively contributed $66,756 [$780,163].[12] The congregation was well aware of the significance of their efforts. They produced three reports annually on the progress of the unassigned system, and each report contained some variation of the sentiment that "the country is paying attention to how we are progressing."[13]

The financial success of Rodef Shalom was instrumental in pushing other congregations to consider the change. If unassigned seating was financially viable, then this undercut the main critique of the system, which was that it could not raise the same amount of money as selling seats. Rabbi Harry Levy of Temple Israel in Boston trumpeted Rodef Shalom's financial success as a model for Temple Israel. Like Rodef Shalom, Temple Israel was limited in their growth by the number of seats, so unassigned seating would lead to unfettered growth, as it did in Pittsburgh. "Increased membership means larger strength, larger influence, larger possibilities. And there is no limit to the number of members we can secure."[14]

Levy was careful to articulate the practical implications of unassigned seating. If Temple Israel had more members than seats, the High Holidays would pose a special problem as the time when all the members would come. Levy proposed the congregation hold two High Holiday services, either concurrently in separate spaces or sequentially, with the same service being repeated. He also made clear that only members would be issued special cards for the holidays, ensuring them a seat but just not ensuring them a special seat. These would be minor issues, though, compared to the general vitality that the unassigned pew would give the congregation.

The financial success of this model was important news, not just for congregations that were growing but also for congregations that had seen pew sales slide and were concerned what to do next. Temple Adath Israel in Louisville, cited at the beginning of this chapter, was one such congregation. The president of the congregation noted that one of the central factors driving him to propose the elimination of selling pews was the simple fact that people did not want to buy pews anymore, and that "numerous pews are being surrendered to the congregation, and . . . if we increase the assessment upon the pews, many other members would surrender their pews."[15] The reason he believed that people were no longer interested in buying pews or paying for them was quite simple — democracy:

> The time has now come for Adath Israel to take one more step forward
> in its reform and its democracy by asking that each and every pewholder
> in the congregation surrender his pew. You hear much about democracy
> these days; democracy everywhere, but it occurs to me that there is no
> place on earth where there should be so much of democracy as in the
> house of God. There should be in the temple no distinction of wealth or
> class; there should be no rich men's section and no poor man's corner.
> There should be that equality in the privilege of worship that we believe
> all men do have when eventually they are called to face their Maker. There
> should be no great, no small, no rich, no poor. Every man should be
> permitted to enter a temple and take whatsoever seat he may desire that
> may be unoccupied at the time of his entrance.[16]

For the most part, the president of Adath Israel was echoing Leo Franklin's claims from fifteen years earlier that the selling of seats was anti-egalitarian, but the important distinction between this iteration and Franklin's was the specific focus on democracy. Franklin argued for unassigned seating on the basis of a democratic ideal, but he did not actually use the term *democracy*. Whereas in 1919, democracy seems to be the central idea for everyone pushing for eliminating pew sales.

The UAHC's resolution urging congregations to adopt the unassigned pew places democracy as the singular issue involved: "Whereas, Judaism is a religion in which the principle of democracy finds distinct expression, and whereas, in actuality this principle has failed to receive the fullest expression and practice in the congregational organization of most of the congregations belonging to the Union, be it resolved that this Union of American Congregations take steps to encourage among its members such changes in their constitutions as will establish the unassigned pew and the elimination of the minimum due."[17]

Rabbi Levy in Boston argued similarly, saying, "What are the advantages of the unassigned pew? It makes the synagogue what it ought and must be, democratic."[18] Rabbi Henry Berkowitz of Philadelphia's Rodeph Shalom argued at the UAHC convention that in olden times, the synagogue was democratic but in modern times it became aristocratic. The unassigned pew would return the synagogue to a democratic state.[19] Temple Emanu-El in Milwaukee abolished "the time-worn pew system" and did "away with the undemocratic method of classifying its membership by any standard of preferment."[20]

While unassigned seating attracted far more attention in the Reform movement, some Orthodox synagogues debated its merits, and there too, the discussion was about democracy. In 1919, David De Sola Pool, rabbi of Shearith Israel, spoke in favor of the system. He claimed that the unassigned system would inevitably come with the democratizing of the churches and synagogues. De Sola Pool argued that the system would soon be adopted universally and pew owners would have to give up their attachment to their pews for the greater good.[21] When the Brooklyn Jewish Center was conceived in that same year, some argued to establish it on the basis of unassigned seating, because selling pews "seemed to be on the way out in favor of democracy."[22] Seemingly every argument and every mention of the unassigned seating system in the immediate post–World War I era was wrapped up with references to democracy.

The synagogue emphasis on democracy simply mirrored the wider cultural atmosphere, where discussion of democracy was rampant. In 1917, Woodrow Wilson requested a declaration of war with the famous aim of making the world safe for democracy. At precisely that same period, women were fighting for suffrage and using the language of democracy. In fact, some women would use quotes from the president's own language of democracy to embarrass him and make their point. The suffragettes would march with banners that read, "We shall fight for the things which we have always held nearest our hearts — for democracy, for the right of those who submit to authority to have a voice in their own government."[23] W. E. B. Dubois used a similarly ironic rhetoric to talk about expanded democracy for African Americans, saying, "We return from fighting. We return fighting. Make way for Democracy."[24]

The president of Adath Israel said democracy was everywhere, and it seemingly was. Postwar America was awash in discussions of democracy, and within this context the pew system seemed outmoded. And because it was outmoded, members were less interested in buying seats. This postwar cultural atmosphere explains why Leo Franklin's efforts to promote unassigned seating at the turn of the twentieth century did not lead to change, while the calls for unassigned seating after the war did. The democratic nature of unassigned seating had a strong cultural resonance in 1919. Its time had come in an American society acutely discussing the meaning of democracy.

As an interesting aside, the president of Adath Israel linked the democracy of unassigned seating with a democratic call for greater women's participation in the synagogue. Right after he called on the synagogue to eliminate pew sales, he asked for women to sit on the board of the congregation:

> Another personal recommendation I desire to make is that women should be placed upon the Board of the Congregation. In every sphere of secular life women are today being accepted in their proper position. . . . She is receiving that recognition which all too many years she has been denied, and if in the secular world she is entitled to place and privilege which are accorded men, surely in the congregation, in the matter of religion, she is properly entitled to consideration. . . . The greater part of the activities of this Congregation are directed by women; by far the greater attendance is on the part of women. The concern manifested in congregational affairs by women is infinitely greater than that manifested by the men. It seems to me undemocratic, unfair, and not in keeping with the broad principles of Israel or of our country to deny to women that representation for which I am herein pleading.[25]

In the example of Adath Israel, one can see with unusual clarity the in-fluence of the broader culture on the internal dynamics of the synagogue. The cultural expectations of increased democracy pushed the congregation to change its financial and governance structures in order to align the congregation with changing American mores.

Ultimately, a number of synagogues followed Rodeph Shalom and elim-inated pews in the postwar era. These included Temple Adath Israel in Louisville, Temple Beth Zion in Buffalo, Temple Israel in New Rochelle, Temple Israel in Memphis, Temple Emanu-El in Milwaukee, Congregation Achduth Vesholom in Ft. Wayne, and Congregation Beth Israel in Houston, where "an individual exception was made to this ruling [eliminating pew sales], and for many years a dainty foot stool marked the place which was reserved as a tribute to one slightly, erect lady."[26]

For other congregations, the process took decades. In 1921, Temple Israel's Special Committee on Unassigned Pews made a recommendation in favor of eliminating pew sales, which the temple board approved. They explicitly followed the model of Rodeph Shalom and proposed that the unassigned pew system be instituted for a two-year trial. If after two years 80 percent of pew owners decided that the system was not beneficial to the synagogue, the congregation would go back to pew sales; otherwise, the unassigned system would remain in place and pew owners would turn over their pews.[27] It seems that the system was never enacted, though, because one year later the president wrote in his annual message that "the unassigned pew system . . . had not become a reality as yet, due mainly to the fact that many of our members seemed rather indifferent about it. Many others, however, expressed themselves as being in favor of it, [but] not enough to cover the necessary quota. . . . It has [therefore] been dropped for the time being."[28] The congregation did not end up moving to the unassigned pew system until the mid-1950s.[29]

The move to unassigned seating spread slowly but inexorably through American Judaism. In 1936, the Union of American Hebrew Congregations estimated that large Reform congregations were roughly split between unas-signed pews and assigned pews, while smaller congregations were a majority using unassigned pews. A small number of congregations, they noted, were using the voluntary model of Stephen Wise. "The unassigned pew system, which is steadily gaining in favor, is an indication of a definite tendency in the direction of more democratic methods in seating as well as in the scale of payments," Jacob Schwartz wrote in *Financial Security for Your Synagogue*.[30] By 1940, nearly two hundred synagogues had adopted some form of free seating.[31] Although there are no full-scale statistics on the matter, by the 1960s it appears that most synagogues of all denominations had moved to unassigned seating with the exception of the High Holidays. Jonathan Sarna notes that one of the most interesting facets of the move to free seating was that the debate remained largely on the local congregational level. Each congregation weighed the decision for themselves and the issue did not become a broader point of contention between the different movements. Despite the UAHC's national endorsement of unassigned seating, there is no evidence that the other movements raised any ideological opposition to it, and as noted earlier, David De Sola Pool, rabbi of Shearith Israel, an Orthodox synagogue, was an early voice in favor of the change — in theory, at least, as his synagogue did not eliminate pew sales for decades.[32]

The move to free seating was driven by the ideological commitment to democracy, but it was also driven by the stories of financial success from Rodeph Shalom. American synagogue history is a constant tug between idealism and financial practicality. For some synagogues, despite all of the rhetoric around democracy, unassigned seating came with a large exception — during the High Holidays there would be assigned seats. Some congregations assigned seats arbitrarily and some congregations maintained stratified seating prices for the High Holidays. It was a compromise between the democratic ideal that individuals should not own prized seats in the house of worship and a nod to the reality that members wanted to be assured of proper seats on the most important days of the year, lest they have to run around looking for an empty seat. Congregations rarely filled up outside the High Holidays, so the practical implications of not having an assigned seat on other days were effectively limited. But when the throngs of worshippers came for the holidays, the congregation needed to assure its members there would be some tangible benefit to having paid their dues.

The High Holidays had historically been the focal point of the financial year for congregations. Pews would typically go on sale before the holidays, but with the elimination of pew sales, there was even more focus on the High Holidays. If members did not have their payments in order they would not receive their High Holiday seat. Congregations used, and still use today, the promise of a High Holiday ticket to extract from members all financial commitments to the synagogue.

The switch to dues categories touched on another significant tension in synagogue financing, namely the question of whether members should pay what they are capable of paying based on their income or whether all members should contribute equally regardless of wealth. The first congregations that eliminated pew sales believed in dues categories based on income. Franklin wrote, "The principle that each man should give according to his means, *ke-matenath Yado*,[33] should be basic to the financial system of every well regarded Jewish congregation."[34] In many respects, this made the switch away from pew sales easier to digest. As there were stratified payments under the old system, so there would be under the new system. One could have imagined, though, a democratic, egalitarian argument to be made that everyone should simply pay the same fee.

There seems to have been no real discussion of this possibility, however. Perhaps the passage in 1913 of the Sixteenth Amendment establishing a permanent income tax created the cultural template here. Progressive Era economists argued that the most moral way for the government to raise income was a progressive income tax. Columbia University economist Edwin R. A. Seligman, the son of banker Joseph Seligman and a member of Felix Adler's Ethical Culture Society, was one of the most prominent voices for the income tax. He argued that justice demanded that "each individual should be held to help the state in proportion to his ability to help himself."[35] Seligman also argued that taxation was about duty: "We pay taxes not because we get benefits from the state, but because it as much our duty to support the state as to support ourselves or our family."[36] In short, the democratic ideal put forth by Progressive Era intellectuals was that duty and justice demanded individuals pay according to their means, and they should pay regardless of particular benefits they might be receiving. This ideal seems to fit with the change in synagogue financing away from paying for the benefit of a particular seat and toward paying for the synagogue out of a sense of duty.

But despite the initial push to dues categories and using what would come to be known as the "fair share" system, some synagogues would later move to one uniform dues fee (often with categories based on age but not income).

I have not found evidence suggesting that the change was ideological; it seems more to have been practical. Still, uniform dues underscored the idea that all members of the congregation were treated alike. A uniform dues fee had the added benefit of not entangling the congregation in determining the income of members who preferred to keep their financial information private. The debate over which system — the fair share or the uniform dues system — was more ideologically justified and financially beneficial never really ended. It remains alive and well today, with contemporary synagogues relatively split between the two systems.[37]

The change from pew sales to income-based dues categories was also significant because it meant that members no longer had the agency to decide what to give to their synagogue. One could choose to buy or not buy nicer seats. But there was no choice when it came to income-based dues. The dues system thus stood directly opposite the voluntarism that characterized both the free synagogue movement and most Protestant churches of the time. Synagogue members came to accept the idea of dues as a kind of compulsory and necessary tax. "Dues," Jonathan Sarna has argued, are "the price [Jews] pay for the separation of church and state."[38]

It is noteworthy how divided the Jewish and Protestant financial systems became. By the early twentieth century, as churches continued to move away from pew sales and toward the free church model, they developed a sophisticated corpus of theological and practical reflection — known as stewardship — focused on why members should give voluntarily to their churches. Stewardship became an integral part of Protestant church life. Synagogues developed no similar system. This speaks in large part to how successful synagogues were in the twentieth century in raising necessary funds without recourse to any special theological or homiletical idea. The powerful impulse among Jews to belong to a synagogue for religious and ethnic reasons made dues a success. Jews accepted the "tax" as necessary to belong to the group.

The Boom before the Bust

At the same time that synagogues were debating the move to unassigned seating, they were also building more and more synagogues to have these debates in. Between 1916 and 1921, 400,000 Jews would immigrate to America. The number of synagogue members would swell as a result of this immigration as well as the fact that earlier immigrants now had children in need of a Jewish education. They also had greater means to be able to spend on the synagogue. The U.S. Religious Census of 1926 found that there were over four million members of synagogues.[39] The number of synagogues would go from 1,619 in 1916 to 3,118 in 1926.[40] The total expenditure to create synagogue buildings in this period, both acquiring and refurbishing old buildings as well as new construction, totaled $78,000,000 [$1.3 billion].[41] This was the golden age of synagogue building.

At the center of the building boom was the new synagogue-center. Mordecai Kaplan, the figure most associated with the synagogue-center movement, sought to expand the role of the synagogue in the lives of its members. Influenced by the Institutional Church movement, Kaplan believed that for the synagogue to be relevant, it must touch on all facets of Jewish life; in his words, "It must be the Jew's second home. It must become his club, his theater, and his forum."[42] According to Kaplan, the synagogue-center should provide "Jewish elementary school facilities; recreational facilities such as gymnasia, showers, bowling alleys, pool tables and game rooms; adult study and art groups; communal activities; religious services and festival pageants and plays; informal meetings of friends and associates."[43]

While not all synagogue-centers quite reached this level of activity, many synagogues came close. The Brooklyn Jewish Center, built in 1920, combined a synagogue with a Hebrew school, kosher restaurant, library, pool, gym, bowling alley, and men and women's social rooms. Kaplan himself was the founding rabbi of the Manhattan Jewish Center, which had a synagogue, assembly hall, gym, swimming pool, meeting rooms, and a school.[44]

While Kaplan supplied the ideological foundations for the synagogue-center, there were also socioeconomic factors that pushed these large new synagogues. "Laymen . . . tended to see the synagogue-center in . . . pragmatic terms; as a means to 'sell' the masses on synagogue membership, and even more critically, to 'lure' straying youth back into the fold of the Jewish community," David Kaufman wrote in *Shul with a Pool*.[45] With the combination of ideological and sociological factors, the synagogue-center concept swept across the country. Synagogue-centers were built in almost every American city with a sizable Jewish population.

Just a small sample of these synagogues will illustrate the significant expansion of American synagogues as well as their commensurate costs. In Boston, Congregation Mishkan Tefila's synagogue-center was finished in 1929 and came to a total of $1,050,000 [$14,343,204].[46] In 1926, Temple Emanu-El of San Francisco built a synagogue-center complex with three buildings — a synagogue, an administration building, and a "Temple House" with a social hall and meeting areas. The buildings cost collectively $1,250,000 [$16,533,053]. In 1924, Newark's Temple B'nai Abraham built a synagogue with a 2,000-seat sanctuary, a social center, and a pool at a cost of $1,250,000 [$17,115,843].[47] Beth El in Detroit spent $1,000,000 [$13,967,020] in 1922 to create their synagogue-center, "a marvel of architecture and engineering," according to an article in the *American Israelite*.[48] Temple Tifereth Israel in Cleveland, known as "The Temple," dedicated in 1924, was perhaps the most expensive synagogue built in a period of expensive synagogues. Its final bill was $1,300,000 [$17,800,476]. Tifereth Israel's sanctuary was built to hold 1,900 people. Additionally, there was a gymnasium, a kitchen, a library, a memorial chapel, and an auditorium that could accommodate 1,200. The elaborate main sanctuary was "a seven-sided dome chamber lighted by a group of five windows on each side. At night, artificial lighting comes through these windows, giving the effect of daylight," according to the *American Israelite*. The synagogue proudly declared there would be no need for light fixtures in the sanctuary because of this extraordinary effect. The synagogue was a marvel to the ears as well as the eyes, as audio experts declared the synagogue's acoustics perfect.[49]

The fact that so many synagogue-centers were built was testament to Kaplan and like-minded thinkers who pushed to expand the mission of the synagogue. However, paying for the synagogue-centers may have been more challenging than agreeing on the concept. As Deborah Dash Moore, in her article on the founding of the Brooklyn Jewish Center, writes, "The issue that stirred the most debate [in creating the Center] revolved less around the ... ideal of a Jewish center ... than around its financing."[50]

A close look at the finances of the building of Temple Israel in Boston reflects this truth. In the post–World War I era, Temple Israel was growing by leaps and bounds. Under their beloved rabbi, Harry Levy, the congregation became the most influential Reform synagogue in New England, a "hub of local Jewish life," well known for its communal activism, its patriotism, its interfaith activities, and its modern approach to Jewish life.[51] Between 1920 and 1923, the congregation grew from 433 to 652 families.[52] There were not nearly enough seats for members who wished to purchase them and the president reported that the congregation routinely had to turn away 1,000 people at Sunday services.[53]

The time had come for a significant expansion of the synagogues to accommodate all those who wanted to be a part of them. Interestingly, the president argued that synagogue expansion was necessary not just to accommodate Jews, but also for the many Christians who came to services. The board minutes of 1924 noted, "With only 1,082 seats, we are obliged to turn away as many every Sunday, part of whom are of the Christian faith who might be affected in their attitude towards our people if they were permitted to hear and see a Jewish service as it is."[54] Young Jews "who need the influence of our Rabbi's ideals," and Orthodox Jews who are "seeking something their congregations cannot provide," were also being turned away for want of a larger space.

The congregation followed national trends closely and was keen to create a synagogue-center. The president of the congregation argued, "With the inspiration that comes from seeing all the beautiful Jewish temples of Chicago, Cleveland, Cincinnati, [and] Pittsburgh, I am convinced that Boston is sadly in need of a proper religious center."[55] His wishes for a synagogue-center in Boston would soon be answered, and not just by Temple Israel. Temple Ohabei Shalom, Congregation Kehillath Israel, and Congregation Mishkan Tefila would all build extensive and expensive synagogue-centers in the exact same period as Temple Israel had.[56] The synagogue-center boom was alive and well in Boston in the 1920s.

Boston's synagogue building "craze" fit into the general economic expansion of the time. New construction in the mid-1920s was happening all around the synagogue, as the president noted, "Buildings are going up every day — we can see them in every direction, but my friends, they are merely buildings to live in or do business in, while we are concerned with buildings for religious need."[57] All of these factors — the national religious trends, the booming local economy, and the increased demand to be a part of the synagogue — pushed Temple Israel to plan for a large new home.

In 1923, Temple Israel's board passed a resolution that called for the synagogue to build a new "Temple Israel Center."[58] The finances of the congregation, however, were not quite as robust as their vision. Their income roughly matched their expenses at this time, but the ways and means committee prophesied future trouble. Even if the congregation could raise the money to construct the new building, the ongoing cost of such a massive new structure would demand significant new revenue sources.

The congregation had expenses of $42,899.91 [$588,589]; around 60 percent went to salaries, with the largest salary being that of Rabbi Levy, who earned $10,000 [$136,927].[59] The biggest financial issue, besides the new building, was the recent commitment the congregation had made to pay the Union of American Hebrew Congregations 10 percent of the congregation's expenses, or roughly $4,000 [$54,771]. Temple Israel's board passed along the bill to its membership. They charged each member a special 10 percent assessment on their dues earmarked for the UAHC.[60] On the income side, the congregation earned $41,876.76 [$574,552], made up almost entirely — 99 percent — of dues and seat assessments.

The initial fund-raising for the Temple Israel Center went successfully for the congregation, with 406 members pledging $235,000 [$3,217,778] in the first year. This meant an average gift of $578.82 [$7,926], an impressive outpouring of resources, reflective of the general wealth of the congregation and its commitment to the project. Synagogue records show that the giving was well spread among members and not concentrated among a few very wealthy individuals. The building committee chairperson did note at the annual 1924 meeting that 223 members had not yet pledged, but he was optimistic that these members would soon join the campaign.[61]

The congregation purchased a plot of land for $150,000 [$2,058,009], for which it took out a $90,000 [$1,234,805] mortgage and put down $60,000 [$823,204] in cash.[62] The congregation's initial plan called for a campus to include "a grand sanctuary," along with a school to accommodate 1,000 students, as well as an auditorium, administrative offices, and space for meetings. The first phase of the building would cost $400,000 [$5,488,024], which meant the congregation would need to raise an additional $150,000 [$2,058,009]. The initial optimism about the fund-raising, however, seems to have withered quickly, as the president in his 1925 annual message struck a piqued tone: "The pledges received so far have been made by one-half of our members and I sometimes wonder what the other half is waiting for. . . . As compared with other large cities, and . . . with other congregations in our own city, we seem to be rather slow in coming forward. Many have given and given liberally, but there are others who have not done their share."[63] On top of this, the ways and means committee of the congregation again warned that nothing was being done to prepare for the increased ongoing expenses for a new synagogue-center beyond the cost of the building.[64]

The president of the synagogue, Felix Vorenberg, became so disenchanted with the progress of fund-raising that he resigned his post out of his feeling that "it was best for all concerned to make a change."[65] On January 1, 1927, the congregation was still trying to raise the money for the first part of the building. The brotherhood and the sisterhood collectively pledged to raise $35,000 [$471,891].[66] In post–World War I synagogues, these auxiliary organizations would become crucial in providing funds for building projects.

The congregation finally achieved enough revenue from fund-raising to be able to take out a five-year, $600,000 [$8,080,567] loan at 5.25 percent interest with the intention of completing the first two phases of a construction project whose total cost was now projected to be roughly $1,000,000 [$13,482,612].[67] The congregation had raised by this point close to $400,000 [$5,393,055], so the repayment of the loan would still entail significant effort for the congregation.

To address the need for greater revenue for both mortgage repayment and the increased expenditures associated with the new campus, estimated to be $104,500 [$1,408,932], the congregation instituted a significant new financial plan. The Special Committee on Revenue and Maintenance called for the congregation to increase its dues by 100 percent. They also recommended that the children of nonmembers in religious school be charged $30 [$404] (if they could afford it). Finally, they called for the temple's payments to the UAHC to be reduced from 10 percent of expenses to 5 percent. The committee also reported, "Our present membership should be increased so as to give us added financial strength to carry out our program."[68]

Within these recommendations, one can see some of the basic financing issues for synagogues of the time and which remain issues for synagogues to this day. Temple Israel's decision to halve its payment to the UAHC represented a loss of approximately $3,000 [$40,448] to the national movement. Further, Temple Israel was (and still remains) a flagship Reform synagogue whose decisions were watched by other congregations. The UAHC's response to Temple Israel is not extant, but one can only imagine the national movement reacted with significant dismay not only to the loss of revenue but also to the fear that others might follow suit. The funding of the national offices and seminaries for all of the denominations would be an important issue in synagogue finance throughout the twentieth century. The issue has taken on even greater significance in contemporary financing as more congregations balk at passing money "upstream" to the national organizations, threatening the very existence of those institutions.

The inadequate plan for financing that led to the decision to double the cost of membership while simultaneously calling for new members to join the synagogue represents another (albeit problematic) pattern in synagogue finance. The board minutes of the synagogue make clear that the ways and means committee, a small cadre of people who truly understood the finances of the synagogue, warned for a number of years that a significant increase in revenue would be necessary, but a serious plan was put off until the building project was well under way. In the first few years of the fund-raising campaign, neither the president nor the rabbi made any mention of significant new costs for members to absorb beyond the capital campaign. The doubling of dues may have had the disincentive of pushing members away precisely when the congregation needed members the most. Temple Israel was far from alone, though, in following this exact pattern. In a speech to the Rabbinical Assembly of the Conservative Movement in 1931 on "Lessons from the Economic Crisis," Rabbi Alter Landesman said, "In many cases magnificent structures were built which were not paid for, and now their mortgages are a source of continual worry to their membership. . . . No plans were made beyond the immediate future. No means were devised for their support after these buildings were erected."[69]

Temple Israel would ultimately manage to build the first phase of the building in 1928, but the difficulties of fund-raising were soon compounded by the Depression, and it would be roughly two more decades before the religious school was built in the 1940s. The sanctuary was not completed until the early 1970s. Almost one hundred years after the decision to build a synagogue-center, Temple Israel remains a nationally recognized leader of social justice and synagogue outreach. But the fact that it took over forty years to bring the building to completion suggests the difficulty the synagogue faced in matching its financial realities to its vision.

One of the lasting consequences for synagogues in building such enlarged institutions was the increase of financial demands on members. As seen in Temple Israel's story, the synagogue-center idea necessitated more resources and created barriers to those with lesser means from joining the synagogue. Ironically, perhaps in an era that was so suffused with discussion of democracy, synagogues risked becoming more elite. For Temple Israel, this may have been an unintended consequence, but for other synagogue-centers elitism was an explicit decision.

One of the first synagogue-centers was the Brooklyn Jewish Center (BJC). As noted above, it included not just a large sanctuary and social spaces but also a full gym, swimming pool, and restaurant. The BJC began with the intention of being a closed institution. The creation of the BJC came from a small circle of men who committed to limiting the membership to those able to afford an initial $500 [$5,843] initiation fee and minimum dues of $100 [$1,169] per member.[70] There would be 750 seats in the synagogue sold collectively for the cost of the building, which they initially pegged at $250,000 [$2,922,500].[71] The limitation of its membership to the well-off meant that the congregation eschewed any commitment to being a broad *kehillah* (community), and functioned effectively as a kind of club. "A 1925 survey of the center's membership . . . showed that the largest single group, almost 25 percent, were manufacturers, followed by professionals, mostly lawyers and doctors," writes Deborah Dash Moore in "A Synagogue Center Grows in Brooklyn." "Together with merchants, realtors and building contractors, these occupational categories accounted for over 50 percent of the membership. The leaders considered their membership 'truly democratic,' despite the absence of the working class, and thought that 'with its cosmopolitan complexion' it 'does indeed typify American Jewish communal life.' Certainly it typified those affluent and upwardly mobile bourgeoisie, committed Jews who were attracted to the synagogue-center."[72]

The affluence of the Brooklyn Jewish Center reflected the economic rise of the Jewish community and its concern for issues of status. But there was certainly a tension between their perceptions of themselves as a democratic institution and the restrictive approach to membership.

This tension was also played out in the BJC's initial dispute over whether to sell seats or have unassigned seating. Samuel Rottenberg, one of the largest manufacturers of knit goods in New York City and one of the founders of the center, believed it was a financial necessity to sell seats.[73] "Rottenberg protested that since they couldn't sit in a circle during services, there had to be front rows and back rows. He favored democracy in the rest of the building but not in the synagogue. There some would have better seats, and these men should be willing to pay more for the honor," Moore writes.[74]

The financial elitism of the synagogue-centers could also be seen in who served on their boards. Mordecai Kaplan noted cynically that to serve on the board of the Jewish Center in Manhattan one needed to contribute $1,000 [$11,690], five times the annual dues to the synagogue.[75] Jenna Joselit, in her book on New York City's Orthodox Jewish community between the wars, described the board of the Manhattan Jewish Center in the 1920s: "Exclusively male in composition, the officers and the board were made up of the moneyed interests of the congregation, who were expected to transfer the skills that had won them considerable financial success in the outside world to the more intimate confines of the sanctuary. 'We have the greatest cloakmakers in the world here,' observed a Jewish Center congregant of his fellow worshippers and trustees. 'We have the greatest collarmaker in the world here. We have the greatest banker, etc. etc.'"[76]

This concentration of wealth and power did not go without critique. Rabbi Barnett Brickner, who served Holy Blossom Temple in Toronto and Congregation Anshe Chesed in Cleveland, in an editorial called "The Socialized Synagogue," implored rabbis to democratize synagogues and their leadership: "The Synagog [sic] cannot influence democracy until it is democratic. This implies free pulpit, free pews, democratic representation on its board, etc. Too long have the Reformed Temples of our country been privileged possessions. Too long has membership in these Temples been the mark of social distinction.... Open the Temple to rich and poor alike."[77]

Progressive activists like Brickner clashed ideologically with businessmen like Rottenberg over the basic mission of a synagogue. Brickner believed the synagogue was meant to promote progressive social values and its financial and governance structures should reflect those values. Rottenberg wanted a synagogue to "be everything that a man needs in the way of recreation, physical and mental,"[78] and the financial structures of the synagogue should be pragmatic to raise the necessary money to accomplish this mission. Ultimately, the debate about the primary mission of a synagogue was put on hold as the boom of the golden era of synagogue building crashed into the Depression.

Cutting to the Bone but Not the Heart:
Synagogues and the Depression

And then all that building debt came due. The golden age of synagogue building came to an abrupt end with the Depression. All synagogues experienced some level of financial distress during this period, but for those who had just built expensive new campuses the timing was particularly difficult. Not only had these synagogues taken out significant loans that now came due, but they were also dependent upon membership growth to finance the campuses, and the Depression saw membership drop or stagnate at almost all synagogues. A 1932 report to the Rabbinical Assembly on synagogue-centers stated:

> Synagogue-Center construction suffered from lack of adequate financing. Many structures were erected without regard to available funds for construction and maintenance. Too much money was expended in the purchase of choice locations and too large a financial commitment was made for architecturally magnificent and huge Synagogue structures.... The ill effects of overbuilding and underfinancing are manifold. The membership is appeal-ridden and becomes critical. The attractive program that was promised cannot, under the circumstances, be realized. The rabbi wears himself out in making appeals for funds. The community sometimes becomes resentful because the preoccupation of the group that sponsored the new building makes the support of that group unavailable for other necessary communal endeavors. In short, the attention of rabbi, trustees, and membership is diverted from the legitimate functions of the Synagogue Center and the joy of participation in the work itself, to the never-ending task of meeting the perplexing and pressing financial obligations.[79]

The Brooklyn Jewish Center responded to the Depression by eliminating staff and reducing wages for those who stayed, operating on a "starvation diet."[80] As noted above, the BJC started with visions of an economically well-to-do closed membership, but the financial difficulties of the Depression removed any vestige of such thinking as they slashed their annual membership fee in half in a desperate effort to fill the synagogue. "This radical step was taken to lighten the burden of many of our members who are suffering from the prolonged, bitter depression. However we [also] hoped that the smaller dues would attract many new members."[81]

It was of course not only the large new synagogue-centers that experienced financial turmoil as a result of the Depression. A sampling of synagogues large and small from across the country revealed membership decline and subsequent loss of dues and seats revenue. This in turn led to staff layoffs, salary freezes, and the curtailment of programs. Congregation Beth Israel in Atlantic City sent out an SOS to its congregation at the height of the Depression. The letter to its members literally said "SOS" at the top, and then followed with, "Due to conditions many of which are beyond control, our Congregation finds itself in a most serious situation. . . . We only seek your counsel and guidance. That we shall cease to function is unthinkable. . . . You must not fail us in this crisis. Heed our distress call and let the meeting next Tuesday evening take precedence over all else."[82]

The problem for the congregation, as it was for so many synagogues, was a steady loss of membership through the Depression. In 1930, the congregation's budget was down only minimally from the previous year. Its expenses that year totaled $26,912.22 [$377,052], which was higher than the national average for urban congregations at the time, which was $16,000 [$224,167] — but it was typical for a congregation of its size.[83] The rabbi was paid $10,000 [$140,105]; the secretary, choir, and janitor collectively made $9,000 [$126,094]; they paid $1,300 [$18,214] to support Hebrew Union College; and the rest was made up of building expenses. Three years later, in 1933, expenses were $11,790 [212,771], or a decrease of 56 percent. The rabbi's salary was cut by $3,500 [$63,164], the secretary's salary was halved, the choir's collective salary was reduced 300 percent, and the donation to Hebrew Union College was eliminated.[84] The SOS meeting produced a profusion of possible ideas: make personal urgent appeals to all members; raise dues 10 percent; put someone at the door for the High Holidays to ensure that no one was allowed in unless they had fully paid their dues; eliminate the choir; ask all teachers to teach voluntarily; and send dues notices monthly as opposed to yearly.[85] The congregation ultimately put some of these in place, such as sending dues statements more regularly, but mostly the congregation limped through until the economy turned.

The small congregation of Rodeph Sholom in Johnstown, Pennsylvania, had been following national trends and resolved in 1924 to build its own small version of the synagogue-centers being built all over the country. The Jewish Community Center would house a traditional synagogue and meeting rooms. The congregation made a down payment on a $1,500 [$20,539] lot, but the plan was abandoned because in 1934 only 25 percent of the congregation paid their dues and pledges on time.[86]

Congregation Beth Ahabah in Richmond, Virginia, weathered the Depression better than most. In 1923, the congregation had income of $23,295 [$319,609] and expenses of $21,478.58 [$294,687]. The rabbi made $10,000 [$137,201], and the rest was spent on music and building expenses. Ten years later, in 1933, during the Depression, the budget did not look terribly different. The income from dues and seats dropped 25 percent because of a loss of membership, but the congregation managed to receive $1,000 [$18,047] from a generous donor, who mollified what could have been a more difficult situation. As a result, the only change in the budget was a cut in the rabbi's salary to $8,500 [$153,397].[87]

Temple Beth El in Utica, New York, completed their $205,000 [$2,800,340] building four months before the Depression hit. They were indebted for $130,000 [$1,775,825]. In a too familiar story, Solomon Kohn writes in *The Jewish Community of Utica*, "The leaders of the synagogue had expected many new members to join the new and beautiful institution. . . . The membership could hardly support the normal cost of maintaining so large an institution."[88] The congregation had dues categories. The highest category was $250 [$3,415] and the lowest $75 [$1,024]. In 1932, to stem the loss of membership, the synagogue dropped its dues fee to $25 [$428] and separate school fees were instituted at $40 [$685] per child. "This change stabilized the financial situation for a few years. For now the congregation knew its financial limits and ceased to count on large dues-payers who could not fulfill their obligations," Kohn writes.[89]

Temple Adath Israel in Louisville, Kentucky, held their annual meeting on Tuesday, October 24, 1929 — a most ominous sign, as it was the very day of the stock market crash. The congregation voted an expected budget of $31,300 [$427,564] in income. Two years later, in 1931, the actual income of the congregation had dropped to $23,102.68 [$315,587]. The rabbi's salary was cut, the payment to the UAHC was cut, and the congregation put off almost all repairs to their building. The president's annual message to the congregation in 1932 was a mix of compassion and annoyance: "The financial cataclysm of November 1929 and the ensuing growth of pessimism and depression have been tragically reflected in our membership and dues. Many of our most earnest and loyal members found it really necessary either to resign or else to make a drastic reduction in their dues. Other members, not so earnest and not so loyal, have taken advantage of the situation and substantially decreased their contribution."

The congregation ended up raising $2,098.24 [$35,935] less than they expected, and their expectations had already been tempered by a few years of the Depression. Only $6,000 [$102,758] in unexpected income from cemetery plot sales saved the congregation from real calamity.[90]

In the midst of all of this synagogue turmoil, there was no shortage of thinking about how to deal with the effects of the Depression. In 1936, the Union of American Hebrew Congregations put out a publication, *Financial Security for Your Synagogue*, a handbook on the best practices for synagogues to respond to the economic crisis. The book noted that congregations, no matter whether they were using an assigned or an unassigned pew system, were experiencing problems collecting dues. Some members had stopped paying, some members were paying less than their assessment, and some members had left altogether. The primary solution they advocated was that congregations should deal with people individually and do what they could to keep them from leaving the temple. "After various experiments," *Financial Security for Your Synagogue* reported, "congregations have been adopting more and more the policy of preventing by every possible means the withdrawal of members either permanently or temporarily. The method of 'personal adjustment,' that is to say handling each case separately, has been meeting with increasing favor."[91]

In handling each case separately, the UAHC advocated trying to meet with individuals when possible. They suggested forgiving past debt or allowing seat owners to just pay dues but not seat assessments. The singular goal was to do what was necessary to maintain membership. The book continues:

> Concessions are made in the way of granting time to pay what they can as
> soon as they can. . . . In all of these adjusted cases there is no curtailment
> of privileges. By constantly maintaining such a policy, the congregation in
> the first place retains the good-will of the member and the member retains
> his self-respect; in the second place, lapses of membership resulting

purely from financial stringency are prevented; in the third place, in the large cities desertion from one congregation, and application to another, which invariably results in injury to congregational morale, is likewise prevented.[92]

Interestingly, while arguing for individual reduction of payments when necessary, the UAHC strongly urged congregations not to reduce dues generally. They described a case where a large congregation reduced dues by 20 percent but all that occurred was for the congregation to lose 20 percent of revenue over and above the losses it was already experiencing. This advice seems to contradict evidence from congregations like Beth El in Utica, described above, where a large reduction of dues led to a stabilization of finances as it brought members back to the synagogue. Beth El was not alone in reducing dues; most synagogues in this period tried some decrease in dues to draw in members.[93]

Besides working out deals, the other practical advice in the book was the suggestion of an "envelope plan," which was utilized "successfully by one Midwestern congregation." The envelope plan was simple: members were encouraged to give $1 every week at Friday night services. They would put the $1 in an envelope and leave it at the temple office. The idea was that if members gave a little bit every week, they were less likely to fall behind payments. The plan was straightforward, but it contained one rather surprising element. Members would not only leave $1 before services, but also "a general collection is also taken at the Friday evening services and the members are informed that any contributions they make will be credited to their dues."[94] This is an extraordinary statement because the UAHC was advocating for the collection of money on the Sabbath during services, an act that contradicts the Jewish law prohibiting the handling of money on Shabbat.

The Reform movement did not feel themselves bound to follow Jewish law, so it is not the contravening of Jewish law in general that is so surprising, but the particular custom of not handling money during services was a significant boundary. I would contend that it is precisely because the practice of passing the plate during services became so identifiable with Christianity that it became such a bright boundary for Jewish groups even in liberal Jewish circles. But there was at least one voice echoing the UAHC and calling for synagogues to collect envelopes during services.

Rabbi S. Felix Mendelsohn was the author of a number of books on Jewish humor and the rabbi of Beth Israel in Chicago for thirty-four years. He was also a regular contributor to Chicago's Jewish newspaper, the *Chicago Sentinel*. In an editorial in the *Sentinel* in 1933, Mendelsohn railed against the collection of dues as the financial system for synagogues. "That this method is faulty and inefficient has been proved by current conditions. The wealthy supporters of the synagogue have either lost most of their money or they are panic-stricken and they refuse to contribute."[95] Mendelsohn claimed that sending out a bill to members at the beginning of the fiscal year was ineffective because members inevitably fell behind on their payments and then would stay away or work out a deal where they would pay minimally on what they owed. Mendelsohn believed the answer was clear — to follow the churches that had implemented the envelope plan. Baskets would be passed around during services, members would write in an envelope how much they were giving, and this would be credited against their annual dues. Mendelsohn noted the religious problem: "Of course it will be argued that the weekly collection system cannot be successful because Jews will object to handling money on Friday evenings." But he reasoned that this argument was not valid in Reform and Conservative synagogues, where people regularly handled money on the Sabbath outside of the synagogue, so "there is no earthly reason why they should have any scruples against giving a contribution to the synagogue on the Sabbath."[96]

Ultimately, there is no evidence that any synagogue adopted the envelope plan other than that one successful Midwestern synagogue, but even suggesting the adoption of this system, despite its provocative nature, reflected the panicked desire of the national movement to give congregations something they might be able to utilize.

While the UAHC was advocating engaging members directly and collecting money weekly, the Conservative movement also had a national conversation about combating the Depression. The Rabbinical Assembly devoted a session of their 1931 annual meeting to a discussion of the Depression's impact. Some of the speakers reflected on practical responses while others focused on encouraging the assembled rabbis not to lose heart and to encourage continued fiscal generosity from their members. Israel Goldman, rabbi of Temple Emanu-El in Providence, Rhode Island, urged his fellow rabbis to hold fast: "No matter how well meaning they may be, the main concern of most of our lay-governing bodies is to economize and 'to cut to the bone.' We, the rabbis, must stand on guard so that our religious work be not cut to the heart!"[97]

One of the repeated tropes in the presentations was to defend giving to synagogues and rabbis as opposed to giving to other Jewish institutions. Goldman said:

In a time of economic depression, the natural tendency is to sacrifice and to abandon spiritual and cultural activities and to give precedence to physical needs and to those of our communal institutions which cater to them. It becomes our task and duty, therefore, to emphasize again the undisputed fact that the synagogue is the supreme institution in Jewish life! . . . The synagogue as a morale-molding, character-constructing, spirit-nurturing agency occupies a position of supreme and central importance and must therefore be supported at all times. Who will say then that family welfare, care for the aged, the child, the sick and the unemployed should come first, when the closing of our synagogues will mean discontinuing caring for the normal and the well and the removal of those positive and preventive influences from the Jewish life which have been the pride and the glory of our Jewish communities. Surely, the spiritual needs are at least as great as the physical."[98]

Rabbi Louis Schwefel, who served the Hebrew Institute of New Rochelle, provided an aggressive defense of supporting rabbis even if it meant not supporting other synagogue professionals. He argued that there were several ways synagogues could save on their expenses. The primary way, he contended, was to eliminate Hebrew school principals: "I know I am treading on very delicate ground when I discuss this subject from the point of view I now adopt but I am sincere in my conviction that the 'profession' of Jewish education has been overestimated and has grown puffed up about nothing at all. . . . I am more convinced than ever that the expense and complication [of a Hebrew school principal] has generally not proven worthwhile. Most of our rabbis are fully capable of supervising our synagogue classes as are the principals."[99]

Schwefel claimed that principals were a "luxury" synagogues indulged in during days of prosperity, freeing rabbis to play golf and travel, but given the economic times, such luxuries were no longer sensible. As for the folks he just proposed eliminating, Schwefel had some compassion but not overly much. "What will happen to the trained principals?" he asked. "That is truly a sad situation; but I believe it will be necessary for many of them to find an auxiliary source of income."[100]

Schwefel, however, was not done with his plans for saving synagogues money. His next proposal was to get rid of all part-time employees. Hebrew school teachers should not be paid unless their positions were combined with other positions to create a full-time job. He noted his own congregation hired a secretary who was also a fully qualified Hebrew teacher. He admiringly described how this allowed the congregation to replace two people with one. Cantorial soloists were next on his list. He argued that they too should also be done away with:

> High-priced soloists were very fashionable when United States Steel was selling at $250 a share; but when the same stock sells for $80 a share and the Real Estate of our members is practically unsaleable at any price they begin to wonder why a full salary shall be paid to a cantor who sings his sweet songs on the Sabbath and then disappears for another week. If the Cantor assists in school, is the financial secretary of the congregation or if he has a business on the side which can occupy the rest of the week it may be a perfectly equitable arrangement; but we must rid our synagogue budget of the burden of cantors who are prima-donna luxuries.[101]

Schwefel acknowledged the aggressive nature of his proscriptions:

> Someone hearing these suggestions by a rabbi to dispense with useless or part-time employees may feel that we make these proposals to save our own skin. First of all, our skin, in most cases, has already been seared. None of us is receiving the salary he has become accustomed to, certainly not the salary we would like to receive. If we will succeed in saving our skin it is only because we deserve it, each as an individual. It is our claim that a rabbi is an indispensable functionary in the synagogue and it is up to ourselves to prove that we are indispensable.[102]

Schwefel's survival instincts reflected the difficult environment for rabbis at this time. Many rabbis, according to Israel Goldman, were being asked to take pay cuts or pay moratoriums, or simply told they could no longer be afforded at all.[103] Mordecai Kaplan noted, "Among those who are bound to suffer most keenly from the demoralizing effect of the present economic depression are the rabbis, the superfluousness of whose calling has become more conspicuous than ever. Most of my colleagues are going through torments of hell."[104]

But even given the sense of peril for the rabbinate, Schwefel's plans for synagogues reads most ungenerously. His naked attack on the livelihood of all other synagogue employees reflected the desperation born of the Depression.

Schwefel did have some suggestions for saving money and increasing revenue that did not involve cutting other people's jobs. He encouraged congregations to hold concert and lecture series, charge tuition for Sunday school, and ask wealthier individuals to pay for the tuition of poorer students. He also suggested synagogues seek renters for unused space. "I take it quite for granted that you and your money-raising officers have not overlooked the gold waiting to be picked up at bazaars, theater parties, annual dances and bridges."[105]

Rabbi S. Joshua Kohn of Beth El in Utica, another presenter at the conference, had conducted a national study of the finances of fourteen congregations. From this data set he made some interesting observations. The most significant financial issue for congregations was debt. Kohn found that the total debt of those fourteen congregations compared to their total expenditure was 23 percent, "or almost one dollar out of every five is of no profit culturally or educationally or religiously to our institutions."[106] The major proscription to help congregations he proffered was quite simply to do what they could to reduce their debt. "Our synagogues have done very little — it seems — in prosperous times to liquidate their debts. They have relied on still better times. Only in this period of depression have they paid off indebtedness and pruned the budgets so that the religious and educational work is now interfered with."[107]

To Schwefel's point regarding the "gold" at bazaars and theater parties, Kohn reported that "monies earned from card parties, mah jong, bazaars, dances, strawberry festivals, rental of facilities for meetings and dances" amounted to 14 percent of the budget of synagogues. "In other words one out of every seven dollars must be earned with our noses to the grindstone. No small wonder we are busy business men."[108] While dances and bazaars had been long-standing ways for synagogues to raise money, my own analysis of synagogue budgets from the 1920s suggests that 14 percent represents a significant increase from earlier budgets. This was not surprising given the loss of membership. Congregations needed to turn elsewhere to make up revenue. But as Kohn suggested, keeping one's nose to the grindstone is no easy feat, and as the Depression wore on, congregations turned to different sources to try and find income.

Beth Wenger, in her illuminating study of New York Jewry during the Depression, points to the increased reliance on synagogue sisterhoods to make up lost revenue from membership decreases. Sisterhoods shouldered an increasing burden for fund-raising. Wenger writes, "So great was the preoccupation with fund-raising, that [the National Federation of Temple Sisterhoods] expressed concern that 'sisterhoods have been so engrossed in decreasing the indebtedness of their Houses of Worship that that they have not had the opportunity of increasing those spiritual activities for which these Houses of Worship stand.'"[109] Wenger noted as an example the Kane Street Synagogue Sisterhood, which contributed $1,750 [$30,543] in 1934 to keep the synagogue afloat.

While synagogues struggled to make debt payments and raise money, the impact of the economy was felt beyond the financial statements. Rabbis themselves took a much more strident tone regarding the difficulties they saw around them. Whereas in the nineteenth century rabbis were reticent to take positions regarding the accumulation of wealth,[110] the Depression era engendered a robust critique of the basic structure of American capitalism. Some rabbis argued for the general proposition that the economy needed to be guided by justice and morality and not simply the invisible hand of the market. Rabbi Alter Landesman, head of the Hebrew Educational Society of Brooklyn, argued:

> To the extent that we have tacitly accepted the status quo of social and eco-
> nomic organization, and have made no vigorous effort to assert the princi-
> ples of divine justice and righteousness as applied to the practical problems
> of economic and social life, we must be charged with great neglect of duty
> in these spheres of life. When we realize that the moral conditions under
> which men live are vitally affected by economic conditions, it becomes
> evident why the synagogue should interest itself in all questions touching
> these conditions, no matter how many other problems are facing us.[111]

As the Depression wore on, though, the critique of capitalism sharpened significantly. In 1934, with the Depression still hanging over the country, the Rabbinical Assembly passed a "Pronouncement on Social Justice." It began with a general statement affirming "that the discussion of problems of social and economic justice and the evaluation of movements to abolish exploitation, poverty, and war and other social evils are not only legitimate but even necessary concerns of the synagogue." The document than called for a series of progressive initiatives, including minimum wage laws, the right to unionize, free public schools and colleges, and direct government aid to the unemployed. But the Rabbinical Assembly did not stop at liberal policies aimed to ameliorate the plight of workers; it went on to address something much more far reaching — it called for an end to the market economy and an embrace of what might be termed democratic socialism:

> We hold that only a cooperative economy, only one which has for its objective the enrichment of all rather than the profit of a few — only such an economy can be moral, can elevate man and function successfully. . . . Only when our economy is socially controlled throughout and only when its control is used to the end that all share equitably in the world's goods, will the problem of unemployment be solved. It is with us a matter of moral principle that an individualistic profit economy is as sinful as it has proved a failure. Our faith in our ideals and in human nature impels us to look to a cooperative economy directed to the good of all men. . . . We call upon the State to use its power of taxation to correct this gross inequity in the distribution of wealth. We ask for sharply increased taxes on land values, income, gifts, inheritances, corporation surpluses, and capital levies which shall use the power of taxation to redistribute the social resources of our society. . . . We regard all private ownership of natural resources and machinery of large-scale production as involving injustice, [although] we recognize the impracticability of an immediate transfer of all capital from private to public.[112]

The Central Conference of American Rabbis was similarly moved to action by the plight of Americans. It adopted a declaration at its 1932 national conference that shared a great deal with the Rabbinical Assembly's pronouncement. "There has been a tendency among those who are satisfied with the status quo to regard, particularly today, the pulpit's function to be to raise charity funds to patch up social ills, while keeping silent concerning the wounds which fester underneath the patches," it declared. Like the Rabbinical Assembly, the CCAR called for specific progressive initiatives, including increased taxes on the wealthy to provide relief for the unemployed and increased quality public housing. It then provided a broader critique of capitalism:

> We recommend to all people our modern rabbinical Program of Social Justice as a basis of action for the solution of these problems which are devastating our physical and spiritual existence. The chief aspects of this program refer not only to such palliatives as compulsory unemployment insurance but the farther reaching demands of a more adequate distribution of the profits of industry. From many angles, present day capitalism is under grim suspicion as to its ability ever to achieve a satisfactory sense of social responsibility. It has in effect placed the safeguarding of investments above the safeguarding of human life. With few conspicuous exceptions, it has constantly fought labor's right to organize and to have a decent voice in the administration of the basic pursuit of a livelihood. It has, in some instances, exploited the masses by reducing wages or eliminating employment in cases where such action was not at all justified on the basis of the financial status of industry. . . .
>
> Any system which can be so characterized is neither economically sound nor can it be sanctioned morally. We therefore advocate immediate legislative action in the direction of changes whereby social control will place the instruments of production and distribution as well as the system of profits increasingly within the powers of society as a whole.[113]

While a few rabbis were uncomfortable with the CCAR going on record in support of something approaching socialism, the vast majority of rabbis supported the resolution, indicating the extent of rabbinic support for positions that previously would have been considered far too radical.

Not all rabbis were enthusiastic about mixing economics with religion, however. The *Orthodox Union*, for example, dismissed this prevailing trend: "[The rabbi] is not a teacher of economics, but of religion. What we need today is to make our people understand that our economic, social and political problems are basically personal religious ones."[114] Other approaches did not deny the right of rabbis to speak about economics, but believed that the spiritual crisis engendered by the Depression was more pressing than the material crisis. Solomon Freehof, in a 1931 editorial, "The Spiritual Depression," argued that the Depression had created a climate of fear and anxiety where individuals focused solely on themselves and their families. This "terrible selfishness" unnecessarily threatened the survival of synagogues and charities, because people were not giving, and it also created a sense of despair: "The spiritual depression . . . may grow into a complete psychic panic which neither facts, experience nor reason can control . . . lest a temporary business depression become a permanent spiritual calamity. We must rediscover our courage and grow sensitive again to the human needs for education, spirituality and mutual aid."[115]

Although there were some rabbis who were uncomfortable with an overtly economic and political stance, the predominate view held a significant moral critique of the American economic system. In articulating this critique, rabbis were allying themselves with the working classes, which, particularly for Reform rabbis, were not the predominate group in their synagogues. But it is not clear that in taking radical positions they were endangering their own authority. Roosevelt's New Deal was immensely popular in the Jewish community.[116] Transferring private property into the hands of the government was not the radical assessment it would be seen as today. But it was also the case that the Progressive Era had already created the expectation that synagogues were meant to be active in ameliorating the conditions of the poor. The devastating economic conditions wrought by the Depression pushed that impulse to a broader and more systematic approach to the economy.

Ultimately, synagogues survived the Depression. Despite the fact that a number of synagogues built synagogue-centers just as the Depression hit, most synagogues were able to muddle through. Many had to cut expenses dramatically to do so, but given the difficulties of the economy, the overall strength of synagogues may be more surprising than their struggles. The 1936 Religious Census showed, in fact, that the number of synagogues actually rose during the Depression, increasing from 3,118 in 1926 to 3,728 in 1936, but the number of members per synagogue dropped.[117] And although synagogues as an institution were surviving, the people who worked in those institutions did not fare as well. Kaplan's contention that rabbis were "going through hell" may have been hyperbolic, but there was ample testimony to the difficulties they faced.

An article from the *Jewish Daily Bulletin* in 1930 gave testimony to both of these ideas — the increase in the number of synagogues and the struggles of rabbis. The article noted that four rabbis had resigned from their synagogues in a single month. All of the resignations were the result of disagreements with the board related to money. "This, however, does not cut down on the number of synagogues; on the contrary, it usually means additional institutions," as each rabbi was looking to start a new congregation.[118] It may be counterintuitive to think of the Depression as a time when new congregations were created, but the challenges of the Depression created the need for smaller synagogues with more manageable budgets.

Wenger summarizes the impact of the Depression on synagogues as a "time of both crisis and consolidation . . . less a dramatic turning point than a period of hardship that accelerated ongoing trends in congregational life."[119] Synagogues, she claims, were already experiencing membership decline and significant apathy in the 1920s. "The Depression revealed the narrow base of synagogue support and brought to light the precariousness of relying on a small group to sustain these institutions."[120]

The lessons regarding this danger were short-lived, however. After the recovery of the economy following World War II, there was another explosion of synagogue building comparable to the building boom of the 1920s. The Depression thus represented a pause between two periods of significant economic expansion for synagogues.

FIVE

"If It Has to Be Done, It Should at Least Be Done in a Dignified Way" *[1945–Today]*

In 1958, Congregation B'nai Jehudah, a large Reform congregation in Kansas City, faced a significant challenge that threatened its viability. The congregation appointed a special committee "to study and recommend what steps should be taken with respect to the growth of the congregation."[1] The problem that so vexed the congregation was not the normal complaint from synagogues that they needed more growth. The problem, rather, was far too much growth. The congregation was inundated with members, and "any material increase in members will aggravate an already critical shortage of personnel."[2] In 1957, the congregation built a massive school building with thirty-one classrooms to accommodate their enrollment of 794 students. One year later, they had 924 students. They projected that by 1960, even if not a single new family joined the synagogue, school enrollment would reach 1,065, an increase of over 30 percent in just two years.[3]

The solution the committee recommended was to seed a new congregation. They proposed giving a group of families that were potentially interested in joining B'nai Jehudah a gift of $5,000 [$41,399] to start a new congregation. The congregation literally proposed paying people to go to another synagogue. Perhaps even more surprisingly, the committee reported that they were not alone in considering such a plan. Congregations in Pittsburgh, Boston, Newark, and Long Island all had a hand in setting up newer congregations because of overcrowding. In Toronto, Holy Blossom Temple gave a $25,000 [$206,996] loan to organize Temple Sinai and to help it with a building.[4]

B'nai Jehudah was just part of the astonishing growth of synagogues in postwar America. Between 1949 and 1956, the number of new Reform and

Conservative synagogues increased by 33 percent.[5] The vast majority of those new synagogues were located in the suburbs. In a front-page article in 1959 entitled, "Judaism on Rise in Suburbs," the *New York Times* reported that since World War II, 57 Reform, 68 Conservative, and 35 Orthodox congregations had been newly established in suburban New York.[6] In just the three-year period from 1953 to 1956, the Conservative movement, which saw the largest growth from the Jewish move to suburbia, reported that 150 new synagogue buildings were being planned or constructed in suburbs around the country.[7]

Many of the new suburban synagogues began as Jewish Community Centers or fellowship groups — places for Jews to gather socially in their new environment. When those Jews felt the need to provide for the religious education of their children, they then established synagogues.[8] The costs associated with the school thus took on a much greater significance than it had in previous generations of synagogue finance. Other funding sources outside of dues and school fees — such as bingo — would, as we shall see, play fascinating but ultimately ancillary roles in the financial life of the congregation. Ultimately, synagogue finance in this era was about financing expansion — new buildings, more members, more professional staff, and increased salaries for rabbis.

"The Synagogue Is a Third Partner in Our Household": The Expanding Synagogue Budget

Beth Emet the Free Synagogue in Evanston, Illinois, like so many other synagogues of the time, grew phenomenally in the 1950s. The congregation began in January 1950 with 40 families and by the end of the year the congregation boasted 200 families. By 1955 they had 350 families and more than 400 children in their religious school. The congregation was the first synagogue in Evanston, a suburb of Chicago.[9] The congregation bought a building as soon as it was organized, but the number of school children immediately outstripped the capacity of the building. The congregation thus began a capital campaign for a new building almost as soon as it organized as a synagogue.

The congregation initially had a funding structure that had a minimum dues level of $50 [$498] and encouraged voluntary giving over and above that minimum amount. This structure was somewhat unusual for the time, but the congregation prided itself on its affordable and straightforward plan. The congregation soon found, though, that it needed more resources. The budget committee proposed that the congregation charge an additional $15 [$134] for school registration, with the revenue to go into the general fund. Most families had two children, and thus a raise in school registration fees represented a significant amount of money. The board, however, decided that this was an inequitable way of raising money for the general fund. If the congregation needed money for general operating expenses, then it should raise dues on everyone and not unfairly burden families. It ultimately raised dues to $155 [$1,386], a 200 percent increase in five years.[10]

The debate at Beth Emet mirrored debates going on in new suburban synagogues across the country. The influx of families with children seeking religious school raised the question of how the financial burden of congregational Jewish education should be apportioned. Synagogues wrestled with the question of how much of the cost of running a synagogue should be borne particularly by the religious school families, versus how much should be an overall communal expense. One point of view was that since religious school created the increase in costs, families using those services should be the ones to give the lion's share of support in the form of school fees. On the other hand, the task of passing on Jewish education was seen by many as a primary, if not *the* primary, task of synagogues, and thus the costs should be carried by the entire membership.

In a small survey of the four other North Shore congregations in Chicago that Beth Emet conducted, they found a basic split. Two of the congregations had relatively high dues levels — $130 [$1,162] and $185 [$1,654] — but low school fees of $15 [$134] and free; the other two congregations had relatively low dues levels — $80 [$715] and $75 [$671] — but high school fees of $40 [$358] and $30 [$268]. Congregations were thus generally divided over the best way to approach the question of how much the shul should pay for the school.

A more dramatic example of this split can be seen in comparing two synagogues — the previously noted B'nai Jehudah in Kansas City, and Temple Israel of Natick, a smaller suburban Conservative synagogue near Boston, which, like so many other synagogues, experienced exponential growth in the 1950s. B'nai Jehudah, which did not charge religious school fees, had total income in 1956 of $138,400 [$1,219,238], with dues accounting for $131,000 [$1,154,048], or 95 percent of the synagogue budget.[11] In that same period, Temple Israel of Natick had income of $56,000 [$452,748], of which dues accounted for $18,750 [$151,590], or just 33 percent of the budget. School fees at Temple Israel made up the same percentage of the budget as dues, $18,600 [$150,377], or 33 percent. The synagogue was charging $75 [$606] for annual dues, but $75 for school fees per child. Families with two children in school were thus paying three times as much to the synagogue as families without children.[12]

The congregational budgetary differences did not end with the school. B'nai Jehudah's budget was overwhelmingly geared toward dues, and they made up most of the rest of their income primarily from an endowment fund, which generated $5,500 [$48,452] annually for the congregation. Endowment funds in the 1950s, much as today, were primarily utilized by larger, wealthier congregations, and their contribution to the synagogue coffers was rather limited. The creation of trusts and endowments to benefit synagogues was certainly not new. In 1820, Abraham Touro had set up a trust in his will that allocated $15,000 [$256,466] to the state of Rhode Island for the synagogue's perpetual upkeep (which caused the state legislature to refer to the synagogue from that point forward as the Touro Synagogue).[13] But the Touro gift was somewhat anomalous in synagogue history, as most synagogues through the 1950s rarely had significant endowments.

Temple Israel in Natick, as a synagogue only a few years old, certainly did not have an endowment to help its budget. As noted above, one-third of the congregational budget came from dues, one-third from school fees, and the final third was made up primarily through the High Holidays. The congregation sold High Holiday seats (which did not come with membership), raising $8,000 [$64,678]; they sold High Holiday honors, which raised $750 [$6,064]; and they held a Yom Kippur appeal, which raised another $5,000 [$40,424]. A member of the congregation recalls that the appeal was undertaken on Kol Nidre, when during a break in the liturgy, the president of the congregation would hand out pledge cards. Members would fold down a tab on the card indicating their pledge to the synagogue. The president would then read aloud the names of each member and their pledge during services.[14] Such a practice would be condemned in today's milieu, but it is worth noting that announcing pledges out loud was a common fund-raising practice at the time for other Jewish organizations.

The difference between B'nai Jehudah and Temple Israel reflected two different approaches to membership. B'nai Jehudah was singularly focused on dues, and when a member paid their dues, they were buying a "package" that included the school and High Holiday tickets. Temple Israel, by contrast, approached synagogue membership effectively in an à la carte fashion. When a member paid their dues, which were set relatively low, they were allowed to be part of the regular worship and programming of the community, but school and High Holidays were "extras" to be paid for separately.

Most synagogues settled between these two poles, with dues making up between 60 and 80 percent of the congregational budget. Beth Emet the Free Synagogue in Evanston derived 70 percent of their budget from dues, with school fees making up roughly 15 percent and the rest of their income coming from fund-raisers. The school cost more than the 15 percent of the budget it was bringing in, though. This meant that the congregation was subsidizing the school to some degree. The fees would cover some but certainly not all expenses associated with the school. The choice was effectively a compromise between models. For most synagogues then and now, charging school fees that do not entirely bear the cost of the school represents a compromise between the "all-inclusive package" and the "à la carte — pay for what you use option."

The model chosen by a synagogue had downstream effects on the composition of the community, because a dues-heavy model created a barrier for the less wealthy. When Beth Emet the Free Synagogue chose to take the middle path and raise dues and not increase school fees, the board took pains to recommit itself to the principles of compassion and egalitarianism. They noted that if the rise in dues meant financial hardship for any member, the situation would be worked out on a confidential basis, and the synagogue reassured its members that "membership will be regarded for all on the same basis and no distinction will be raised because of the dues."[15] Although Beth Emet sought to sustain an egalitarian notion of membership, the significant expansion of dues inevitably meant that the community would become somewhat more elitist in its membership. As a result of the dues increase, seventeen families resigned from the synagogue.[16]

Just as the construction of large synagogue-centers in the 1920s effectively limited membership to those with means, so too the suburban synagogues of the 1950s created financial barriers to membership.

Another example of this phenomenon was Congregation Mishkan Tefila, one of Boston's most prominent synagogues. The synagogue had established itself in 1905 in the heavily Jewish Roxbury section of Boston. But when the Jewish community began leaving Roxbury for the suburbs, the congregation followed suit and left for the Boston suburb of Newton in the 1950s. There was much debate regarding the move, as members of the congregation were split between those living near the synagogue in Roxbury and those who had already moved to the suburbs. The congregants who advocated for the transition argued the move to the suburbs was the only way to ensure a future for the congregation. There were also promises of maintaining a Roxbury presence as well as welcoming the Roxbury members into the transplanted synagogue. Ultimately, the congregation moved to Newton and left behind much of its Roxbury membership. While the synagogue attracted a diverse economic group when it was in Roxbury, "the Newton membership was exclusively upper middle class not only because of the demography of Newton, but also because of the Temple's dues structure," which required a $100 [$894] minimum dues fee and also a $1,000 [$8,940] building fund commitment in order to join.[17]

Increasing the level of dues was repeated at synagogue after synagogue in the 1950s. In some sense, this is economically counterintuitive. If many new families join a synagogue, the synagogue's revenue line should increase, thus bringing down the cost of the synagogue per family and the need to raise dues. Yet in almost every growing suburban synagogue, dues went up and the cost per family rose. In 1957, Adath Jeshurun, a Conservative synagogue in Minnetonka, had 74 new families join the congregation, which represented a 10 percent increase in one year and brought the total membership to 830 families. But the congregation still ran a $4,000 [$34,014] deficit. In keeping with the spirit of the times, the president of the congregation called for, not surprisingly, an increase in dues. "Costs have risen sharply, but dues income has gone up at a snail's pace," he said.[18] Inflation certainly accounts for some of the cost increase. Salaries rose precipitously at Adath Jeshurun. But fundamentally the increase in membership meant an expansion in resources — the adding of new teachers and youth directors at a minimum, but for so many congregations it was building a new building or renovating an old one that drove the budgets of congregations. Building campaigns were the order of the day for synagogues in suburban America.

God's Not Pushing Me Like My Other Creditors: Building Campaigns

In 1953, the *Jewish Criterion*, Pittsburgh's Jewish newspaper, had a back page section of jokes that included the following:

> The committee was out collecting funds for the new synagogue and they approached Levin, who refused them.
>
> "But you could give something," they insisted.
>
> "No," was the firm reply, "I owe too many other people; debts before charity, you know."
>
> "But don't you think you owe God a larger debt than anyone?" gray-bearded Reb Meyer pointed out.
>
> "Maybe so. But He's not pushing me like my other creditors."[19]

The joke was clearly written for an audience that was accustomed to building campaigns. But the punch line may not be correct, as synagogue building committees pushed members pretty hard to raise money.

At Beth Emet in Evanston, the group of men who ran the campaign to raise money for a new building borrowed heavily from the language of politics. They called themselves the "campaign cabinet," they urged people to call "campaign headquarters" as soon as a pledge was made, and one of their significant initiatives was to pass out "victory" cards to those men (and indeed it was all men) who agreed to pledge or solicit pledges for the building fund.[20] The language of the building campaign had much more in common with a highly calculated political election campaign than a religious endeavor.

At Shaare Zion, the Syrian Orthodox synagogue in Brooklyn, the building of a new edifice was a legal as well as a financial struggle. The synagogue began in 1941 and ten years later planned for a large building. They collected $250,000 [$2,305,140], signed a prominent architect, and hired a contractor. Two years later, after only the foundation was built, the contractor went bankrupt and the various subcontractors put liens on the building project.

The plumber claimed he had a contract for $40,000 [$368,821], the electrician was owed $35,000 [$322,729], and so forth. The congregation was ready to give up when a small cadre of wealthy donors got together and began to hold fund-raisers, approached other wealthy donors, and cajoled the subcontractors to come back to work. The congregation then turned to a traditional method for synagogues to raise money for a new building: they sold seats. This was a new practice for the congregation, as by this point most American congregations no longer sold seats. The head of the building committee reported, "Buying specific seats was a first in our community, and it was a hard sell. Half the seats were priced at $500 [$4,610] per couple, which was a lot of money at a time when houses in the synagogue's area were priced at around $35,000 [$322,729]."[21] The congregation eventually sold $20,000 [$184,410] in seats, but this was not enough to pay for the building. Finally, the congregation sold a private house that it owned at $90,000 [$829,847], and this enabled the membership to complete their new synagogue and move into the building in 1959.[22]

To evaluate the capital campaigns of this period, Beth Emet's experience in Evanston provides a useful paradigm. In 1953, Beth Emet had 370 members and needed to raise $300,000 [$2,766,156] for a new building. They began their campaign in 1951 and had successfully raised $200,000 [$1,844,104] through gifts from 227 members, or 61 percent of the congregation.[23] The largest single gift was $15,000 [$138,308], the next largest was $6,500 [$59,933], and there were fifty-nine pledges of $1,000 [$9,221] or more. The final $100,000 [$922,052] was harder for the congregation to raise. The synagogue found forty-eight members who pledged to solicit members who had not yet given, but would ultimately make good themselves on any shortfall. It was to these gentlemen that the victory cards would be given.[24]

In the six months after the announcement to solicit members who had not yet given, fifty-one members left the synagogue while only forty-two joined. Given its phenomenal previous growth, the net loss of membership can only be attributable to the financial pressure that some members felt to contribute to the new building. The contributions that the congregation was looking for were significant. Although there was a range, the median gift to the synagogue for the building fund was $750 [$6,713], paid over three years.

To give context to this figure, we can approximate the percentage of an annual salary a gift of $750 over three years would comprise. Although we do not have data for the average salary of a Jewish suburbanite in Chicago, we do have data from a unique study of Washington, D.C., Jewry that can serve as a reasonable approximation of Jewish Chicago.[25] In 1957, the Jewish Community Council of Greater Washington, D.C., conducted a study, the results of which testify to the success of the Jewish community at the time and a generally thriving economy. Unemployment, for example, was extremely low — less than 1 percent of Jewish men under forty-five were unemployed. Because of the conflict in Korea, 40 percent of Jewish men between twenty and twenty-four years old were employed in the military. One-quarter of Jewish women were in the workforce.[26] More than a third of Jewish men were employed as "technical and professional workers," one-quarter worked as "managers, officials, proprietors," another 20 percent were clerical workers, and 10 percent were manual workers.[27] The data placed the median family income for Jews in Greater D.C. at between $7,000 and $10,000 [$59,524 and $85,034], with one-quarter reporting income over $10,000.[28] If the data are examined for just Jews in the suburbs, the average income is higher. In the northwest suburbs of D.C. the median income was between $10,000 and $15,000 [$85,034 and $127,551].[29]

If we presume then a suburban Jewish family income of $12,500 [$106,293], and the median gift at Beth Emet was $250 [$2,123] annually for three years, this would mean members were giving roughly 2 percent of their annual income to the building fund. This was on top of the dues and school fees that for families at Beth Emet averaged $175 [$1,488]. Families were thus giving roughly 3.4 percent of their income to their synagogues during capital campaigns.

As a point of comparison, we can look to church capital campaigns. Synagogues were not the only religious institution that saw massive growth with suburbanization. Protestant churches were also being built at a phenomenal pace. According to surveys by the Department of Commerce, the annual value of new religious construction grew from $126,000,000 [$1.67 trillion] in 1945 to $700,000,000 [$6.2 trillion] in 1955, a growth of over 500 percent in ten years.[30] A 1955 article in *McCall's Magazine* said, "Not since Solomon have people lavished so much on housing for God and those who would worship Him."[31] Another demonstration of church growth is seen in the percentage of Americans who claimed religious affiliation. In 1930, 47 percent of Americans claimed affiliation; in 1954 that number was 79 percent. In just one year from 1956 to 1957, there was an estimated increase of 3,000,000 churchgoers.[32]

To meet the massive new demand for churches, Protestant churches became sophisticated in their approach. They targeted wealthy donors for large advance pledges, created campaign materials, and had rituals designed to increase participation in the campaign. They also held bazaars, dinners, auctions, and special Sabbaths for pledging[33] — techniques, not coincidentally, also utilized by Beth Emet in Evanston. Some churches hired development professionals to run capital campaigns for their congregations. There were at least twelve major fund-raising counsel firms in the 1950s. They charged anywhere from $1,800 [$16,095] for a small church to $10,000 [$89, 417] for large churches.[34]

To follow the same calculations as we made for the Jewish congregation, in 1957, estimates of the average annual per capita contribution of church members was $54 [$459].[35] According to a census report, the average American family income that year was $4,800 [$40,816].[36] If we presume that the average American family was a good proxy for Protestant churchgoers, this means Christians averaged a contribution of 1.1 percent of their income to churches.[37]

To look at one particular example, we have data for the First Presbyterian Church in Gary, Indiana, in this period, which confirms this general finding. In 1957, the church had roughly 850 families and raised $75,139 [$638,937] for an average of $88 [$748] per adult member.[38] The median salary of white urban Americans in the Midwest — the demographics of the Gary congregation — was $5,557 [$47,253],[39] so $88 represents 1.5 percent of income.

The same church, though, saw a significantly higher percentage of giving for a capital campaign. In 1947, the church in Gary burned down and the congregation needed to rebuild. They ultimately raised $250,000 [$2,680,972], in addition to $100,000 [$1,072,388] of insurance money, for a new building. The congregation had at this point approximately 800 families. They gave an average of $312 [$3,346] over three years, or $104 [$1,115] per year. This means members were giving 3.5 percent of their annual income during capital campaigns.

All of these numbers are rough estimates, but they point to a similar story that Jews and Christians gave between 3 and 4 percent of their income to their congregation during capital campaigns, and roughly half that rate for regular congregational support. The other implication of these statistics is the uniformity between Christians and Jews in their giving patterns. Despite different approaches, with synagogues stressing the practical need for new buildings to meet growing demand, and churches incorporating steward-ship themes of God's rightful ownership of one's resources, they both drew roughly the same percentage of their congregants' incomes.

Rabbinic Pay

The increased wealth of suburban synagogues was also reflected in clergy pay. As discussed previously, the creation of American rabbinic seminaries and rabbinic organizations in the early twentieth century professionalized the rabbinate and put forth the notion that rabbis should be paid upper-mid-dle-class salaries in line with the growing wealth of their members.[40] As the Jewish community moved to the suburbs and became more well-to-do, the salary of rabbis kept pace with these changes. A 1972 report on the condition of the rabbinate for the Central Conference of American Rabbis (CCAR) found a median salary for all Reform rabbis of roughly $17,500 [$97,690]. The report confirmed, "Compared with salaried professionals in business, industry and academe, Reform rabbis do well."[41] The growth of rabbinic salaries has continued to keep pace with other professions. In a 2015 survey by the CCAR, 455 Reform rabbis serving as solo or senior rabbis had a me-dian income of roughly $130,000. Salaries at larger synagogues ranged even higher, with all rabbis serving congregations of over 800 families earning salaries of at least $200,000.[42] The median rabbinic salary places rabbis in the top 5 percent of American earners.[43]

Rabbinic salaries are on average significantly higher than those of their Christian ministerial counterparts. The 1972 CCAR report noted that just 35 percent of rabbis earned less than $15,000 [$85,853], compared with 98 percent of Protestant ministers. It also noted, "Two out of every hundred ministers have salaries comparable with those of two out of every three rabbis."[44] In 2000, a survey of Protestant ministers found an average salary of $40,000 [$55,689], or less than half of what the average rabbi earns.[45]

There are a few factors that may explain some of the cleavage between rabbinic and ministerial salaries. Clergy of both faiths that serve rural areas are paid less than their suburban or urban counterparts. Because there are so many ministers in rural areas, these salaries skew the comparison. Similarly, there are many more churches than synagogues with smaller memberships, which also skews the comparison. Even correcting for these factors, though, rabbinic salaries remain significantly higher than ministerial ones.

A 2010 article in *The Forward* on the subject of rabbinic and ministerial salaries quoted leaders of all the Jewish denominations suggesting that the reason for the higher rabbinic salaries is the desire for rabbis to live in the same community with their members, who often live in upper-middle-class suburban neighborhoods.[46] But this cannot entirely explain the differentiation in pay. One would then expect equal pay among rabbis and ministers who reside in the same community, but that is generally not the case.

The difference in pay is most attributable to the idea that rabbis are part of the professional class and should be compensated accordingly. Synagogues throughout the twentieth century believed that rabbis were professionals and sought to attract talented individuals to the profession with the promise of high wages. Meanwhile, Protestant ministers have slowly and steadily de-professionalized themselves. Hudnut-Beumler explains the decline of ministerial compensation over the twentieth century as follows: "Protestant clergy throughout the last two hundred years were more comfortable with the idea of having a calling rather than being in a profession. As such, they became captive to the willing acceptance of an economic lot that a more professionally motivated group in society would not have accepted. . . . Seeking to abandon the image of ministers as managers, they took on the mantle of servant leaders. Partly as a consequence, in the year 2000, they found themselves paid in many places accordingly — as servants."[47] While the Protestant ministry accepted their "economic lot," rabbis pushed to maintain their economic status.

And Bingo Was Its Name-O

Although the topic may seem frivolous, no synagogue finance issue in the post–World War II era engendered as much controversy as bingo. Bingo was the flashpoint for controversial state legislation, interfaith discord, dueling opinions of Jewish law, and even the expulsion of sixteen synagogues from the Conservative movement. Bingo also provides an excellent paradigm in which to view one of the central issues of this book — the extent to which synagogues were pragmatic in their approach to financing.

Bingo's popularity emerged during the Great Depression when many Americans had more idle time, less income to spend on other leisure activity, and a heightened desire for quick money.[48] Players were predominately middle-aged women who were so enthusiastic for the game that they were said to have been afflicted with "bingoitis." Initially, games were held in cinemas and social halls, but Catholic churches began hosting games to make up for the decrease in pledge revenue due to the Depression. New York City mayor Fiorello La Guardia feared that organized crime would take control of the games and he ordered a ban on bingo in 1938. The New York State Legislature followed suit and outlawed bingo as a form of gambling except when played for charitable purposes and under certain circumstances.[49]

Throughout the 1940s, some synagogues utilized bingo, though it proves difficult to ascertain how many did so. The popularity of charitable bingo games continued to grow to the point that the New York State Legislature proposed a constitutional amendment in 1957 to legalize the game for nonprofit institutions. Specifically, the amendment would grant each town or city the right to decide whether to legalize nonprofit games within its own district.

In the run-up to the 1957 vote, the state's religious community was divided on the propriety of bingo. The *New York Times* reported, "Bingo has split Catholics and Protestants more thoroughly than any point of doctrine. Though an occasional bishop has banned it, no Catholic moralist has ever found the game anathema. To most Protestant authorities however, gambling in any form is repulsive."[50] The Protestant opposition to bingo was absolute and aggressive. Before the vote, the New York State Council of Churches distributed anti-bingo flyers and circulars to 3,500 churches, and conducted door-to-door canvasing in some areas to stop the bingo amendment.[51]

Numerous Protestant leaders publicly characterized bingo as a gateway to more serious forms of gambling. One Brooklyn pastor claimed bingo was "a sin against man, against society, and against God. . . . No institution has the moral right to exploit the cupidity of its fellowmen for the church or for any other cause."[52] Alongside the condemnation of bingo was a strong denunciation of the Catholic Church for their support of legalized gambling. Reformation Sunday, which was described by contemporary newspapers as a day for services "stressing aspects of faith and morals that distinguish Protestant from the Roman Catholic viewpoint," occurred during the run-up to the bingo vote. Protestant leaders throughout the state took the opportunity to condemn the Catholic Church for their support of gambling, with one prominent minister likening the Catholic Church to the money changers in the Temple.[53]

The Christian debate over gambling provided the context for the Jewish responses to bingo, as Jewish religious leaders closely watched the debate and decided to follow the lead of their Protestant neighbors. A 1936 responsa written by the Central Conference of American Rabbis concerning the propriety of using games of chance to fund synagogues argued that Jewish legal tradition was ambiguous on the question, but noted a report of the United Lutheran synod of New York that condemned games of chance. The Reform responsa argued that synagogues should be wary of games of chance because "such Jewish affairs, especially if much publicized, may lower the respect for Judaism in the eyes of non-Jews. Hence, discretion is advisable even from this angle alone."[54] Because Protestants opposed gambling, Reform leaders felt Jews should oppose it as well in order to maintain their reputation with Protestant religious leaders.

Thus, despite the presence of bingo at some synagogues, in the run-up to the 1957 New York vote Jewish religious authorities expressed staunch opposition to the bingo amendment. The New York Board of Rabbis issued a statement urging Jews to vote against bingo: "The raising of funds through bingo games, even for worthwhile causes, is not consonant with the high standards of morality and dignity which the synagogue sets for the general community."[55] The New York Federation of Reform Synagogues agreed, saying, "When bingo and like games of chance become the source of synagogue support they will . . . cause the decline of the synagogue as the spiritual center of our community and the lives of the people who dwell in them."[56] The Orthodox movement's Rabbinical Council of America and the Union of Orthodox Jewish Congregations both came out against bingo as well.[57]

The substantial opposition to bingo from the rabbinic organizations was by no means a given considering the traditional Jewish sources related to gambling. Jewish sources are unequivocal in their condemnation of professional gamblers, but much more fluid when it comes to the occasional game of chance when played for fun. The basic Jewish legal source on gambling is found in the Babylonian Talmud (the source text for Jewish law), which states that games of chance are improper only when those participating have no other jobs and are not productive members of society.[58] Medieval Jewish sources repeatedly reaffirm the condemnation of gambling by professional gamblers as well as any gambling involving significant amounts of money.[59] Maimonides, the great Jewish medieval scholar, went so far as to declare gambling a form of robbery.[60]

But despite the repeated condemnation of gambling, Judaism also offered times and places when gambling was permitted as long as high stakes were not involved and the gambling would not lead people to become professional gamblers. For centuries, holidays like Hanukkah and Purim represented occasions when Jews played games of chance.[61] Another historical precedent was the surge in popularity of lotteries in Europe in the seventeenth and eighteenth centuries. Not only did some synagogues hold lotteries, but some Jewish communities also encouraged members to purchase lottery tickets with the expectation that the winner would donate a portion of the winnings to charity.[62] This encouragement built on the established Jewish legal precedent that allowed synagogues to receive money from questionable sources. Moses Isserles, a preeminent Jewish legal authority, permitted money from gamblers and prostitutes to support a synagogue with the understanding that such people should be allowed to support sacred causes, even if their money was gotten through illicit means.

In other words, Jewish sources supported both sides of the bingo debate. The sources could be read stringently to say that using bingo to support synagogues might encourage people to gamble more heavily, thus making the game unethical, or the sources could be interpreted in a lenient manner to say that as long as good was coming from it, games of chance could be permitted.

In the 1950s, as the religious leaders of all non-Catholic denominations opposed the bingo amendment, the Conservative movement became the center of significant bingo tension. In 1957, the movement's Committee on Law and Standards wrote a legal opinion exploring some of the textual arguments noted above, ultimately declaring that they could find no traditional Jewish legal basis to bar bingo from being used for synagogue fund-raising.

"Nonetheless," they wrote, "the spirit of the age and of our land, created spiritual standards" and upon that basis the committee declared its opposition.[63] Although the committee's decision was not unprecedented, it was highly unusual for it to ignore traditional practice and rule on the basis of "spiritual standards" alone.

Nonetheless, despite the religious objections to the bingo amendment, the public had a large appetite for bingo and the amendment won 60 percent of the total New York vote, with 70 percent approval in New York City.[64] After the passage of the bill, more than 500 towns and cities voted in favor of legalizing local bingo games, and statewide proceeds from bingo games were expected to exceed $1 million in the first year alone.[65] Across the river in New Jersey the figures were even more startling. Bingo for charitable purposes had been legalized in 1954 and by 1957 it was reported that more than 5 million people played in bingo games with receipts totaling $19 million.[66]

Despite the overwhelming public support, the Conservative movement continued its opposition to bingo. In 1961, the United Synagogue (the synagogue arm of the Conservative movement) passed a constitutional amendment decreeing that synagogues could not utilize bingo for synagogue finances. Basing their decision on the Committee on Law and Standards, a United Synagogue committee concluded:

> In the Jewish tradition the raising of funds for synagogue or charitable purposes is in itself an act of sanctity and therefore must have the same spiritual quality as the ends to which the funds are to be employed. Synagogues shall therefore not permit any form of fund-raising under their auspices, on or off their premises, which is not in keeping with the spirit of Judaism, or the practice of which is likely to bring discredit and disrepute upon the synagogue, even though such activity may be sanctioned by civil law.[67]

This statement is fascinating in its representation of Jewish tradition. As noted above, Jewish legal authorities had long held that funds could be obtained for the synagogue from gambling, and the Conservative movement itself just four years previously had held that there was no Jewish legal basis for not allowing bingo. Nonetheless, the movement grounded its anti-bingo stance in what it claimed was Jewish traditional values. One might see the influence of the Protestant anti-bingo crusade as to why the Conservative movement was claiming a Jewish value that it had earlier said did not exist.

In 1967, Rabbi Leon Fink, a proponent of bingo, wrote, "Even the most dispassionate observer would have to conclude that our movement's involvement with bingo during the past few years must not be qualified as a simple concern for standards, but as an obsession."[68] The Conservative movement's "obsession" with stamping out bingo led to the unprecedented act of expelling sixteen synagogues from the movement. In the history of the movement only two synagogues had ever been expelled, and those were related to not keeping a kosher kitchen, so the charge of "obsession" seems well founded. Though Protestant churches had led the failed crusade against bingo in New York in 1957, Conservative Judaism appeared ready to take the mantle as a vehemently anti-gambling religious denomination.

However, in 1967, just ten years after it ruled that bingo violated "spiritual standards," the turmoil over bingo led the Committee on Law and Standards to revisit the question of bingo's propriety. Rabbi Fink authored an opinion, passed by the committee, overturning their previous finding against bingo. Rabbi Fink began by reviewing the legal tradition around gambling, but soon moved on to what he believed was the essential point. He contended that the ban on bingo was discriminatory against urban congregations, which, he claimed, were less well-off and more dependent upon bingo income than suburban congregations. "It should also be noted that at United Synagogue conventions where national policies . . . are adopted, we seldom encounter delegates from lower income groups. Their voices are not heard."[69] Significantly, Fink's argument did not rest on a theological argument for or against gambling. Rather, he focused on the economic and political effects of the ban, claiming that prohibition's inequity — rather than its treatment of gambling — presented the grounds for it to be overturned.

Rabbi Fink's argument was compelling enough for the movement to do an about-face on bingo. Fink's opinion concluded by noting that bingo was not an ideal solution for synagogue fund-raising, but neither did it deserve to be outlawed. Based on the Fink responsum, the movement pulled back on its bingo "obsession" and simply encouraged congregations to seek other sources of revenue.

However, even this opinion did not end the bingo story for the movement. In 1981, the Committee on Law and Standards revisited both of their previous rulings and reinstated its initial response, thereby rejecting bingo as a form of gambling antithetical to Jewish values. The committee claimed that Fink's main argument that bingo was vital to the economic well-being of urban congregations was demonstrably wrong. The committee concluded, "In our secular society, we Jews cannot afford any rationalization which would permit us to ignore the sanctity of the synagogue."[70]

The experience of one Conservative synagogue that embraced bingo following the Fink responsum may illuminate the issues involved. Temple Reyim was a 350-family congregation, founded in 1951, and located in Newton, Massachusetts, in the suburbs of Boston.[71] Typical for expanding suburban synagogues, Reyim wanted to present itself as more than simply a place for services, so it added a large religious education wing as well as a gift shop at a cost of $350,000.[72] Between the construction of the sanctuary, social hall, and religious school, the synagogue was carrying in 1969 a mortgage of $290,000. Income from dues and building pledges were not sufficient to pay off expenses and the congregation ran a chronic short-term deficit that it financed with yearly short-term loans.[73]

In 1971, the president of the congregation reported to the synagogue board that the Conservative movement had dropped its sanctions against synagogues that utilized bingo (subsequent to the Fink responsum) and some conversation was had about Reyim conducting bingo following the lead of other local congregations. The proposal was temporarily dropped, but the congregational deficit increased in 1973 when fifty-two families did not rejoin the congregation, and the high expense of membership was cited as the major factor for congregants leaving. To address the financial problems, the congregation froze payments to the Conservative movement and tried a variety of cost-cutting measures, including lowering the heat during Hebrew school hours.[74]

In 1974 the congregation was forced to further raise dues and school fees to cover ongoing expenses, but the building now needed significant repair. With serious financial distress setting in, the board ultimately agreed to hold Thursday bingo nights on a trial basis, with the rabbi urging, "If it had to be done it should at least be done in a dignified way."

Bingo was an immediate success. It raised $22,000 in its first year. This represented more than 10 percent of a total budget of $187,000. Over the

next fifteen years, revenue from bingo would hover between $20,000 and
$60,000. In the early 1990s, with the addition of the sale of Massachusetts
lottery tickets, bingo night revenue rose dramatically, reaching a height of
$160,000 in 1995.[75] With bingo providing consistently between 10 and 20
percent of budgetary revenue, it is not hard to understand why the game
was attractive to a small congregation that was paying a full complement
of synagogue professionals as well as the upkeep of an expensive building.

But just three years after its peak revenue for the congregation, bingo
night at Reyim ended. Two major factors underlay its demise. The first was
competition. Other groups started holding bingo nights in Newton and
other gambling opportunities, such as the opening of Foxwoods Casino
in Connecticut, decreased the appetite for Reyim's version of bingo. The
second factor was the human resources it took to run the game. Twenty
people were necessary to run bingo night, and the congregation had for
years needed to plead for members to staff the games. When the person
responsible for running bingo resigned unexpectedly, the congregation
could not find someone to take his place. Despite the creation of an Ad Hoc
Committee to Save Bingo, which pushed the congregation to create a special
program whereby anyone who staffed bingo would receive a $200 rebate on
dues, bingo at Reyim came to an abrupt end.[76] This meant the congregation
had to make up substantial revenue. It promptly raised membership dues
and reduced expenses. But the bingo revenue was sorely missed.

Temple Reyim's story is not unique. Although bingo games were a main-
stay of synagogue financing for a number of congregations in the second
half of the twentieth century, it is the rare synagogue today that relies on
regular bingo for funding. Bingo was so attractive for synagogues for the
simple reason that it gave them revenue from nonmembers. Synagogues
are often stymied by their reliance on their own membership for the en-
tirety of the budget. If expenses rise more than expected, they are forced
to either raise the membership rates or go back to the same donors who
have funded them before. Reyim tried both of those tactics to overcome its
chronic short-term budget deficits. But bingo meant that synagogues had
access to revenue from beyond their own membership — in many respects
"the holy grail" of synagogue financing.

The end of bingo at Temple Reyim, similar to many bingo synagogues,
was a result of financial and cultural factors. With the increased number of

casinos and lotteries, people could go to more appealing locations than the social hall of a synagogue.[77] But the moral factor against bingo also played a significant role. The increase in gambling ventures was accompanied by a heightened awareness of gambling as an addiction. As American culture began to use the language of gambling "addiction" akin to drug or alcohol addiction, there was a strong sense that synagogues should not be aiding and abetting addictive behavior. The morally neutral language that Rabbi Fink of the Conservative movement's Committee on Law and Standards used to describe bingo in the late 1960s would not pass muster thirty years later at the end of the century. The gap between bingo and the values people believed a synagogue should stand for became too wide to bridge. Mindy Abramowitz, who was the last person to run bingo at Temple Reyim, re-signed, saying that all the time it took to run the game distorted what she sought from her synagogue membership.[78]

This was not the first time in American history that synagogues turned to games of chance to solve budget deficits. As discussed in the first chapter, Congregation Mikveh Israel held a lottery to retire its building debt in the 1790s. There were voices back then who questioned the moral propriety of a religious institution utilizing a form of gambling to retire its debt. In both the colonial case and the more recent past, synagogues were following the lead of churches in utilizing games of chance as a funding resource. In both cases, congregations were choosing the path of financial pragmatism over morality. But in the ongoing historic tension between pragmatic ways to fund a synagogue and the ideal moral way to fund one, bingo was perhaps so far on the pragmatic side that it was unsustainable.

Conclusion
[*Today–Tomorrow*]

The first American synagogue documents we have date back to 1720 from Shearith Israel in New York City and they are, perhaps not surprisingly, primarily financial records.[1] From then until now Jews have been in some sense tinkering with how to raise the money to sustain communities. As we have seen, that process has been far from static. While the main story on the revenue side has been the change from selling seats to charging dues, the ancillary stories of free synagogues, mushroom synagogues, bingo, High Holiday appeals, Purim balls, and all other manner of revenue-raising ideas seem to be endless. But there are some basic themes that emerge from looking at the entire history of synagogue finance.

Synagogues, unlike churches, rarely used theological language to raise money, relying instead on the call to community and Jewish identity to inspire giving. Not only was theological language not used, but also synagogues rarely made overtures to overtly Jewish values or ideas when it came to money. Discussions of fairness or values happened within the context of American ideas of fairness. With the exception of Rabbi Stephen Wise, who argued for the prophetic nobility of the voluntaristic spirit, one would search in vain for a mention of tithing or any kind of biblical or rabbinic precept for giving. Synagogue giving was thus for the most part a pragmatic endeavor.

It was also a democratic endeavor. Synagogues were rarely funded by a handful of wealthy families; they saw themselves and still see themselves as broad-based institutions where each member is expected to contribute some share toward the bottom line. This democratic pragmatism has served synagogues enormously well for these hundreds of years. Particularly in the twentieth century, the Jewish community successfully poured large resources into creating synagogue buildings and communities. But the question that many synagogues today face with anxiety is whether this democratic pragmatism is sustainable.

Below I provide some sketches of what I imagine the near future might be for synagogue finance. I have tried to convey the major trends and where they point to on the basic issues that this book covered: rabbinic salaries, paying for buildings, and funding models. I have also included some comments regarding the close interrelationship between American economic cycles and the cycle of American synagogue growth. Understanding this relationship is important in seeing the larger picture of the future of American synagogues.

Rabbinic Pay

As traced throughout this book, pay for Jewish clergy placed them firmly in the middle to upper class of American society. While certainly not every rabbi at all times enjoyed this income, from the first Jewish spiritual leaders in America until today, the average rabbinic salary was on par with professionals of the time. The biggest challenge to this status came during the late nineteenth century, with the large influx of rabbis from Eastern Europe creating an overabundance of supply for synagogues.

This challenge was eventually overcome by the establishment of seminaries and rabbinic unions that created professional standards for the field. These unions effectively monopolized the supply of rabbis, and synagogues were forced to go along with this structure because there was no credible alternative supply chain. For a good part of the twentieth century until today, if a Conservative synagogue was searching for a rabbi, the congregation hired through the Rabbinical Assembly (the rabbinic organization of the Conservative movement), and there would be penalties for the congregation imposed by the movement if they went outside this structure. This allowed the rabbinic unions to push salaries higher, commensurate with growing Jewish economic prosperity. The argument to congregations was that rabbis were a highly professionalized class with extensive schooling and thus required a middle- to upper-middle-class salary. Further, it was argued that it was simply appropriate that the religious leader of the community be treated well economically, and be paid commensurately with the membership they were serving.

But there have been numerous challenges to this system of late. New rabbinical seminaries like Hebrew College in Boston and Aleph: The Alliance for Jewish Renewal, as well as competition from rabbis ordained by Chabad, have created an alternative supply chain for congregations seeking rabbis. Congregations, for their part, have been willing to challenge the rabbinic unions as denominational affiliation has waned, making alternative rabbinic schools more attractive suppliers.

There have also been some conspicuous attempts to undo the power of rabbinic organizations to penalize congregations seeking rabbis from outside those organizations. Barak Richman, an anti-trust law professor at Duke University, has argued that the rabbinic movements are in fact acting illegally. In an extensive legal opinion that he followed up with popular articles, Richman argued that the Conservative and Reform movements' hiring systems are illegal cartels that unduly restrict competition and "flagrantly violate" the Sherman Act.[2] The *New York Times* featured Richman in a provocatively titled article, "Seeing and Battling a 'Cartel' in the Hiring of Rabbis."[3] As of the writing of this book, there has been no legal action to see whether Richman is correct in his assessment of the rabbinic hiring system, but he has certainly put the rabbinic unions on notice.

Both the creation of the new seminaries and the move to end the rabbinic unions' hiring system are reflections of the weakening of denominations in American Jewish life. Many congregations are no longer as ideologically committed to a movement, and this has opened up the doors to hiring outside the traditional supply of rabbis. Further, the economic struggles facing congregations that began in earnest with the recession in 2007 have pushed some congregations to question their ability to hire Jewish clergy at upper-middle-class salaries.

With these factors at work, it may be unlikely that rabbinical salaries will continue their longtime upward trajectory. On the other hand, the sense of the rabbinate as a profession has deeply engrained itself in the American Jewish worldview.

This next period of American Jewish history will presumably see these forces competing with each other. One could imagine a future for rabbis whereby a good portion serve prosperous congregations and continue to receive salaries commensurate with upper-middle-class incomes, thereby honoring that traditional American understanding of the rabbi as professional. At the same time, the end of the monopolization of the supply chain and the growing economic struggle of congregations may create more rabbinic jobs that will pay closer to ministerial salaries than what rabbis have been accustomed to making.

Buildings

The future is smaller. Or at least a significantly more efficient use of space. Where there is some evidence that synagogues will continue to build large new buildings — Temple Beth Elohim in Wellesley, Massachusetts, a highly successful congregation, constructed a building at a cost of over $25,000,000 in 2010 — there is far more evidence that synagogues are figuring out ways to combat the high price of their own buildings.

Since the late nineteenth century, but particularly in the 1920s and the 1950s, synagogues undertook large building projects. In both of these time periods, the general economy was strong, general construction and building were booming, and the Jewish community was anxious to create edifices that reflected a newfound stature in the American landscape. But the building of large structures inevitably presents ongoing financial expenses. As outlined in the experience of Temple Israel in the 1920s, the building of large structures often does not anticipate the full cost of new buildings, and thus synagogues are forced to raise dues and keep them high precisely when the synagogue needs to find more members.

In the suburbanization period, most congregations instituted a building fund as part of the price of joining a synagogue to help defray some of the cost of buildings. The fund was typically payable over five years. The rationale for this fee was that new members were benefiting from previous members' contributions that paid for the building. The fee would balance this issue and provide additional revenue for the synagogue. Of course, these funds were instituted when synagogues were growing and did not need to worry about membership in the way that contemporary synagogues do. Some synagogues today are now phasing out these fees as they represent an impediment to members interested in joining.

But the most pressing issue for synagogues is often the size and use of the building. Synagogues are spaces that are irregularly used. Sanctuaries might only be used once a week for Shabbat services. A social hall may similarly only be utilized once a week for a celebration. Religious school classrooms might also only be used once or twice a week. And even when they are used, many synagogues were built for the High Holidays and not for regular Sabbath usage. As an editorial from a Jewish newspaper asked in 1986, "Why is it necessary to have a million dollar building for 10 or 12 people to say their Sabbath prayers?"[4] For many synagogues, the cost of large buildings that are not utilized regularly has become onerous. Some synagogues have responded by finding renters who use the space regularly, but finding appropriate tenants has by no means been easy for synagogues.

It may be helpful for synagogues to know that they are not alone in having overbuilt; some churches are similarly suffering. Hudnut-Beumler writes of the twentieth-century Protestant impulse to build churches larger than necessary: "What underlies this urge to build what is described by contemporary clerical critics as the 'edifice complexes'? First it is the deep need to make a mark in the environment — to fashion with one's hands still more perfect structures. . . . Second is a felt need to do something for God. Places of worship are symbolically close to where the action of the holy occurs."[5]

There is, of course, a long history of building majestic worship spaces. Be it Notre Dame Cathedral in Paris, Gaudi's Sagrada Familia in Barcelona, or Temple Emanu-El in New York City, the religious impulse throughout history seems to call out for massive spaces meant to inspire awe. Yet this sense of grandeur makes it difficult for synagogues to consider how to downsize their physical spaces. How does one create a space that can be an offering to God and at the same time be economically sensible? Renting, rather than owning, space has been one response, especially in cities where being a renter is seen as culturally and economically compatible with urban living. Merging with other Jewish institutions to create some economies of scale has been another response. Chabad has been especially creative in designing mixed-use synagogues, where prayer spaces, learning spaces, play spaces, and eating spaces can be interchanged. The near future for synagogues must be to maximize flexible space and limit the underutilization of the building.

Cycles of Synagogue Growth and Decline and Broader American Economic Cycles

The cycle of synagogue building leads to an important insight in the inter-relationship between synagogues and the general economy. In the 1920s, the 1950s, and the 1990s, the number of new synagogue buildings grew dramatically. And in these periods, the buildings themselves were often large complexes that entailed a significant outpouring of resources and expanded synagogue budgets. By contrast, the era of the Great Depression and the more recent Great Recession witnessed large reductions in synagogue af-filiation and resulting budgetary constraints. Synagogues grew during eras of general economic expansion and contracted when economies stagnated. There is a direct correlation between the cycles of synagogue growth and the cycles of the American economy. Recession leads to diminishing syna-gogue membership and budgets, and prosperity leads to synagogue growth.

Jonathan Sarna has forcefully argued that American Jewish history should be seen as cyclical. As opposed to a theory of declension, which says that commitment to Jewish institutions has withered away over the genera-tions, the cyclical theory holds that there are periods of "revivals" where there is "Jewish institutional growth, increased involvement in ritual and worship, and a heightened interest in Jewish education and culture."[6] Sarna suggests that the revivals are often precipitated by events like the rise of nineteenth-century antisemitism, or the menace of Nazism, events that have "disrupted the order of life" and Jews are forced to seek out a new sense of meaning.

I would suggest a version of Sarna's theory of cycles but one focused on American economics as a precipitating factor. Since the turn of the twentieth century, there have been periods of revival in synagogues (1920s, 1950s, and 1990s) and there have been periods of stagnation (the 1930s and presently). And while there are particular cultural events that would ex-plain some of the Jewish institutional vibrancy (the publication of the 1990 National Jewish Population Survey, for example, catalyzed growth in the 1990s), the American economy is ultimately the underlying determinative factor.[7] The economy is never the sole issue precipitating growth or decline, but to miss the importance of the economy would be to ignore the clear historical pattern. Seeing the interrelationship of the broader economy and the synagogue should inform our understanding of American synagogue history. It also explains to some degree the contemporary situation for synagogues and their present struggle to remain vital in the face of a protracted economic downturn.

Four Alternative Trends in Funding Synagogues

Throughout the postwar suburbanization era, synagogue financing was relatively uniform. The dues system was utilized by almost all synagogues. Synagogues raised additional money through annual appeals, fund-raisers, and in some cases bingo. On the expense side, the pay of rabbis and the cost of synagogue buildings continued to rise in concert with the growing wealth of the Jewish community. But this uniformity has of late been challenged. The following is a brief description of new synagogue funding models that have begun to compete with the traditional dues-based one.

CHABAD   The success of Chabad, a branch of Hasidism that utilizes emissaries and outreach in a missionary-type approach to connecting Jews with Jewish practice, has been phenomenal. There are Chabad synagogues in every corner of the globe, as well as in most cities and college campuses in America. One 2002 estimate suggested that worldwide expenses for Chabad approached $1 billion.[8]

From an economic perspective, the Chabad synagogue model differs significantly from traditional synagogues in four respects. First, while most American synagogues pay money "upstream" to support denominations, Chabad is the opposite. Each Chabad synagogue receives help and support from the denomination. Second, while American synagogues have historically been democratically funded by their membership through dues or selling seats, Chabad focuses on development from larger donors to effectively support the whole community. Their successful fund-raising means that for the majority of Jews who go to Chabad, Jewish activities, including religious school, are free. Third, Chabad rabbis have a reputation for being entrepreneurial in their approach, in part because there is no board to which the rabbi is answerable. Because the model is not based on the democratic communal model or corporate model of typical synagogues, Chabad rabbis have the flexibility for risk taking that might be stymied in a traditional setting. Fourth, the rabbis themselves make significantly lower salaries than rabbis at standard American synagogues.[9] Given that rabbinic salaries can make up 20 to 30 percent of a synagogue budget, this means that Chabad synagogues run a leaner budget. The success of the "Chabad model" has made a substantial impact in the Jewish world and has many non-Chabad synagogues considering ways in which it can imitate or more successfully compete with Chabad synagogues for membership.

INDEPENDENT MINYANIM   Located primarily in urban settings and attracting a younger demographic than typical synagogues, independent minyanim have also made a significant impact on the Jewish landscape. An independent minyan is typically lay-led (no paid rabbinic leadership), nondenominational, and focused on "authentic" prayer experiences.[10] They often mix a commitment to Jewish law and community with an inclusive approach to Jewish life.

From an economic standpoint, independent minyanim represent a significant challenge to the traditional model. With no paid clergy, and often no building, expenses at such synagogues are minimal compared to traditional synagogues. With fewer expenses, membership dues are low, so belonging to an independent minyan is much more affordable. The spread of independent minyanim may be limited by their need for committed and knowledgeable laypeople to steer them. But at the same time, the DIY (do-it-yourself) grassroots spirit of these synagogues is in alignment with the contemporary zeitgeist.

THE FREE SYNAGOGUE (THE VOLUNTARY COMMITMENT SYNA-GOGUE)   Between 2009 and 2017, more than sixty synagogues have switched from a dues-based financial model to a free synagogue model where congregants themselves determine how much they will give to support their synagogue without oversight.[11] These synagogues are all in the non-Orthodox movements and are geographically spread around the country.

The voluntaristic principle of giving that Stephen Wise advocated over a century ago has reemerged as an intriguing new model for synagogues. Strong anecdotal evidence suggests that the number of synagogues using this model will continue to increase, as free synagogues have almost uniformly reported modest success in raising revenue and finding new members.[12] The rise of the number of free synagogues is directly tied to the recession that began in 2007. The economic downturn ignited a significant loss of membership in non-Orthodox synagogues, often as much as 20 percent. As a result of this membership loss and a decrease in dues payments from remaining members, synagogue revenues dropped, and synagogues could not raise dues rates without fearing more membership resignations. The dues model was seen by some as outdated and not flexible enough to deal with this new reality.

In looking for a new model, these synagogues returned to an old idea of the free synagogue that made dues voluntary. Such synagogues stress financial transparency and engagement with membership as crucial to encouraging members to give sufficiently to support the synagogue. The free synagogue model has garnered significant attention from established synagogues and if it continues to show successful results, may well represent the next major phase of synagogue finance.

THE COMMUNITY SYNAGOGUE   Since 1825, when the Jews of Charleston and New York City founded alternative synagogues to the established congregations, competition between synagogues for membership has existed. But throughout American Jewish history much of that competition was dampened by denominationalism. The ideological divide between the denominations limited the extent to which some Jews were willing to move between Reform, Conservative, and Orthodox synagogues. As noted above, the diminishing importance of denominations and the blurring of their ideological distinctions, particularly between the liberal movements, has meant that Jews are now more apt than ever before to move between denominations. The same trend has been noted among American Protestants, who are similarly more likely than ever before to change denominations.

The result of denominational hopping and the increase in independent synagogues means an increase in competition among synagogues. Additionally, synagogues are seeing new competition for members from a variety of other sources: a growing number of independent Hebrew schools; independent rabbis who perform life cycle events; and the World Wide Web, whereby Jewish educational resources previously only available through a synagogue or through a movement can now be obtained at home via the Internet.

In a number of locations, the response of heightened competition has been to merge congregations of different denominations into "community synagogues."[13] A merged community synagogue might have a Reform-inspired service on Friday night, a Conservative service on Saturday morning, and a Reconstructionist service monthly. Basic economics suggests that when an industry sees new players enter the market, the effect of competition is to push the existing institutions to be more economically efficient. In the case of the "synagogue industry," this has meant mergers to seek efficiencies through having one building and/or one rabbi. Diminishing denominational differences has certainly made these mergers more possible. It is unlikely that American Judaism will witness a return to the old model of one synagogue per community, but as the economics of synagogue life become more difficult, it is likely that the trend to merge or share resources will only increase.

═══

The writing of this book coincides with a significantly heightened interest in the subject of synagogues and money because so many synagogues are feeling financially challenged. Many of the issues covered in this book, such as paying clergy upper-middle-class salaries, which at one time may have seemed settled, have now been reopened. Some commentators on religion have even wondered about the synagogue itself as a viable organization given the rise of Internet culture and the perceived disinterest among millennials in paying for Jewish life. It is, of course, dangerous to practice prophecy, but reflecting on the pragmatic adaptability of synagogues in this country over the past 360 years, I am quite confident that synagogues will rise to this financial challenge. The ancient institution of the synagogue has proved itself remarkably adaptable to American life.

Notes

Introduction

1. There are of course exceptions to the general rule that synagogue histories ignore economics. For works that do include a significant economic perspective on synagogues, see the following: Hyman Grinstein, *The Rise of the Jewish Community of New York* (Philadelphia: Jewish Publication Society, 1945); Leon Jick, *The Americanization of the Synagogue* (Hanover, NH: Brandeis University Press, 1976); Beth Wenger, *New York Jews and the Great Depression* (New Haven, CT: Yale University Press, 1996); David and Tamar de Sola Pool, *An Old Faith in the New World: Portrait of Shearith Israel, 1654–1954* (New York: Columbia University Press, 1955); Frank Adler, *Roots in a Moving Stream: The Centennial History of the Congregation B'nai Jehudah of Kansas City, 1870–1970* (Kansas City, MO: Congregation of B'nai Jehudah, 1972); Jonathan Sarna, "Seating and the American Synagogue," in *Belief and Behavior: Essays in the New Religious History*, eds. Philip Vandermeer and Robert Swierenga (New Brunswick, NJ: Rutgers University Press, 1991); and Kimmy Caplan, "In God We Trust: Salaries and Income of American Orthodox Rabbis, 1881–1924," *American Jewish History* 86 (1998): 77–106.

2. Jonathan Karp, "It's the Economy Schmendrick: An 'Economic Turn' in Jewish Studies?" *AJS Perspectives* (Fall 2009): 8–11. Recent books like Rebecca Kobrin's edited volume, *Chosen Capital: The Jewish Encounter with American Capitalism* (New Brunswick, NJ: Rutgers University Press, 2012), are explicitly placing economics at the center.

3. James Hudnut-Beumler, *In Pursuit of the Almighty's Dollar: A History of Money and American Protestantism* (Chapel Hill, NC: University of North Carolina Press, 2007), xi.

4. Moses Weinberger, *People Walk on Their Heads*, ed. and trans. Jonathan Sarna (New York: Holmes & Meier, 1982), 43.

5. "President's Message," Board Minutes of Congregation Adath Israel, November 18, 1919, AJA.

6. Leo Franklin, "A New Congregational Policy," *American Israelite*, November 17, 1904.

7. "Temple Israel May Adopt New Pew System," *The Jewish Advocate*, February 17, 1921.

8. On the free synagogue movement, see Melvin Urofsky, *A Voice That Spoke for Justice: The Life and Times of Stephen Wise* (Albany: SUNY Press, 1982); Stephen Wise, *Challenging Years: The Autobiography of Stephen Wise* (New York: G.P. Putnam's Sons, 1949); and Stephen Wise, "What Is a Free Pulpit?" in *Free Synagogue Pulpit* (New York: Bloch, 1908). On the free church movement, see Garth M. Rossel and Richard A. G. Dupois, eds., *The Memoirs of Charles G. Finney* (Grand Rapids, MI: Academie Books, 1989), 290–97; Charles C. Cole. "The Free Church Movement in New York City," *New York History* 34 (1953): 284–97; and *The Congregationalist* 77 (December 29, 1892): 219–21. On the relationship of the free church to the free synagogue, see Jonathan Sarna, "Seating and the American Synagogue," 189–206.

9. On mushroom synagogues, see Daniel Judson, "A History of Mushroom Synagogues," *American Jewish Archives Journal* (forthcoming); Jeffrey Gurock, *Orthodox Jews in America* (Bloomington: Indiana University Press, 2009), 104–6; Deborah Dash Moore, *At Home in America: Second Generation New York Jews* (New York: Columbia University Press, 1981), 139–140; and Arthur Goren, *New York Jews and the Quest for Community* (New York: Columbia University Press, 1970), 76–79.

10. On the synagogue-center movement, see See David Kaufman, *Shul with a Pool: The "Synagogue Center" in American Jewish History* (Hanover, NH: Brandeis University Press, 1999), 242–74; and Deborah Dash Moore, "A Synagogue Center Grows in Brooklyn," in *The American Synagogue: A Sanctuary Transformed*, ed. Jack Wertheimer (Hanover, NH: Brandeis University Press, 1987), 297–326.

11. On the hazan craze, see A. R. Malachi, "*Hahazanim Harishonim Ba'Amerika,*" *Hadoar*, September 3, 1937 [Hebrew]; Abraham Karp, "An Eastern European Congregation on American Soil: Beth Israel, Rochester, New York, 1874–1886," in *A Bicentennial Festschrift for Jacob Rader Marcus*, ed. Bertram Korn (Waltham, MA: American Jewish Historical Society, 1976), 271–72; Mark Slobin, *Chosen Voices: The Story of the American Cantorate* (Urbana: University of Illinois Press, 1989); and Kimmy Caplan, "In God We Trust."

12. For discussion of this term, see Robin Klay and John Lunn, "Protestants and the American Economy in the Postcolonial Period: An Overview," in *God and Mammon: Protestants, Money, and the Market, 1790–1860*, ed. Mark Noll (New York: Oxford University Press, 201), 49.

13. "Minute Book of the Congregation Shearith Israel," *Publications of the American Jewish Historical Society* 21 (1913).

14. Cited in Hudnut-Beumler, *In Pursuit of the Almighty's Dollar*, 81.

15. Hudnut-Beumler, *In Pursuit of the Almighty's Dollar*, 94.

16. Maimonides was a famous dissenter from this position. He took a strident position against rabbis being paid. He warns in his commentary to *Pirkei Avot*,

chapter 4 (*Teachings of the Fathers*), "Don't use the Torah as a spade to dig with," which means that you must not use the Torah as a means to make a living. He writes quite dramatically, "One who derives personal benefit from the Torah removes his life force from the world." Isadore Twersky suggests that Maimonides's vehement objections to the payment of scholars was not necessarily because the act of being paid itself was inherently problematic; rather, the prevailing religious leadership had become corrupt and no longer deserved to be paid. Isadore Twersky, *Introduction to the Code of Maimonides* (New Haven, CT: Yale University Press, 1980), 82–83. See also Aryeh Leibowitz, "The Pursuit of Scholarship and Economic Self-Sufficiency: Revisiting Maimonides's Commentary on Pirkei Avot," *Tradition* 40, 3 (2007): 31–41, in which Leibowitz cites genizah documents from the synagogue of Fustat during Maimonides's time that suggest the synagogue was spending seven times as much on the upkeep of scholars and officials than it was on true cases of charity. Perhaps, as a once impoverished immigrant to Fustat himself, Maimonides felt that scholars' dependence on charity forced the community to be ungenerous to those in need.

17. See Philip Segal, "Games of Chance on Synagogue Premises," *Proceedings of the Committee on Jewish Law and Standards of the Conservative Movement* (New York: The Rabbinical Assembly, 1997), 537–38; and Leon Fink, "Games of Chance," *Proceedings of the Committee on Jewish Law and Standards of the Conservative Movement, 1927–1970* (New York: The Rabbinical Assembly, 1997), 1507.

18. See Roger Finke and Rodney Stark, *The Churching of America, 1776–2005: Winners and Losers in Our Religious Economy* (New Brunswick, NJ: Rutgers University Press, 2005), for a discussion of religious markets in American religious history.

19. Jonathan Sarna, *American Judaism* (New Haven, CT: Yale University Press, 2004), 60.

20. Combined Jewish Philanthropies, "Greater Boston Jewish Community Study," 2017, https://cdn.fedweb.org/fed-34/2/Cohen%2520Center%2520Report%2520Final%2520Clickable.pdf?v=1479484614. Traditional "brick and mortar" synagogues refers to synagogues that are neither Chabad nor places like Kavod House, which is devoted to young Jews doing social justice work but also has religious services.

21. Michael Paulson, "The 'Pay What You Want' Experiment at Synagogues," *New York Times*, February 2, 2015.

22. Steven A. Rosenberg, "Temples Trading Dues for Pledges," *Boston Globe*, April 20, 2014.

23. Lisa Miller, "Young Jews Rebelling Against Paying Dues," *Washington Post*, January 18, 2013.

24. See Dan Judson and Lianna Levine Reisner, "Connection, Cultivation, and

Commitment: New Insights on Voluntary Dues," *Synergy* 14 (May 2017), www. ujafedny.org/assets/787642. Contemporary congregations typically use the term "voluntary dues" to describe their model, but it is identical to the Free Synagogue envisioned by Stephen Wise.

25. John McCusker, *How Much Is That in Real Money?: A Historical Commodity Price Index for Use as a Deflator of Money Values in the Economy of the United States* (Worcester, MA: American Antiquarian Society, 2001).

ONE   "The Foundation Stones Are Now For Sale" | *1728–1805*

1. Edwin Wolf and Maxwell Whiteman, *The History of the Jews of Philadelphia from Colonial Times to the Age of Jackson* (Philadelphia: Jewish Publication Society, 1957), 142–45.

2. Ibid., 224.

3. For a discussion of the Amsterdam Jewish community as a model for worldwide Jewish communities, see Jonathan Sarna, *American Judaism*, 12.

4. Arnold Wiznitzer, *The Records of the Earliest Jewish Community in the New World* (New York: American Jewish Historical Society, 1954), 28–29.

5. Ibid., 30–32, 79–80.

6. Sarna, *American Judaism*, 20.

7. Because the vast majority of New York citizens at the beginning of the eighteenth century were members of various dissenting denominations, establishing the Anglican Church was a source of significant controversy. The counties surrounding New York City either did not have an established church or fought its imposition. See Patricia Bonomi, *Under the Cope of Heaven: Religion, Society, and Politics in Colonial America* (New York: Oxford University Press, 2003), 50–54.

8. E. Brooks Holifield, *God's Ambassadors* (Grand Rapids, MI: William B. Eerdmans Publishing Company, 2007), 95–99.

9. Donald Scott, *From Office to Profession: The New England Ministry, 1750–1850* (Philadelphia: University of Pennsylvania Press, 1978), 3.

10. Luther Powell, *Money and the Church* (New York: Association Press, 1962), 120.

11. Holifield, *God's Ambassadors*, 97; Powell, *Money and the Church*, 108.

12. Powell, *Money and the Church*, 91–103.

13. Ibid., 128–35.

14. The selling of synagogue seats was an old custom that went back to medieval Europe. Salo Baron, in his magisterial *Jewish History*, cites records from the fourteenth century in France, Spain, and Germany that testify to synagogues selling seats. Isaac ben Sheshet, a fourteenth-century Spanish Talmudic authority, reported a case of a speculator who had bought numerous synagogue seats and was profiting

from renting them out. When Jews who owned seats went into debt to Christian creditors and their property was seized, it meant that Christians would ironically own synagogue seats. In such cases, the seats were usually resold to Jews and the money given to the Christian creditor. Salo Baron, *The Jewish Community: Its History and Structure to the American Revolution*, vol. 2 (Philadelphia, PA: The Jewish Publication Society of America, 1945), 124–125.

15. Stephen Wise, *Challenging Years*, 45.

16. On Finney and his disparagement of pew rentals, see Keith Hardman, *Charles Grandison Finney, 1792–1875: Revivalist and Reformer* (New York: Syracuse University Press, 1986). On the democratizing elements of the Second Great Awakening, see Nathan Hatch, *The Democratization of American Christianity* (New Haven, CT: Yale University Press, 1991).

17. "Minute Book of the Congregation Shearith Israel," *Publications of the American Jewish Historical Society*, 21 (1913): 31.

18. Giving wood was a common form of payment both within the congregation and the culture at large, which had a significant level of bartering.

19. "Minute Book of the Congregation Shearith Israel," 29–30.

20. Holifield, *God's Ambassadors*, 98.

21. Despite all colonial currency being denoted in pounds, each colony before the Revolution printed its own money, so a pound held different value depending upon the state. For example, 1 pound sterling of New York currency in 1731 was almost twice as valuable as 1 pound sterling of Massachusetts currency. Thus, although the hazan was paid £50 and the New England clergy £60, the hazan was making substantially more. See McCusker, *How Much Is That in Real Money*, 34.

22. Simon Middleton, *From Privilege to Rights: Work and Politics in Colonial New York City* (Philadelphia: University of Pennsylvania Press, 2006), 266–67, notes 63, 65.

23. Editorial, A Supplement to the New-York Weekly Journal, March 28, 1737.

24. *History of Wages in the United States from Colonial Times to the Present*, Bulletin of the U.S. Bureau of Labor Statistics, No. 604 (1934): 118.

25. Jacob Rader Marcus writes that "it can hardly be doubted" that Lopez de Fonseca continued to work as a trader while acting as a hazan. There is, however, no evidence of this and Marcus may have presumed the salary was low, which would have necessitated de Fonseca continuing to work. Jacob Rader Marcus, *The Colonial American Jew, 1492–1776* (Detroit: Wayne State University Press, 1970), 866.

26. "Minute Book of the Congregation Shearith Israel," 36. The synagogue increased his salary to £50 the following year, removing the tzedakah fund proviso. The hazan, David Machado, was a merchant who continued working as a merchant while acting as hazan; see Leo Hershkowitz, *Wills of Early New York Jews* (New York: American Jewish Historical Society, 1967), 51, which details how Machado is named

as executor for the will of Shearith Israel member Rachel Luis, who cites Machado as a "New York City merchant," and is not identified as hazan of the synagogue.

27. Ibid., 35–38.

28. Hudnut-Beumler, *In Pursuit of the Almighty's Dollar*, 81.

29. See footnote 16 in the introduction for a discussion of Maimonides's position on this issue.

30. "Minute Book of Congregation Shearith Israel," 3. In pre-Revolutionary budgets, the congregation often uses the Spanish phrase *obras pias* (religious works) to indicate money given to the poor, while the entire budget is called "The Holy Sedaka of Shearith Israel."

31. Ibid., 86.

32. Ibid., 69–70.

33. Hyman Grinstein, *The Rise of the Jewish Community of New York* (Philadelphia: Jewish Publication Society, 1945), 134.

34. "Minute Book of Congregation Shearith Israel," 56.

35. Marcus, *The Colonial American Jew*, 1050.

36. "Minute Book of Congregation Shearith Israel," 2–3.

37. Marcus, *The Colonial American Jew*, 1033.

38. Edwin Burrows and Mike Wallace, *Gotham: A History of New York City to 1898* (New York: Oxford University Press, 1999), 145.

39. Marcus, *The Colonial American Jew*, 1049.

40. Wolf and Whiteman, *The History of the Jews of Philadelphia*, 136.

41. Ibid., 139.

42. David de Sola Pool, *Portraits Etched in Stone* (New York: Columbia University Press, 1955), 94–104.

43. David and Tamar de Sola Pool, *An Old Faith in the New World: Portrait of Shearith Israel, 1654–1954* (New York: Columbia University Press, 1955), 352–54. See also Jacob Rader Marcus, "The Handsome Young Priest in the Black Gown: The Personal World of Gershom Seixas," *Hebrew Union College Annual* 40/41 (1969–1970): 416–17, where he notes that Seixas's decision to start the tzedakah fund when all of the members of the adjunta had left the city suggests an unusual level of decisiveness and independence on Seixas's part.

44. See Jacob Rader Marcus, "The Oldest Known Synagogue Record Book of Continental North America, 1720–1721," in *Studies in American Jewish History: Studies and Addresses* (Cincinnati: Hebrew Union College Press, 1969), 44–53.

45. Marcus, *The Colonial American Jew*, 912–15.

46. "Minute Book of the Congregation Shearith Israel," 3. The minutes are silent as to why the selling of mitzvot was not convenient, but the selling of mitzvot would in a later period lead to significant congregational disputes. See chapter 2 for how

the dispute around the selling of mitzvot would ultimately lead to a congregational split.

47. Ibid., 14.

48. Ibid., 97–98.

49. See chapter 2.

50. "Minute Book of Shearith Israel," 36.

51. Ibid., 53.

52. Ibid., 63.

53. De Sola Pool, *An Old Faith*, 293.

54. Ibid., 263.

55. "Minute Book of Congregation Shearith Israel," 2.

56. Ibid., 57.

57. Ibid., 61.

58. Ibid., 69.

59. Ibid., 89.

60. Ibid., 66–67.

61. Ibid., 81–84.

62. Ibid., 154.

63. De Sola Pool, *An Old Faith*, 272–73.

64. Hershkowitz, *Wills of Early New York Jews*, 208. Interestingly, the very next bequest in Myers's will is the gift of a slave boy "Harry" to his loving wife, and upon her death the slave was to be manumitted.

65. It is still the custom among the surviving colonial synagogues for people to pay for *hashkavot* — Mikveh Israel asks for $500 for such a service. See www.mikvehisrael.org/e2_cms_display.php?p=hashcabot.

66. "Minute Book of Congregation Shearith Israel," 102.

67. Hershkowitz, *Wills of Early New York Jews*, 70.

68. De Sola Pool, *An Old Faith*, 41. See also Burrows and Wallace, *Gotham*, 133; and Marcus, *The Colonial Jew*, 406–11. Marcus notes that 1727 was the legalization of a practice in place since at least 1718 of Jews omitting the vow of Christian fealty in the oath of naturalization. Naturalization was significant, as it made Jews eligible to participate in trade and own property.

69. See Joyce Goodfriend, *Before the Melting Pot: Society and Culture in Colonial New York City, 1664–1730* (Princeton, NJ: Princeton University Press, 1992), 187–216, for a description of the growth of Lutheran, Presbyterian, and Quaker churches in New York City between 1700 and 1730.

70. Michael Kammen, *New York: A Colonial History* (New York: Charles Scribner's Sons, 1975), 191.

71. See Burrows and Wallace, 118–34.

72. Ibid., 134. For a more detailed discussion of Nathan Simson's trading, see Marcus, *The Colonial American Jew*, 634–41.

73. "Minute Book of the Congregation Shearith Israel," 40.

74. A black Chinese tea considered a luxury item in eighteenth-century America.

75. The congregation initially was named Shearith Jacob and transitioned to Shearith Israel in the 1720s. See Marcus, "The Oldest Known Synagogue Record Book," for a discussion of the name change.

76. "Items Relating to Shearith Israel," *Publications of the American Historical Society*, 27 (1920): 2–3.

77. Ibid., 3–4.

78. Mordechai Arbell, *The Jewish Nation of the Caribbean* (Jerusalem: Gefen Publishing House, 2002), 163.

79. Marcus, *The Colonial American Jew*, 177.

80. Solomon Breibart, "The Synagogues of Kahal Kadosh Beth Elohim, Charleston," *South Carolina Historical Magazine* 80, 3 (July 1979): 218.

81. Daniel Ackerman, "The 1794 Synagogue of Kahal Kadosh Beth Elohim," *American Jewish History* 93 (2007): 174. Ackerman notes that the cost of the building was £4000 but previous sources reported it as $20,000, which he disputes.

82. "Minute Book of Congregation Shearith Israel," 19–25.

83. Ibid.,12.

84. Ibid., 12.

85. De Sola Pool, *An Old Faith*, 42.

86. Sarna, *American Judaism*, 17.

87. Ackerman, "The 1794 Synagogue," 163–65.

88. Nathaniel Levin, "The Jewish Congregation of Charleston," *Occident* 1 (November 1843).

89. James Hagy, *This Happy Land: The Jews of Colonial and Antebellum Charleston* (Tuscaloosa: University of Alabama Press, 1993), 14.

90. Ibid., 190–91.

91. Ackerman, "The 1794 Synagogue," 163.

92. *City Gazette and Daily Advertiser*, December 6, 1794.

93. Wolf and Whiteman, *The History of the Jews of Philadelphia*, 114.

94. Ibid., 142–43.

95. Congregation Mikveh Israel Letter 1788, AJA.

96. A "mite" according to *Webster's* is a small sum of money.

97. Benjamin Franklin, *The Autobiography of Benjamin Franklin* (New York: Cosimo Classics, 2007), 63.

98. Asa Martin, "Lotteries in Pennsylvania Prior to 1833 [part 2]," *The Pennsylvania Magazine of History and Biography* 48 (January 1924): 67. See also Powell, *Money and the Church*, 144.

99. C. P. B. Jeffries, "The Provincial and Revolutionary History of St. Peter's Church, Philadelphia, 1753–1783," *The Pennsylvania Magazine of History and Biography* 48 (January 1924): 45.

100. Martin, "Lotteries in Pennsylvania," 81–84.

101. Asa Martin, "Lotteries in Pennsylvania Prior to 1833 [part 1]," *The Pennsylvania Magazine of History and Biography* 47 (October 1923): 320.

102. Cited in Wolf and Whiteman, *The History of the Jews of Philadelphia*, 232.

103. Minute Book of Mikveh Israel, AJA. See also Wolf and Whiteman, *The History of the Jews of Philadelphia*, 144–45.

TWO "So Paltry a Way of Support" | *1805–1865*

1. Minutes of KKBI Board of Trustees, August 30, 1853, AJA.

2. Cited in de Sola Pool, *An Old Faith*, 263.

3. Constitution of Mikveh Israel, 1823, AJA.

4. For a history of the congregation, see Jonathan Sarna and Karla Goldman, "From Synagogue Community to Citadel of Reform," in *American Congregations*, eds. James Lewis and James Wind (Chicago: Chicago University Press, 1994); and Joseph Jonas, "The Jews in Ohio," *Occident* 1, 11 (1844) and continuing in serialized form in additional issues.

5. Minutes of KKBI, 1845.

6. Israel Goldstein, *A Century of Judaism in New York: B'nai Jeshurun, 1825–1925* (New York: Congregation B'nai Jeshurun, 1930), 133–34.

7. "Report of the Temple Emanu-El Congregation," *American Israelite*, April 6, 1855. See also Grinstein, *The Rise of the Jewish Community*, 482.

8. Minutes of Mikveh Israel, September 7, 1845, AJA.

9. "Report of the Temple Emanu-El Congregation," April 6, 1855.

10. Selig Adler and Thomas Connolly, *From Ararat to Suburbia: The History of the Jewish Community of Buffalo* (Philadelphia: Jewish Publication Society, 1960), 62.

11. Minutes of Congregation Keneseth Israel Board of Trustees, September 24, 1850; April 20, 1851, AJA.

12. Minutes of Congregation Ahavath Achim Board of Trustees, December 16, 1849, AJA.

13. Chicago Sinai Constitution, 1861, AJA.

14. Minutes of Keneseth Israel, October 23, 1853, and March 1, 1859, for rental policy, AJA.

15. Minutes of Mikveh Israel, September 7, 1845, AJA.

16. Ibid.

17. Minutes of KKBI, August 1, 1846, AJA.

18. Minutes of Mikveh Israel, August 25, 1833, AJA.

19. Stephen Mostov, "A 'Jerusalem' on the Ohio: The Social and Economic History of Cincinnati's Jewish Community, 1840–1875" (PhD diss., Brandeis University, 1981), 126.

20. KKBI Constitution, 1889, AJA.

21. Minutes of Keneseth Israel, January 24, 1858, AJA, for introduction of family pews. See also Jonathan Sarna, "The Debate over Mixed Seating in the American Synagogue," in *The American Synagogue: A Sanctuary Transformed*, ed. Jack Wertheimer (New York: Cambridge University Press, 1987), 363–94.

22. Minutes of Keneseth Israel, January 17, 1858, AJA.

23. Ibid., April 22, 1856, AJA.

24. Ibid., October 23, 1853, AJA.

25. Ibid., September 3, 1861, AJA.

26. Ibid., July 27, 1856, AJA.

27. Isaac Fein, *The Making of an American Jewish Community: The History of Baltimore Jewry from 1773 to 1920* (Philadelphia: Jewish Publication Society, 1971), 50–51.

28. Minutes of Keneseth Israel, August 3–10, 1858, AJA.

29. Ibid., April 13, 1856, AJA.

30. Ibid., February 1, 1852, AJA.

31. See Max Lilienthal, "The Taxes in Our Congregation," *The Israelite*, December 21, 1855, quoted below, where Lilienthal makes this point explicitly.

32. Max Lilienthal, "The Taxes in Our Congregation," *The Israelite*, November 30, 1855.

33. Sarna and Goldman, "From Synagogue Community," 173.

34. Lilienthal, "The Taxes in Our Congregation."

35. Ibid.

36. Justitia, "A Reply to the Taxes in Our Congregation," *The Israelite*, December 14, 1855.

37. Ibid.

38. Max Lilienthal, "The Taxes in Our Congregation," *The Israelite*, December 21, 1855.

39. Cited in Grinstein, *The Rise of the Jewish Community*, 483.

40. Isaac Leeser, "Synagogue Reforms," *The Occident*, November 1847, 379.

41. See chapter 3 on the free synagogue and chapter 4 on free seating to see these same arguments continued.

42. A "Cohen" refers to someone with patrilineal lineage linking him to the biblical Jewish priesthood.

43. That is, Simchat Torah.

44. Joseph Colon, *Shealot U'tsheuvot*, no. 9.

45. Ismar Elbogen, *Jewish Liturgy: A Comprehensive History,* tr. Raymond Scheindlin (Philadelphia: Jewish Publication Society, 1993), 142 and 424, n. 117.

46. Ibid., 424, n. 117.

47. Quoted in Lance Sussman, *Isaac Leeser and the Making of American Judaism* (Detroit: Wayne State University Press, 1995), 135.

48. Robert Liberles, "Conflict over Reform: The Case of Congregation Beth Elohim in Charleston," in *The American Synagogue: A Sanctuary Transformed*, ed. Jack Wertheimer (New York: Cambridge University Press, 1987), 280.

49. Sarna, *American Judaism*, 58.

50. "'Memorial': A Petition to the Parent Congregation, 1824," reprinted in L. C. Moise, *Biography of Isaac Harby with an Account of the Reformed Society of Israelites of Charleston, S.C.* (Columbia, SC: R. L. Bryan, 1931), 52.

51. Ibid., 55.

52. Ibid., 56.

53. Lou Silberman, *American Impact: Judaism in the United States in the Early Nineteenth Century* (Syracuse, NY: Syracuse University Press, 1964).

54. The church would only officially become Unitarian some years later, but it was Unitarian in spirit at this time.

55. "Review of *The Constitution of the Reformed Society of Israelites, for Promoting True Principles of Judaism According to Its Purity and Spirit*," *The North American Review* 23, 52 (July 1826). The author of the review is anonymous, but Silberman notes in the above cited article that the review is certainly by Reverend Gilman.

56. George Edwards, *A History of the Independent or Congregational Church of Charleston, South Carolina* (Boston: Pilgrim Press, 1947), 66.

57. Leonard Dinnerstein, a historian of antisemitism, quotes the governor of Mississippi in 1837 speaking in reference to Baron Rothschild as saying, "The blood of Judas and Shylock flows through his veins, and he unites the qualities of both his countrymen." Leonard Dinnerstein, "A Note on Southern Attitudes Towards Jews," *Jewish Social Studies* 32, 1 (1970): 44.

58. Gary Zola, *Isaac Harby of Charleston, 1788–1828: Jewish Reformer and Intellectual* (Tuscaloosa: University of Alabama Press, 1994), 117.

59. Moise, *Biography of Isaac Harby*, 63, n. 193.

60. Philadelphia also had two congregations with the creation of Rodeph Shalom in 1802, an Ashkenazi synagogue. Sarna suggests, however, that the appearance of Rodeph Shalom was not meaningfully an alternative to Mikveh Israel, as Mikveh Israel was in such dire straits at that point that "the rise of a new synagogue [Rhodeph Shalom] ... represented less a challenge to [Mikveh Israel's] authority than a response to its languid feebleness." Sarna, *American Judaism*, 53.

61. De Sola Pool, *An Old Faith*, 294–96.

62. Grinstein, *The Rise of the Jewish Community*, 532 n. 9.

63. Minutes of Congregation Shearith Israel, 149–80, AJA. See also Grinstein, *The Rise of the Jewish Community*, 41–49.

64. "The Constitution and Bye-laws of the *Hebra Hinuch Nearim*," in Joseph L. Blau and Salo W. Baron, *The Jews of the United States: A Documentary History, 1790–1840*, 3 vols. (New York: Columbia University Press, 1963), 2: 542–45.

65. Leeser, "Synagogue Reforms," November 1847, 377–78.

66. See Leon Jick's classic work on synagogue change, *The Americanization of the Synagogue, 1820–1870* (Hanover, NH: Brandeis University Press, 1992). The disputes over paying for Torah honors fit precisely into his thesis of synagogue change and Americanization.

67. Sarna, *American Judaism*, 60.

68. Cited in Hudnut-Beumler, *In Pursuit of the Almighty's Dollar*, 13.

69. Ibid., 16.

70. Ibid., 31.

71. Richard Pointer, "Philadelphia Presbyterians, Capitalism, and the Morality of Economic Success, 1825–1855," *The Pennsylvania Magazine of History and Biography*, 112, 3 (July 1988): 350.

72. George Marsden, *The Evangelical Mind and the New School Presbyterian Experience: A Case Study of Thought and Theology in Nineteenth-Century America* (New Haven, CT: Yale University Press, 1970).

73. Mark Noll, "Protestant Reasoning about Money and the Economy," in Noll, *God and Mammon*, 273.

74. Ibid., 272.

75. Ibid., 276.

76. Ibid., 279.

77. Kenneth Startup, "'A Mere Calculation of Profits and Loss': The Southern Clergy and the Economic Culture of the Antebellum North," in Noll, *God and Mammon*, 217.

78. Ibid., 218.

79. Isaac Mayer Wise, "The Age of Corruptions II: Mammonism and Science," *The Israelite*, January 30, 1857.

80. Isaac Mayer Wise, "To Our Subscribers," *The Israelite*, November 30, 1860.

81. Jacob Rader Marcus, *The Americanization of Isaac Mayer Wise* (Cincinnati: American Jewish Archives, 1969), 12.

82. Cited in Marcus, *The Americanization*, 12.

83. Cited in Harold Sharfman, *The First Rabbi: Origins of Conflict Between Orthodox and Reform: Jewish Polemic Warfare in a Pre-Civil War America: A Biographical History* (Malibu, CA: Pangloss, 1988), 244–45.

84. Ibid., 245–47; see also Fein, *The Making of an American Jewish Community*, 55–57.

85. Mostov, "A 'Jerusalem,'" 127–29.

86. Fein, *The Making of an American Jewish Community*, 136.

87. Lloyd Gartner and Louis Swichkow, *The History of the Jews of Milwaukee* (Philadelphia: Jewish Publication Society, 1963), 47.

88. Adler and Connolly, *From Ararat to Suburbia*, 63–69.

89. Rebecca Kobrin, "The Chosen People in the Chosen Land: The Jewish Encounter with American Capitalism," in *Chosen Capital: The Jewish Encounter with American Capitalism,* ed. Rebecca Kobrin (New Brunswick, NJ: University of Rutgers Press, 2012), 1.

90. For reflections on Sombart's essay, see Werner Mosse, "Judaism, Jews and Capitalism: Weber, Sombart and Beyond," *Leo Baeck Institute Yearbook* 24 (1979): 3–15; Paul Mendes-Flohr, "Werner Sombart's 'The Jews and Modern Capitalism': An Analysis of Its Ideological Premises," *Leo Baeck Institute Yearbook* 21 (1976): 87–107; and Salo Baron, "Modern Capitalism and Jewish Fate," *Menorah Journal* 30 (Summer 1942): 116–38.

91. Fein, *The Making of an American Jewish Community,* 54–55.

92. Adler and Connolly, *From Ararat to Suburbia*, 70.

93. Leeser, "Synagogue Reforms," November 1847, 380–81.

94. Minutes of Mikveh Israel, February 9, 1804, AJA.

95. Wolf and Whiteman, *The History of the Jews of Philadelphia,* 246.

96. See Sussman, *Isaac Leeser,* 55–57, for a description of negotiations in Leeser's hiring by Mikveh Israel.

97. Fein, *The Making of an American Jewish Community,* 110.

98. Donald Adams Jr., "Wage Rates in the Early National Period: Philadelphia, 1785–1830," *The Journal of Economic History* 28 (September 1968): 406.

99. Ibid., 422.

100. Sarna, *American Judaism,* 52–53.

101. De Sola Pool, *An Old Faith,* 177.

102. Minutes of Shearith Israel, July 31, 1828, AJA. Also see Robert Margo, "The Rental Price of Housing in New York City, 1830–1860," *The Journal of Economic History,* 56 (September 1996): 621, where he shows the average yearly rent on a house in the Lower East Side in the 1830s was $150.

103. Minutes of Shearith Israel, September 21, 1829, AJA.

104. De Sola Pool, *An Old Faith,* 177.

105. David Hempton, "A Tale of Beggars and Preachers: Methodism and Money in the Great Age of Transatlantic Expansion, 1780–1830," in Noll, *God and Mammon,* 143.

106. Sefton Temkin, "Isaac Mayer Wise: A Biographical Sketch," in *A Guide to the Writings of Isaac Mayer Wise,* ed. Doris C. Sturzenberger (Cincinnati: American Jewish Archives, 1981), 18.

107. Grinstein, *The Rise of the Jewish Community of New York,* 91.

108. Minutes of KKBI, November 28, 1855, AJA.

109. Goldstein, *A Century of Judaism in New York*, 112.

110. *The Occident* 8, 1 (April 1850); see also Bertram Korn, *The Early Jews of New Orleans* (Waltham, MA: American Jewish Historical Society, 1969), 252–53.

111. Touro's complete will with explanatory notes is found in *A Documentary History of the Jews in the United States, 1654–1855*, ed. Morris Schappes (New York: Citadel Press, 1952), 332–41, 657–62.

112. Minutes of Congregation Beth Shalome, February 8, 1857; August 31, 1868, AJA. On Jacobs owning a slave, see Myron Berman, *Richmond's Jewry, 1769–1976: Shabbat in Shockoe* (Charlottesville: University of Virginia Press, 1979), 177.

113. Minutes of Keneseth Israel, April 10, 1859, AJA.

114. There is no official data that support these figures; these numbers are based on my own unpublished research in contemporary synagogue finances and represent budgets from numerous synagogues.

115. Minutes of Keneseth Israel, February 10, 1860, AJA.

116. Fein, *The Making of an American Jewish Community*, 111.

117. Bertram Korn, "An American Jewish Leader in 1860 Voices His Frustration," in *Michael: On the History of Jews in the Diaspora*, ed. Lloyd P. Gartner (Tel Aviv: The Diaspora Research Institute, 1975), 45–46.

118. J. D. Eisenstein, "The History of the First Russian-American Jewish Congregation," *Publications of the American Jewish Historical Society*, 9 (1901): 64–65. See also Jeffrey Gurock, *Orthodox Jews in America* (Bloomington: Indiana University Press, 2009), 56.

119. There were exceptions to this. Jacques Judah Lyons at Shearith Israel was earning $1,500 yearly and occupied a more prominent position in the synagogue than Dr. Adolph Fisher, who was engaged as preacher. See Grinstein, *The Rise of the Jewish Community of New York*, 93. For a brief period in the 1880s the "hazan craze" also pushed the salaries of star cantors higher than their rabbinic counterparts.

120. Grinstein, *The Rise of the Jewish Community of New York*, 87.

121. See "Congregation Emanuel, San Francisco," *The Israelite*, November 16, 1855; and "'No Ear for Lectures': Rabbi Julius Eckman, 1855," in *Jewish Voices of the Gold Rush: A Documentary History, 1849–1880*, ed. Ava F. Kahn (Detroit: Wayne State University Press, 2002), 173–175.

122. *The Jewish Messenger*, May 21, 1858.

123. *The Israelite*, September 29, 1854.

124. *The Jewish Messenger*, September 10, 1858.

125. Minutes of Ahavath Achim, September 22, 1849; May 30, 1852; April 1854, AJA.

126. *The Israelite*, September 22, 1854.

127. Minutes of KKBI, November 28, 1855, AJA.

128. E. Brooks Holifield, "The Penurious Preacher?: Nineteenth-Century Clerical

Wealth: North and South," *Journal of the American Academy of Religion* 58, 1 (Spring 1990): 24.

129. Ibid.

130. Ibid., 19.

131. Scott, *From Office to Profession*, 113.

132. Ibid.

133. Jonas, "Jews of Ohio," *Occident* 2, 3 (June 1844).

134. Ibid. The gift came with the proviso that if the congregation stopped using the chandeliers they would be returned to Shearith Israel.

135. Ibid.

136. Ibid. 2, 5 (August 1844).

137. Lee Weisbach, *The Synagogues of Kentucky* (Lexington: University Press of Kentucky, 1995), 24.

138. Bertram Korn, "A Reappraisal of Judah Touro," *The Jewish Quarterly Review* 45, 4 (April 1855): 571.

139. Minutes of Mikveh Israel, April 25, 1824, AJA.

140. Wolf and Whiteman, The History of the Jews of Philadelphia, 367.

141. Minutes of Mikveh Israel, April 15, 1860, AJA.

142. "Consecration of the New Synagogue, Keneseth Shalom, at Syracuse, New York," *The Occident*, October 1851, 372–73. See also Bernard Rudolph, *From a Minyan to a Community: The Jews of Syracuse, New York* (Syracuse, NY: Syracuse University Press, 1970), 37–43.

143. Minutes of KKBI, July 11, 1852, AJA.

144. Minutes of Keneseth Israel, May 15, 1853; June 19, 1853; July 24, 1853; July 31, 1853, AJA.

145. In the way that all good ideas just come around again, a synagogue in the Philadelphia area has recently gained some notoriety for advertising to its members that they should become "investors" in the synagogue and buy shares. In private correspondence, the rabbi of this synagogue has noted that because so many of his members are involved in finance professionally, the language of "investing" and "shareholding" is resonant and has made a financial difference in the well-being of the congregation. See the website for Congregation Beth Hillel Beth Torah at tbhbe.org.

146. "Nashville, April 28, 5620/1860," found in the minutes of Mikveh Israel for 1860, AJA.

147. "Hebrew Congregation," found in the minutes of Mikveh Israel for 1838, AJA.

148. "Generous and Honorable Fellow Citizens," Minutes of Congregation Tifereth Israel, AJA. The circular is undated, but it mentions the passing of Judah Touro (misspelled as Judah Toure), so we can safely date the letter to the mid-1850s.

149. See Bertram Korn, "A Reappraisal of Judah Touro," *The Jewish Quarterly Review* 45, 4 (April 1955): 571; Bertram Korn, *The Early Jews of New Orleans* (Waltham,

MA: American Jewish Historical Society, 1969), 245–258; and Leon Huhner, *The Life of Judah Touro* (Philadelphia: Jewish Publication Society, 1946).

150. Schappes, *A Documentary History*, 332–41.

151. Minutes of Congregation Beth Shalome, October 21, 1863, AJA.

152. Ibid.

153. See Bertam Korn, *American Jewry and the Civil War* (Philadelphia: Jewish Publication Society, 1951).

154. *Richmond Examiner,* January 15, 1863, cited in Gary Bunker and John Appel, "'Shoddy' Antisemitism and the Civil War," in *Jews and the Civil War*, eds. Jonathan Sarna and Adam Mendelsohn (New York: New York University Press, 2010), 323–24.

155. Cited in Berman, *Richmond's Jewry*, 185–86.

156. Korn, *American Jewry*, 104–5.

157. Minutes of Congregation Beth Shalome, January 31, 1864, AJA.

158. The congregation's August 31, 1856, minutes had a budget of $1,652, while the 1863 budget was $3,109. Minutes of Congregation Beth Shalome, AJA.

159. Ibid. I presume the railroad stock was a gift to the congregation, as it would have been unusual in peace or wartime for a congregation to invest in railroad stock.

160. Minutes of Congregation Beth Shalome, September 1, 1863, AJA.

161. Minutes of Congregation Keneseth Israel, December 13, 1863, AJA.

162. Minutes of KKBI, September 1869, AJA.

163. "Receipts on Account of Building," Minutes of KKBI, February 1865, AJA.

164. James G. Heller, *Isaac M. Wise: His Life, Work, and Thought* (New York: Union of American Hebrew Congregations Press, 1965), 375–79.

165. Allan Tarshish, "The Economic Life of the American Jew in the Middle Nineteenth Century," in *Essays in American Jewish History* (Cincinnati: American Jewish Archives, 1958): 272.

166. Michael Rich, "Henry Mack: An Important Figure in Nineteenth-Century Jewish America," *American Jewish Archives* 47, 2 (1995): 261–79. See also Adam Mendolsohn, *The Rag Race: How the Jews Sewed Their Way to Success in America and the British Empire* (New York: New York University Press, 2014).

167. Sarna, American Judaism, 124.

168. Thomas Clark, "The Post-Civil War Economy in the South," in Sarna and Mendelsohn, *Jews and the Civil War*, 387–98.

THREE Mushroom Synagogues, Free Synagogues, and the Hazan Craze | *1865–1919*

1. Moses Weinberger, *People Walk on Their Heads*, ed. and trans. Jonathan Sarna (New York: Holmes & Meier, 1982), 105–6.

2. Clifton Levy, "A Necessary Reform," *Jewish Criterion* 2, 1 (February 15, 1895).

3. Weinberger, *People Walk on Their Heads*, 100.

4. A. R. Malachi, "Hahazanim Harishonim Ba'Amerika," *Hadoar*, September 3, 1937.

5. Hayim Zeligson, "The First Jews from Suwalk in America," in *Memorial Book of Suvalk*, ed. Berl Kagen, trans. Ida Schwarcz (New York: The Suvalk and Vicinity Relief Committee of New York, 1961), 567–69.

6. Malachi, "Hahazanim."

7. Ibid.

8. "Local News," *The Jewish Messenger*, August 20, 1886. Malachi's "Hahazanim" says that the Ansche Suvalk was the first synagogue.

9. Malachi, "Hahazanim," reports Michalovsky's salary of $2,000 being raised to $2,500, but "Report from New York," *Hamelitz*, June 5, 1887, puts the salary at $3,000; while Annie Polland claims the salary was initially $4,000. See Annie Polland, *Landmark of the Spirit: The Eldridge Street Synagogue* (New Haven, CT: Yale University Press, 2009), 51.

10. Malachi, "Hahazanim." According to Polland, though, Minkowsky was "only" paid $2,500 annually with $500 annual salary increases and the congregation paid 1,000 rubles, not dollars, to free him from his contract. See also Jeffrey Shandler, "Sanctification of the Brand Name: The Marketing of Cantor Yoselle Rosenblatt," in *Chosen Capital: The Jewish Encounter with American Capitalism*, ed. Rebecca Kobrin (New Brunswick, NJ: Rutgers University Press, 2012), 258.

11. Malachi, "Hahazanim."

12. Polland, *Landmark of the Spirit*, 49.

13. Department of the Interior Census Office, "Report on Manufacturing Industries in the United States at the Eleventh Census: 1890," *United States Census Reports*, xxvi.

14. Board Minutes of Congregation Beth Hamedrash Hagodol, 1884, AJHS, New York City Archives.

15. Ibid., 276.

16. A. Karp, "An Eastern European Congregation on American Soil," 271–72.

17. Mark Slobin, *Chosen Voices: The Story of the American Cantorate* (Urbana: University of Illinois Press, 1989), 54.

18. Kimmy Caplan, "In God We Trust: Salaries and Income of American Orthodox Rabbis, 1881–1924," *American Jewish History* 86 (1998): 89–90.

19. Charles Kindleberger, *Manias, Panics, and Crashes: A History of Financial Crises* (New York: John Wiley & Sons, 2000), 109–16.

20. J. D. Eisenstein, "The History of the First Russian," 72.

21. Polland, *Landmark*, 55.

22. Jeffrey Shandler, "Sanctification," 258.

23. Ibid.

24. Bernard Drachman, *The Unfailing Light: Memoirs of an American Rabbi* (New York: The Rabbinical Council of America, 1948), 282.

25. Caplan, "In God We Trust," 104.

26. Ibid., 95.

27. Y. L. Lazerov, *Der Yiddisher Redner, vol. 2: Oyf En Yaakov* (New York: Y. Z. Bookbinder, 1927), 11–12.

28. Caplan, "In God We Trust," 95; see also Eisenstein, "The History of the First Russian," 74.

29. Hutchins Hapgood, *The Spirit of the Ghetto* (Cambridge, MA: Harvard University Press, 1967), 61.

30. "Haroeh Vehazon," *Hapisgah* 3 (January 15, 1892), cited in Caplan, "In God We Trust," 94.

31. See Samuel Buchler, "An Ambiguous Eulogy," in *"Cohen Comes First" and Other Cases: Stories of Controversies before the New York Jewish Court of Arbitration* (New York: Vanguard Press, 1933), 35–39, for a fascinating case involving a family's refusal to pay a rabbi for a eulogy because the eulogy was thought impersonal and not sufficient.

32. Caplan, "In God We Trust," 95, reports that Israel Kaplan, Mordecai's father, made $576 annually as a judge in R. Jacob Joseph's court.

33. Hapgood, *Spirit*, 61.

34. See Harold Gastwirt, *Fraud, Corruption, and Holiness: The Controversy Over the Supervision of the Jewish Dietary Practice in New York, 1881–1940* (Port Washington, NY: Kennikat Press, 1974), for a description of the kosher food business and the role of rabbinic supervision in the industry.

35. Caplan, "In God We Trust," 98–99.

36. "Agreement, August 17, 1907," Congregation Ahavath Achim, Atlanta, GA, AJA.

37. Adler and Connolly, *From Ararat to Suburbia*, 159.

38. Caplan, "In God We Trust," 96.

39. Abraham Karp, "New York Chooses a Chief Rabbi," *Publications of the American Jewish Historical Society* 44 (1955): 155. See also Caplan, "In God We Trust," who argues that Joseph's salary was actually $3,000; he also notes that Mordecai Kaplan says in his diary that Joseph was paid $4,000, 95.

40. Gedalya Silverstone, *Sukkat Shalom*, vol. 2 (St. Louis, MO: Molnester Printing Co., 1934), 14.

41. Isaac Mayer Wise letter to Henry Lipman, February 21, 1893, Collection for Beth Emeth, Albany, NY, AJA.

42. Adler and Connolly, *From Ararat to Suburbia*, 205.

43. Caplan, "In God We Trust," 87.

44. A. Karp, "New York Chooses a Chief Rabbi," 157.

45. See Chicago Sinai board minutes from February 17, 1899, where one board member says unhappily that the rabbi has been "constantly harping and railing" at the millionaires in the congregation "Sunday after Sunday after Sunday." Board Minutes of Chicago Sinai Congregation, AJA.

46. Ibid., April 2, 1898.

47. Hirsch's reference here is not entirely clear, as his offer from Temple Emanu-El in New York would not officially come until the following year; perhaps this is a reference to an earlier informal conversation with Temple Emanu-El.

48. Board Minutes of Chicago Sinai Congregation, April 28, 1898, AJA.

49. See also Zev Eleff, "Power, Pulpits and Pews: Religious Authority and the Formation of American Judaism, 1816–1885" (PhD diss., Brandeis University, 2015), for a discussion of the changing power dynamics within the synagogue.

50. Caplan, "In God We Trust," 103.

51. "Wayside Etchings," *American Israelite*, July 8, 1881.

52. Max Vorspan and Lloyd Gartner, *History of the Jews of Los Angeles* (Philadelphia: Jewish Publication Society, 1970), 86–87.

53. *American Israelite*, July 10, 1885.

54. Hudnut-Beumler, *In Pursuit of the Almighty's Dollar*, 232.

55. The census was carried out in 1906, 1916, 1926, and 1936, but according to Hudnut-Beumler (*In Pursuit of the Almighty's Dollar*, 84), the religious census was abandoned "because of a combination of funding issues and questions raised about why the government was collecting information concerning numbers of members, church property, and the payment of ministers."

56. U.S. Department of Commerce, Bureau of the Census, *Religious Bodies 1906*, 96–98.

57. Ibid., 96–98.

58. Ibid., 96–98. The census defined non-cities as locations under 25,000.

59. U.S. Department of Commerce, Bureau of the Census, *Historical Statistics of the United States, Colonial Times to 1957* (Washington, D.C.: Superintendent of Documents, 1960), Series D603–617.

60. Thomas Goebel, "The Uneven Rewards of Professional Labor: Wealth and Income in the Chicago Professions, 1870–1920," *Journal of Social History* 29, 4 (Summer 1996): 760.

61. Paul Starr, *The Social Transformation of American Medicine: The Rise of a Sovereign Profession and the Making of a Vast Industry* (New York: Basic Books, 1984).

62. Jonathan Sarna, *JPS: The Americanization of Jewish Culture, 1888–1988* (Philadelphia: The Jewish Publication Society, 1989), 68–72. The *Year Book* only published income information for synagogues in the first two editions. See Sarna for a discussion of the creation of the *Year Book* as well as the need to limit the size of the *Year Book* due to time and financial constraints.

63. *American Jewish Year Book: 5660*, ed. Cyrus Adler (Philadelphia: The Jewish Publication Society, 1899).

64. Many synagogues were presumably rounding their incomes in their report to the *Year Book*. Sometimes this rounding could be significant. Chicago Sinai's 1899 budget report, for example, shows income of $29,000, which is reported to the *American Jewish Year Book* as $30,000. See Board Minutes of Chicago Sinai Congregation, April 29, 1899, AJA.

65. The number is determined simply by dividing the reported income by the number of members. This should not be taken as a perfect figure, as synagogues obtained some income outside of their own membership, but this amount was typically fairly negligible. The Chicago Sinai budget of 1899, for example, showed that only $180 of $30,000 was derived from a source outside its own membership, in this case interest on synagogue investments. See Board Minutes of Chicago Sinai Congregation, April 4, 1898, AJA.

66. *American Jewish Year Book*, 120, 145.

67. Ibid., 142–155. I have counted Reform synagogues as those that were members of the UAHC and placed Chizuk Emunah, which would become a Conservative congregation, in the traditional category.

68. Carol Wright, *Seventh Special Report of the Commissioner of Labor: The Slums of Baltimore, Chicago, New York, and Philadelphia* (Washington, D.C.: Government Printing Office, 1894), 462–63. See also Arcadius Kahan, "Economic Opportunities and Some Pilgrim's Progress," *Essays in Jewish Social and Economic History*, ed. Roger Weiss (Chicago: University of Chicago Press, 1986), 101–17.

69. Fein, "The Making of an American Jewish Community," 295.

70. See Goebel, "The Uneven Rewards of Professional Labor," 749–77.

71. Massachusetts Bureau of Statistics of Labor, *Sixth Annual Report* (Boston: Wright and Potter, 1875). See also Daniel Horowitz, *The Morality of Spending: Attitudes Toward the Consumer Society in America, 1875–1940* (Baltimore: John Hopkins University Press, 1985), 13–14, for a description of the importance of this study. See as well Robin Klay and John Lunn, "Protestants and the American Economy in the Postcolonial Period: An Overview," in Noll, *God and Mammon*, 44, for further uses of the study.

72. This figure may hold until today. The Pew Report of 2013 (pewforum.org /files/2013/10/Jewish-american-beliefs-attitudes-culture-survey-overview.pdf) claims that 25 percent of the Jewish community earns over $150,000 while 20 percent have an income of less than $30,000, suggesting a median income of between $80,000 and $100,000. My own study of a sample of Reform synagogue budgets and a survey of typical synagogue dues levels would both suggest the average gift to synagogues of around $2,500 to $3,000, exactly between 2 and 3 percent of income.

73. Robert Schine, "'Members of This Book': The *Pinkas* of Vermont's First Jewish Congregation," *American Jewish Archives* 60 (2008): 51–98.

74. Ibid., 69–71, for a discussion of raising money through auctioning off of aliyot.

75. Ibid., 75.

76. This is inexpensive for a Torah scroll at this time. An ad in *The Israelite* from June 26, 1868, offers a used Torah for $150.

77. Ibid., 74–78.

78. Board Minutes of Temple Adath Israel, November 3, 1867, TI Archives.

79. Ibid., September 18, 1870.

80. Ibid., October 11, 1868; August 29, 1869, TI Archives. The congregation was also paying a shamas (sexton), but his salary is not detailed.

81. Night soil was the euphemism for human waste.

82. Ibid., February 7, 1871; April 14, 1872, TI Archives.

83. Meaghan Dwyer-Ryan, Susan Porter, and Lisa Davis, *Becoming American Jews: Temple Israel of Boston* (Waltham, MA: Brandeis University Press, 2009), 13.

84. See Grinstein, *The Rise of the Jewish Community of New York*, 103–14.

85. Board Minutes of Chicago Sinai Congregation, October 3, 1897, AJA.

86. Clifton Levy, "A Necessary Reform," *Jewish Criterion* 2, 1 (February 15, 1895).

87. "A New Thing in Congregations," *American Hebrew*, August 28, 1896, 14. Isaac Moses's synagogue ultimately did not come to fruition. Even earlier suggestions of a free synagogue can be found. In 1882, *The Jewish Messenger* suggested that a free synagogue be formed in the city and named after Moses Montefiore, whose one hundredth birthday approached. The editorial expressed concern for the poor masses flooding the Lower East Side, and the need for wealthier Jews to respond to their plight. They called on every Jew in the city to give one dollar to erect a free synagogue on the Lower East Side so immigrant Jews would have a synagogue to pray in. The *American Israelite* thought the plan unwise, that there were plenty of extra seats in synagogues. They also complained that this might attract Montefiore's money when the Union of American Hebrew Congregations was already planning on naming a professorship at Hebrew Union College after him, and this might siphon resources from that plan. See "A Montefiore Memorial," *American Israelite*, November 23, 1883.

88. Sarna, "Seating and the American Synagogue," 195; 202. On the impact of the Social Gospel movement on Judaism, see Egal Feldman, "The Social Gospel and the Jews," *American Jewish Historical Quarterly* 58 (March 1969): 308–22.

89. Quakers, Baptists, Universalists, and Free Methodists were all groups that stressed voluntary donations over pew rents. See Hudnut-Beumler, *In Pursuit of the Almighty's Dollar*, 10.

90. Keith Hardman, *Charles Grandison Finney, 1792–1875, Revivalist and Reformer* (Syracuse, NY: Syracuse University Press, 1987), 175.

91. Charles Cole, "The Free Church Movement in New York City," *New York History* 34, 3 (July 1953): 291.

92. Ibid., 288.

93. Ibid., 293.

94. Ibid., 293–96.

95. Kathryn Long, *The Revival of 1857–1858, Interpreting an American Religious Awakening* (New York: Oxford University Press, 1998), 100.

96. William Rainsford, *The Story of a Varied Life: An Autobiography* (Garden City, NY: Doubleday, Page & Company, 1922), 200.

97. Ibid., 212.

98. Ibid., 213.

99. Kaufman, *Shul with a Pool*, 16–20.

100. Cited in Kaufman, *Shul with a Pool*, 43.

101. *CCAR Yearbook* (1902): 208–12.

102. See Sarna, "Belief and Behavior," 195–97. For full discussion of Beth El and the move from pew rentals to dues, see chapter 4.

103. "President's Report," Minutes of the Congregation Beth Israel Board of Trustees, October 24, 1904, AJA.

104. Ibid., October 5, 1890, AJA.

105. Ibid., November 16, 1894, AJA.

106. Ibid., November 3, 1895, AJA.

107. Ibid., July 18, 1899, AJA.

108. Ibid., undated, 1900, AJA.

109. Ibid., undated, 1901, AJA.

110. Robert Shapiro, "A Reform Rabbi in the Progressive Era: The Early Career of Stephen S. Wise" (PhD diss., Harvard University, 1984), 114.

111. "President's Report," Minutes of Beth Israel, October 24, 1904, AJA.

112. Shapiro, "A Reform Rabbi," 94–100.

113. Cited in Melvin Urofsky, *A Voice That Spoke for Justice: The Life and Times of Stephen S. Wise* (Albany: State University Press of New York, 1982), 35–36.

114. Minutes of Congregation Beth Israel, October 22, 1905, AJA.

115. Ibid., October 4, 1904, AJA.

116. Ibid., October 29, 1911, AJA.

117. Urofsky, *The Voice*, 49.

118. Wise, Challenging Years, 84.

119. Ibid., 91.

120. "Rev. Dr. Wise Surprises Emanu-El Trustees," *New York Times*, January 7, 1906. See also Mark Raider, "The Aristocrat and the Democrat: Louis Marshall, Stephen S. Wise and the Challenge of American Jewish Leadership," *American Jewish History* 94, 1–2 (March–June 2008): 91–113.

121. Wise, *Challenging Years*, 82–94.

122. *The Free Synagogue Constitution*, The Stephen Wise Free Synagogue Archives.

123. Wise, *Challenging Years*, 45.

124. Ibid.

125. "$40,000 Raised to Help Free Synagogue," *Boston Jewish Advocate*, April 9, 1909.

126. Urofsky, *The Voice*, 62.

127. Sydney Goldstein, *The Synagogue and Social Welfare: A Unique Experiment, 1907–1953* (New York: Bloch Publishing Company, 1955), 56–57.

128. "Old Mikveh Israel as Free Synagogue," *Jewish Exponent*, August 20, 1909.

129. Ibid.

130. Henry Morais, "Sale of Mikveh Israel's Old Synagogue," *Jewish Exponent*, November 24, 1911.

131. "Last Services at the Free Synagogue," *Jewish Exponent*, December 29, 1911.

132. "Long Island's Free Synagogue," *Jewish Exponent*, September 22, 1911.

133. "Free Synagog [*sic*] for Los Angeles," *B'nai Brith Messenger*, August 26, 1921.

134. "'Free Pulpit and Free Pew' Basis of Los Angeles Synagogue," *Jewish Daily Bulletin*, October 6, 1930.

135. See Stephen Wise Free Synagogue website at www.swfs.org.

136. See chapter 4 for discussion of contemporary free synagogues.

137. "Interview with Joe Harris, July 25, 1997," Stephen Wise Free Synagogue Archives. Nathan Warshaw was an immigrant from Poland who became a wealthy factory owner in Brooklyn. For an article that describes Warshaw see, "Plain Talk," *The Jewish Transcript*, December 13, 1937.

138. *Jewish Daily Bulletin* (*JDB*), August 17, 1930.

139. For more extensive history of mushroom synagogues, see my forthcoming article, Dan Judson, "Religion at Bargain Prices: The History of Mushroom Synagogues," *American Jewish Archives Journal* (forthcoming).

140. A report by the New York Kehillah cited in Arthur Goren, *New York Jews and the Quest for Community* (New York: Columbia University Press, 1970), 195.

141. Goren, *New York Jews*, 20.

142. For discussion of *landsmanshaftn* synagogues, see Daniel Soyer, *Jewish Immigrant Associations and American Identity in New York, 1880–1939* (Cambridge, MA: Harvard University Press, 1997).

143. Cited in Sarna, *American Judaism*, 161.

144. Jeffrey Gurock, *Orthodox Jews in America* (Bloomington: Indiana University Press, 2009), 104.

145. *American Hebrew*, August 28, 1896.

146. The Tomkin brothers are not found in any standard references of Jewish American history.

147. *American Hebrew*, September 8, 1901.

148. Ibid. The term used to describe mushroom synagogues is "temporary halls of worship" indicating that the term "mushroom synagogue" had not yet been adopted. By 1907, the name "mushroom synagogue" is used extensively to describe this phenomenon, but I could not locate its origins or first usage.

149. Ibid.

150. *Yiddishe Tagblatt*, September 16, 1906.

151. Goren, *New York Jews*, 195.

152. For history of the Kehillah see Goren, *New York Jews*.

153. *New York Times*, July 26, 1909.

154. Jewish Community (Kehillah) of New York City, *Second Annual Report*, 8, American Jewish Historical Society Archives (AJHS).

155. John Whiteclay Chambers, *The Tyranny of Change: America in the Progressive Era* (New Brunswick, NJ: Rutgers University Press, 2000).

156. See A. Karp, "New York Chooses a Chief Rabbi," and Harold Gastwirt, *Fraud, Corruption and Holiness* (Port Washington, NY: National University Publications, 1974), for discussion of earlier failed attempts at organizing the kosher food industry.

157. *JDB*, September 6, 1934.

158. Jewish Community (Kehillah) of New York City, *Third Annual Report*, 12–13, AJHS.

159. Jewish Community (Kehillah) of New York City, *Report to the Executive Committee of the American Jewish Committee*, reprinted in *The American Jewish Year Book, 1913–1914* (Philadelphia: Jewish Publication Society, 1913): 444–45.

160. Jewish Community (Kehillah) of New York City, *Report to the Executive Committee of the American Jewish Committee*, reprinted in *The American Jewish Year Book, 1915–1916* (Philadelphia: Jewish Publication Society, 1915): 378.

161. *New York Times*, September 20, 1914.

162. Kehillah report cited in Goren, *New York Jews*, 195.

163. Kaufman, *Shul with a Pool*, 271.

164. Cited in Moore, *At Home in America*, 140.

165. *JDB*, September 20, 1932.

166. Moore, *At Home in America*, 140–141.

167. *JDB*, August 17, 1930.

168. *JDB*, September 6, 1934.

169. Cited in Wenger, *New York Jews and the Great Depression*, 175.

170. Soyer, *Jewish Immigrant Associations*.

171. A. Karp, "New York Chooses a Chief Rabbi."

172. *JDB*, August 13, 1934.

173. *JDB*, August 17, 1930.

174. *JDB*, September 3, 1933.

175. *JDB*, June 8, 1934.

176. Gastwirt, *Fraud*, 124.

177. For discussion of contemporary legal and regulatory issues regarding kashrut, see Timothy Lytton, *Kosher: Private Regulation in the Age of Industrial Food* (Cambridge, MA: Harvard University Press, 2013).

178. Gastwirt, *Fraud*, 128.

179. See Lytton, *Kosher*, 29, for a discussion of the 1934 Kosher Law Enforcement Bureau. In 2000, however, a federal judge declared New York State kosher food laws unconstitutional. See "Judge Voids Law Certifying Kosher Food," *New York Times*, August 4, 2000.

180. *JDB*, July 13, 1934.

181. *JDB*, July 15, 1934.

182. Marshall Sklare, "Church and Laity Among Jews," *Annals of the American Academy of Political and Social Science* 332 (November 1960): 63.

FOUR   "No Aristocracy and No Snobocracy:
In God's House All Must Be Equal" | *1919–1945*

1. "President's Message," Board Minutes of Congregation Adath Israel, November 18, 1919, AJA.

2. See Sarna, "Seating and the American Synagogue," 194–96, for discussion of American democracy and free seating.

3. The Historical Committee, *A History of Congregation Beth El, Detroit, Michigan, Volume 2, 1900–1910* (Detroit, MI: Winn & Hammond, 1910), 28.

4. Leo Franklin, "A New Congregational Policy," *American Israelite*, November 17, 1904. See also Sarna, "The Debate over Mixed Seating," 363–94, to see how the introduction of mixed seating in synagogues also began through circumstance.

5. *History of Beth El*, 37.

6. Sarna, "Seating and the American Synagogue," 198–199.

7. Franklin, "A New Congregational Policy."

8. Ibid.

9. Ibid.

10. "Temple Israel May Adopt New Pew System," *The Jewish Advocate*, February 17, 1921.

11. "The Unassigned Pew Wins in Pittsburgh," *The American Hebrew & Jewish Messenger*, April 9, 1920.

12. "Temple Israel," *Jewish Advocate*.

13. "Report of the Committee on the Unassigned Pew System," March 7, 1920, Rodef Shalom Archives.

14. "Temple Israel," *Jewish Advocate.*

15. "President's Message," November 18, 1919, Board Minutes of Congregation Adath Israel, AJA.

16. Ibid.

17. Quoted in "Temple Israel." An amendment was added to the resolution that stated: "The Union of American Hebrew Congregations hereby expresses its approval of the resolution presented and ideal and principles therein contained, without attempting in any way to interfere with the autonomy of any congregation or the management and conduct of its affairs."

18. Ibid.

19. Cited in "Adopt Platform of Judaism," *The American Hebrew & Jewish Messenger,* May 30, 1919.

20. "Domestic Notes," *Jewish Exponent,* July 24, 1925.

21. "The Question of Free Pews in Synagogues," *Jewish Exponent,* January 10, 1919.

22. Cited in Moore, "A Synagogue Center Grows in Brooklyn," 299.

23. Cited in A. Scott Berg, *Wilson* (New York: Putnam, 2013), 491.

24. Cited in Thomas Fleming, *The Illusion of Victory: American in World War I* (New York: Basic Books, 2003), 397.

25. "President's Message," November 18, 1919, AJA.

26. See "Start Unassigned Pew System," *The American Hebrew & Jewish Messenger,* October 28, 1921; "Temple Israel, New Rochelle Adopts Unassigned Pews," *The American Hebrew & Jewish Messenger,* December 2, 1921; "Temple Israel May Adopt New Pew System," *The Jewish Advocate,* February 17, 1921; "Domestic Notes," *Jewish Exponent,* July 24, 1925; and Anne Cohen, *The Centenary History: Congregation Beth Israel of Houston, Texas, 1854–1954* (Houston, TX: Congregation Beth Israel, 1954), 50.

27. Board Minutes of Temple Israel, January 16, 1921, TI Archives.

28. Board Minutes of Temple Israel, January 29, 1922, TI Archives.

29. Dwyer-Ryan, Porter, and Davis, *Becoming American Jews,* 72.

30. Jacob Schwartz, *Financial Security for Your Synagogue* (New York: Union of American Hebrew Congregations, 1936), 9.

31. Sarna, "Seating and the American Synagogue," 200.

32. Ibid., 201.

33. The verse is from Deuteronomy 16:17 and it refers to the gifts that pilgrims should offer on the three pilgrimage festivals. "Three times a year — on the Feast of Unleavened Bread, on the Feast of Weeks, and on the Feast of Booths — all of your males shall appear before the Lord your God in the place that He will choose. They shall not appear before the Lord empty-handed, *but each with his own gift,* according to the blessing that the Lord your God has bestowed upon you." (JPS translation, italics mine.) Franklin uses this text because it provides sanction for the entire system of paying for religion based upon one's means.

34. Franklin, "A New Congregational Policy."

35. Cited in Ajay Mehotra, "Envisioning the Modern American Fiscal State: Progressive-Era Economists and the Intellectual Foundations of the U.S. Income Tax," *UCLA Law Review* 52 (2005): 1831.

36. Ibid., 1827.

37. There are no studies to identify how many synagogues use fair share and how many have a uniform dues. My estimation is based on a sample size of approximately thirty Reform and Conservative congregations whose budgets and financial systems I have studied.

38. Nathan Guttman, "High Holy Days Are Free at Some Shuls, and Worshipers Flock," *Forward*, August 12, 2010, https://forward.com/news/130704/high-holy -days-are-free-at-some-shuls-and-worshipe/.

39. U.S. Department of Commerce, Bureau of the Census, *Census of Religious Bodies, 1926* (Washington, D.C.: U.S. Government Printing Office, 1929), 48. The census noted that the 1916 and 1906 statistics for the number of synagogue members could not be compared to 1926, as there was confusion in the earlier censuses on the question of whether to count every member of the family or just the head of household.

40. Ibid., 46.

41. Moore, "A Synagogue Center," 299; Kaufman, *Shul with a Pool*, 244.

42. Mordecai Kaplan, "The Future of Judaism," *Menorah Journal* (June 1916): 160–72. For influence of the Institutional Church model on Kaplan and other Jewish leaders, see Kaufman, *Shul with a Pool*.

43. Mordecai Kaplan, *Judaism as a Civilization* (Philadelphia: Jewish Publication Society, 2010), 428.

44. Abraham Karp, "Overview: The Synagogue in America," in *The American Synagogue: A Sanctuary Transformed*, ed. Jack Wertheimer (Hanover, NH: Brandeis University Press, 1987), 19.

45. Kaufman, *Shul with a Pool*, 243.

46. Ibid., 264–265. See also *The Jewish Advocate*, March 12, 1923, for a series of articles about Mishkan Tefila's plans for a new synagogue-center.

47. "The First 150 Years: A Historical Perspective Created in Celebration of B'nai Israel's 150th Anniversary in 2003," at www.tbanj.org/who-we-are/our-history.

48. "Temple Dedication at Detroit," *American Israelite*, November 16, 1922. See also Kaufman, *Shul with a Pool*, 268.

49. "Temple Israel, Cleveland: Dedication of the Magnificent New Structure," *American Israelite*, September 4, 1924; "Temple Dedications," *American Israelite*, October 2, 1924.

50. Moore, "A Synagogue Center," 299.

51. Dwyer-Ryan, Porter, and Davis, *Becoming American Jews*, 54–72.

52. Ibid., 69.

53. Board Minutes of Temple Israel, April 27, 1924, TI Archives. (Note that Reform synagogues often had large Sunday morning services.)

54. Ibid.

55. Ibid.

56. See Kaufman, *Shul with a Pool,* for a brief description of the building processes for all the congregations.

57. Board Minutes of Temple Israel, November 15, 1927, TI Archives.

58. Board Minutes of Temple Israel, May 11, 1923, TI Archives.

59. "Auditor's Report," Board Minutes of Temple Israel, April 14, 1924, TI Archives.

60. Copy of letter to members found in Board Minutes of Temple Israel, April 1924, TI Archives. The money was specifically to support the Hebrew Union College (the Reform movement's seminary).

61. Board Minutes of Temple Israel, November 4, 1924, TI Archives.

62. "President's Annual Message," Board Minutes of Temple Israel, March 1, 1925, TI Archives.

63. Ibid.

64. "Auditor's Report," Board Minutes of Temple Israel, March 1, 1925, TI Archives.

65. Board Minutes of Temple Israel, November 15, 1925, TI Archives. Vorenberg's poor health was also cited as a factor for the resignation. Vorenberg's resignation was ultimately put off, and he would end up spending another two years as president before finally giving up the position.

66. Board Minutes of Temple Israel, January 1, 1927, TI Archives.

67. Board Minutes of Temple Israel, January 28, 1927, and July 14, 1927, TI Archives.

68. Board Minutes of Temple Israel, February 23 and November 15, 1927, TI Archives.

69. Alter Landesman, "Lessons from the Economic Crisis," *Proceedings of the Rabbinical Assembly, 1931* (New Rochelle, NY: The Little Print, 1933), 195.

70. Moore, "A Synagogue Center," 298.

71. Samuel Abelow, *History of Brooklyn Jewry* (Brooklyn, NY: Scheba Publishing Company, 1937), 73–74.

72. Moore, "A Synagogue Center," 304.

73. See Abelow, *History of Brooklyn Jewry,* 81.

74. Moore, "A Synagogue Center," 299.

75. Jenna Weisman Joselit, *New York's Jewish Jews: The Orthodox Community in the Interwar Years* (Bloomington: Indiana University Press, 1990), 50.

76. Ibid., 50.

77. Barnett Brickner, "The Socialized Synagogue," *American Israelite*, May 9, 1918.

78. Cited in Moore, "A Synagogue Center," 299.

79. Harry Glucksman, "The Synagogue Center," *Proceedings of the Rabbinical Assembly, 1932* (New Rochelle, NY: The Little Print, 1933), 273–274.

80. President of BJC, cited in Wenger, *New York Jews*, 170.

81. Ibid., 172.

82. Board Minutes of Congregation Beth Israel, March 28, 1936, AJA.

83. U.S. Department of Commerce, Bureau of the Census, *Religious Bodies, 1936* (Washington, D.C.: Government Printing Office, 1941), 757.

84. Board Minutes of Congregation Beth Israel, 1933, AJA.

85. Board Minutes of Congregation Beth Israel, March 28, 1936, AJA.

86. Ewa Morawska, *Insecure Prosperity: Small Town Jews in Industrial America, 1890–1940* (Princeton, NJ: Princeton University Press, 1996), 141–44.

87. Board Minutes of Congregation Beth Ahabah, August 31, 1923; August 31, 1933, AJA.

88. S. Joshua Kohn, *The Jewish Community of Utica, New York, 1847–1948* (New York: American Jewish Historical Society, 1959), 66.

89. Ibid., 67.

90. Board Minutes of Congregation Adath Israel, October 24, 1929; October 26, 1932, AJA.

91. Schwartz, *Financial Security*, 12.

92. Ibid., 12–13.

93. Wenger, *New York Jews*, 172.

94. Ibid., 14.

95. Felix Mendelsohn, "Synagogues without Money," *Chicago Sentinel*, January 20, 1933.

96. Ibid.

97. Israel Goldman, "Effects of Economic Depression on Jewish Spiritual Life," *Proceedings of the Rabbinical Assembly of America, 1930–1932* (New Rochelle, NY: The Little Print, 1933), 201.

98. Ibid., 101–2.

99. Louis Schwefel, "The Rabbi and the Congregational Budget," *Proceedings of the Rabbinical Assembly of America, 1930–1932* (New Rochelle, NY: The Little Print, 1933), 211.

100. Ibid., 212.

101. Ibid., 213–14.

102. Ibid., 214.

103. Goldman, "Effects," 109.

104. Cited in Wenger, *New York Jews*, 171.

105. Ibid., 216.

106. S. Joshua Kohn, "The Rabbi and the Congregational Budget," *Proceedings of the Rabbinical Assembly of America, 1930–1932* (New Rochelle, NY: The Little Print, 1933), 221.

107. Ibid., 221–22.

108. Ibid., 221.

109. Wenger, *New York Jews*, 176.

110. See "anti-mammonism" in chapter 2.

111. Landesman, "Lessons from the Economic Crisis," 191.

112. "Pronouncement of the Rabbinical Assembly of America on Social Justice, 1934," *Proceedings of the Rabbinical Assembly of America, 1933–1938* (New York: The Ad Press, 1939), 156–64.

113. "Report of Commission on Social Justice," *Central Conference of American Rabbis Yearbook, 1932* (New York: Central Conference of American Rabbis), 94–105.

114. *The Orthodox Union* 3, no. 6 (February 1936): 3.

115. Solomon Freehof, "The Spiritual Depression," *American Israelite*, September 3, 1931.

116. See Richard Breitman and Allan Lichtman, *FDR and the Jews* (Cambridge, MA: Harvard University Press, 2013), for a discussion of FDR's popularity in the Jewish community.

117. U.S. Department of Commerce, Bureau of the Census, *Religious Bodies, 1936* (Washington, D.C.: Government Printing Office, 1941), 757.

118. "Synagogue Question Agitating Jews of Los Angeles," *Jewish Telegraphic Agency*, September 7, 1930.

119. Wenger, *New York Jews*, 195. Wenger builds on the work of Robert Handy, who argued that the growing secularism of the 1920s had weakened religious institutions even before the Depression. Robert Handy, "The American Religious Depression, 1925–1935," *Church History* 29, no. 1 (March 1960): 3–16.

120. Ibid., 184.

FIVE   "If It Has to Be Done, It Should at Least Be Done in a Dignified Way" | *1945–Today*

1. "Report of the Special Committee Appointed to Study and Recommend What Steps Should be Taken with Respect to the Growth of the Congregation, and How Best the Problem of Reform Judaism in Kansas City Can be Met," Board Minutes of Congregation B'nai Jehudah, January 11, 1958, AJA.

2. Ibid.

3. Ibid.

4. Ibid.

5. Albert Gordon, *Jews in Suburbia* (Boston: Beacon Hill Press, 1959), 97.

6. "Judaism on Rise in Suburbs," *New York Times*, April 5, 1939.

7. *American Jewish Year Book*, 57 (Philadelphia: Jewish Publication Society, 1957), 171.

8. Gordon, *Jews in Suburbia*, 86–120; Herbert Gans, "The Origin and Growth of a Jewish Community in the Suburbs," in *The Jews: Social Patterns of an American Group*, ed. Marshall Sklare (New York: Free Press, 1958), 205–48; Marshall Sklare and Joseph Greenbaum, *Jewish Identity on the Suburban Frontier* (New York: Basic Books, 1967).

9. Board Minutes of Beth Emet the Free Synagogue, 1955, AJA. The congregation called itself a "free" synagogue in the sense that the rabbi would be "free in every respect. He shall have complete freedom to teach and to preach." The congregation's founding rabbi, David Polish, was an outspoken Zionist who had been barred from speaking about Israel at a previous congregation.

10. Ibid.

11. "Report of the Budget and Finance Committee, 1955–1956," Board Minutes of Congregation B'nai Jehudah, AJA.

12. "Budget of Temple Israel of Natick, 1960–1961," Board Minutes of Temple Israel of Natick, TI of Natick Archives.

13. "Touro Synagogue History," http://www.tourosynagogue.org/history-learning /synagogue-history. See also chapter 2 for a discussion of Touro's philanthropy.

14. Oral interview with Stu Brandt, July 18, 2016.

15. Board Minutes of Beth Emet the Free Synagogue, May 6, 1953, AJA.

16. "Campaign Director's Report," Board Minutes of Beth Emet the Free Synagogue, October 31, 1953, AJA.

17. Hyman, "From City to Suburb," 200. As an addendum to this story, in 2016 the congregation sold its Newton campus after years of declining membership and has moved to the somewhat more urban setting of Brookline, closer to the city of Boston. The re-urbanizing of the Jewish community is no doubt a significant factor in patterns of synagogue growth today.

18. "President's Report," Board Minutes of Adath Jeshurun Synagogue, June 13, 1957, Upper Midwest Jewish Archives.

19. "Kosher Korn," *Jewish Criterion*, December 18, 1953, 79.

20. "Campaign Director's Report," Board Minutes of Beth Emet the Free Synagogue, October 31, 1953, AJA.

21. Carolyn Rushefsky, "Shaare Zion: The Synagogue That Nearly Wasn't Built," *Community* 11, 8 (May 2012).

22. Ibid.

23. The congregation also received gifts from twenty-three nonmembers, but no explanation is given as to what moved them to give or how they were connected to the synagogue.

24. "Campaign Director's Report," Board Minutes of Beth Emet the Free Synagogue, October 31, 1953, AJA.

25. Stanley Bigman, *The Jewish Population of Greater Washington in 1956* (Washington, D.C.: The Jewish Community Council of Greater Washington, D.C., 1957). The use of income data from Washington, D.C., may be somewhat skewed because 25 percent of the Jewish workforce was employed by the government, a good source of middle-class jobs.

26. Ibid., 26.

27. Ibid., 30.

28. Ibid., 35. The researchers noted that asking for salary data was "sensitive" and 20 percent of respondents did not give this information. The study also noted that family income was probably underreported because the study only asked for salary information and did not ask for income from stocks and investments.

29. Ibid., 36.

30. Cited in *American Jewish Year Book, 1956* (Philadelphia: American Jewish Committee and Jewish Publication Society, 1957), 188.

31. Clarence Hall, "The Churches Rise Again," *McCall's Magazine*, June 1955, 34–37.

32. *American Jewish Year Book, 1958* (Philadelphia: American Jewish Committee and Jewish Publication Society, 1959), 113.

33. Hudnut-Beumler, *In Pursuit of the Almighty's Dollar*, 158.

34. Ibid., 165–66.

35. *American Jewish Year Book*, 1958, 113.

36. U.S. Department of Commerce, Bureau of the Census, *Current Population Reports*, September 9, 1957, https://www2.census.gov/prod2/popscan/p60-030.pdf.

37. See also chapter 2, for discussion of religious giving in the late nineteenth century.

38. James Lewis, *At Home in the City: The Protestant Experience in Gary, Indiana, 1906–1975* (Knoxville: University of Tennessee Press, 1992), 111.

39. U.S. Department of Commerce, Bureau of the Census, *Current Population Reports, Series P-60, Consumer Income*, no. 30, December 1958.

40. See chapters 2 and 3 for discussions of the creation of rabbinic organizations and rabbinic salaries.

41. Theodore Lenn, *Rabbi and Synagogue in Reform Judaism* (West Hartford, CT: Central Conference of American Rabbis, 1972), 24.

42. Central Conference of American Rabbis, *2014–2015 Study of Rabbinic Compensation.*

43. http://www.whatsmypercent.com.

44. Lenn, *Rabbi and Synagogue*, 25.

45. Josh Nathan-Kazis, "Rabbis Earn More Than Christian Clergy," *The Forward*, September 15, 2010.

46. Ibid.

47. Hudnut-Beumler, *In Pursuit of the Almighty's Dollar*, 94.

48. Jenna Joselit, "Bingo's Sacred History," *The Forward*, March 5, 2008.

49. Charitable institutions could hold bingo only if it was not the sole activity of the evening; Robert Daley, "Bingo Binge Is Big Business," *New York Times*, December 8, 1957.

50. Ibid.

51. "Churchgoers Get Anti-Bingo Pleas," *New York Times*, November 4, 1957.

52. "Brooklyn Pastor Denounces Bingo," *New York Times*, September 30, 1957.

53. "Bingo Is Opposed in Some Pulpits," *New York Times*, October 28, 1957.

54. "Games of Chance in Connection with Fundraising," *American Reform Responsa* 46 (1936): 126.

55. "Bingo Plan Opposed," *New York Times*, October 31, 1957.

56. "Reform Jews Score Fund-Raising Bingo," *New York Times*, May 21, 1958.

57. Boris Smolar, "Between You and Me," *Jewish Advocate*, January 15, 1959.

58. See Talmud, Sanhedrin 24b–25a.

59. See Leo Landman, "Jewish Attitudes Toward Gambling II: Individual & Communal Efforts to Curb Gambling," *Jewish Quarterly Review* 58, 1 (July, 1967): 34–62, for an overview of Jewish approaches to gambling.

60. Maimonides, *Hilchot Gezela*, 7:7.

61. Landman, "Jewish Attitudes Toward Gambling II," 46–47.

62. Leo Landman, "Jewish Attitudes Toward Gambling: The Professional and Compulsive Gambler," *Jewish Quarterly Review* 57, 4 (April 1967): 310.

63. Philip Segal, "Games of Chance on Synagogue Premises," *Proceedings of the Committee on Jewish Law and Standards of the Conservative Movement* (New York: The Rabbinical Assembly, 1997), 537–38.

64. Robert A. Poteete, "Bingo Wins as a State Amendment," *New York Tribune*, November 6, 1957, 1.

65. "Bingo Bill for City Appears on Ballot; Permits Games for Charitable Purposes," *New York Times*, November 3, 1958.

66. "Legal Bingo Sets Records in New Jersey," *New York Times*, February 13, 1958.

67. Cited in Fink, "Games of Chance," 1507.

68. Ibid., 1510.

69. Ibid., 1512.

70. Henry Sosland, "A Statement on Gambling," *Proceedings of the Committee on Jewish Law and Standards of the Conservative Movement, 1980–1985* (New York: The Rabbinical Assembly, 1988), 125.

71. "Sunday Program Marks Dedication of New Temple," *The Jewish Advocate*, March 27, 1952.

72. "Reyim Dedicates New Religious School Building," *The Jewish Advocate*, October 29, 1964.

73. "The Big Bingo Rescue," unpublished essay, Temple Reyim Archives, Newton, MA. With gratitude to Andy Offit for bringing this to my attention.

74. Ibid., 2–3.

75. Ibid., 4.

76. Ibid., 6.

77. Smoking may also have been a factor in bingo's decline at synagogues. As the health threat of secondhand smoke became apparent, a number of churches and synagogues banned smoking, while large bingo parlors still permitted it. Because many people smoked while playing, they left bingo at religious institutions for parlors. See "Bingo," *Rochester City Newspaper*, October 16, 2002, for the impact of smoking on church bingo in Rochester, New York.

78. "Big Bingo Rescue," 6.

Conclusion | *Today–Tomorrow*

1. Jacob Rader Marcus, "The Oldest Known Synagogue Record Book of Continental North America, 1720–1721," *Studies in American Jewish History: Studies and Addresses* (Cincinnati: Hebrew Union College Press, 1969), 44–53.

2. Barak Richman, "Saving the First Amendment from Itself: Relief from the Sherman Act Against the Rabbinic Cartels," *Pepperdine Law Review* 39 (January 2013); Barak Richman, "Rabbi Searches Are Tough, But Are They Illegal?" *The Forward*, September 29, 2010.

3. "Seeing and Battling a 'Cartel' in the Hiring of Rabbis," *New York Times*, August 24, 2012.

4. Bernard Alpert, "Comeback Time for the Maggid," *The Jewish Advocate*, July 31, 1986.

5. Hudnut-Beumler, *In Pursuit of the Almighty's Dollar*, 148.

6. Sarna, *American Judaism*, xviii.

7. In a seminal article on religion and the Depression, Robert Handy argued that churches were already weakened by growing American secularism before the Depression. Beth Wenger extended this argument to synagogues, suggesting the Depression simply accelerated negative synagogue trends. But this argument is questionable. The large synagogue building boom of the 1920s is testimony to the strength of synagogues in this period. See Robert Handy, "The American Religious Depression, 1925–1935," *Church History* 29, 1 (March 1960): 3–16; and Wenger, *New York Jews*, 166–196.

8. Sue Fishkoff, *The Rebbe's Army: Inside the World of Chabad-Lubavitch* (New York: Schocken Books, 2003), 12–13.

9. Based on anecdotal evidence, I would estimate Chabad rabbinic salaries at roughly half of rabbinic salaries at similarly sized non-Chabad synagogues. See Dan Judson, "What One Chabad Rabbi Can Teach Synagogues about Money," http://ejewishphilanthropy.com/what-one-chabad-rabbi-can-teach-synagogues-about-money.

10. See Elie Kaunfer, *Empowered Judaism: What Independent Minyanim Can Teach Us about Building Vibrant Communities* (Woodstock, VT: Jewish Lights Publishing, 2010).

11. The free synagogue model is alternatively referred to as the "voluntary dues" model or the "voluntary commitment" model.

12. See Beryl Chernov, Debbie Joseph, and Dan Judson, "Are Voluntary Dues Right for Your Synagogue? A Practical Guide," UJA-NY Federation, 2014, http://www.ujafedny.org/what-we-do/strengthen-organizations/voluntary-dues-report; Dan Judson, "When Jews Chose Their Dues," *Reform Judaism Magazine* (Spring 2014): 16–22; Dan Judson, "Scrapping Synagogue Dues," January 12, 2012, http://ejewishphilanthropy.com/scrapping-synagogue-dues-a-case-study; and "'The Pay What You Want' Experiment at Synagogues," *New York Times*, February 2, 2015.

13. Alice Mann, "Alliances, Mergers, and Partnerships: Lessons from the Journey, 2008–2013," UJA Federation of New York, 2013, http://www.congregationalconsulting.org/wp-content/uploads/2014/03/SYNERGY-Alliances-Mergers-and-Partnerships-Report.pdf.

Bibliography

Archival Sources

American Jewish Archives, Cincinnati, OH
American Jewish Historical Society, Boston, MA
American Jewish Historical Society, New York, NY
Jewish Historical Society of the Upper Midwest Archives, Minneapolis, MN
Rabbi S. Felix Mendelsohn Sermon Archives, Skokie, IL
Rauh Jewish History Program & Archives, Pittsburgh, PA
Rodef Shalom Congregation Archives, Pittsburgh, PA
Stephen Wise Free Synagogue Archives, New York, NY
Temple Israel Archives, Boston, MA
Temple Israel Archives, Natick MA
Temple Reyim Archives, Newton, MA

Other Sources

Abelow, Samuel. *History of Brooklyn Jewry.* Brooklyn: Scheba Publishing Company, 1937.

Ackerman, Daniel. "The 1794 Synagogue of Kahal Kadosh Beth Elohim of Charleston: Reconstructed and Reconsidered." *American Jewish History* 93 (2007): 159–76.

Adams Jr., Donald. "Wage Rates in the Early National Period: Philadelphia, 1785–1830." *The Journal of Economic History* 28 (September 1968): 404–26.

Adler, Frank. *Roots in a Moving Stream: The Centennial History of the Congregation B'nai Jehudah of Kansas City, 1870–1970.* Kansas City, MO: Congregation of B'nai Jehudah, 1972.

Adler, Selig, and Thomas Connolly. *From Ararat to Suburbia: The History of the Jewish Community of Buffalo.* Philadelphia: Jewish Publication Society, 1960.

Arbell, Mordechai. *The Jewish Nation of the Caribbean.* Jerusalem: Gefen Publishing House, 2002.

Baron, Salo. *The Jewish Community, Its History and Structure to the American Revolution.* Philadelphia: Jewish Publication Society, 1948.

————. "Modern Capitalism and Jewish Fate." *Menorah Journal* 30 (Summer 1942): 116–38.

Berman, Myron. *Richmond's Jewry, 1769–1976: Shabbat in Shockoe*. Charlottesville: University of Virginia Press, 1979.

Blau, Joseph L., and Salo W. Baron. *The Jews of the United States, 1790–1840*, 3 vols. New York: Columbia University Press, 1963.

Bonomi, Patricia. *Under the Cope of Heaven: Religion, Society, and Politics in Colonial America*. New York: Oxford University Press, 2003.

Breibart, Solomon. "The Synagogues of Kahal Kadosh Beth Elohim, Charleston." *The South Carolina Historical Magazine* 80, 3 (July 1979): 215–35.

Brinkmann, Tobias. *Sundays at Sinai: A Jewish Congregation in Chicago*. Chicago: University of Chicago Press, 2012.

Buchler, Samuel. *"Cohen Comes First" and Other Cases: Stories of Controversies before the New York Jewish Court of Arbitration*. New York: The Vanguard Press, 1933.

Bunker, Gary, and John Appel. "'Shoddy' Antisemitism and the Civil War." In *Jews and the Civil War*, eds. Jonathan Sarna and Adam Mendelsohn. New York: New York University Press, 2010, 311–34.

Burrows, Edwin, and Mike Wallace. *Gotham: A History of New York City to 1898*. New York: Oxford University Press, 1999.

Bushman, Richard L. *The Refinement of America: Persons, Houses, Cities*. New York: Knopf, 1992.

Caplan, Kimmy. "In God We Trust: Salaries and Income of American Orthodox Rabbis, 1881–1924." *American Jewish History* 86 (1998): 77–106.

Carey, Patrick. *People, Priests and Prelates: Ecclesiastical Democracy and the Tensions of Trusteeism*. South Bend, IN: University of Notre Dame Press, 1987.

Chambers, John Whiteclay. *The Tyranny of Change: America in the Progressive Era*. New Brunswick, NJ: Rutgers University Press, 2000.

Cohen, Anne. *The Centenary History: Congregation Beth Israel of Houston, Texas, 1854–1954*. Houston, TX: Congregation Beth Israel, 1954.

Cohen, Naomi. *Encounter with Emancipation: The German Jews in the United States, 1830–1914*. Philadelphia: Jewish Publication Society, 1984.

Cole, Charles C. "The Free Church Movement in New York City." *New York History* 34 (1953): 284–97.

Colon, Joseph. *Shealot U'Tsheuvot Maharik*. Warsaw: 1884.

Dinnerstein, Leonard. "A Note on Southern Attitudes Towards Jews." *Jewish Social Studies* 32, 1 (1970): 43–49.

————. *Antisemitism in America*. New York: Oxford University Press, 1994.

"Directory of Local Organizations." *American Jewish Year Book, 1 (1899–1900)*: 105–270.

Drachman, Bernard. *The Unfailing Light: Memoirs of an American Rabbi*. New York: The Rabbinical Council of America, 1948.

Dwyer-Ryan, Meaghan, Susan L. Porter, and Lisa Fagin Davis. *Becoming American Jews: Temple Israel of Boston*. Waltham, MA: Brandeis University Press, 2009.

Edwards, George. *A History of the Independent or Congregational Church of Charleston, South Carolina*. Boston: Pilgrim Press, 1947.

Eisenstein, Judah. "The History of the First Russian-American Jewish Congregation: The Beth Hamedrosh Hagadol." *Publications of the American Jewish Historical Society* 9 (1901): 63–74.

Elazar, Daniel, Jonathan Sarna, and Rela Monson. *A Double Bond: The Constitutional Documents of American Jewry*. Lanham, MD: University Press of America, 1992.

Elbogen, Ismar. *Jewish Liturgy: A Comprehensive History*, trans. Raymond Scheindlin. Philadelphia: Jewish Publication Society, 1993.

Eleff, Zev. "Power, Pulpits and Pews: Religious Authority and the Formation of American Judaism, 1816–1885." PhD diss., Brandeis University, 2015.

Elzas, Barnett A. *The Jews of South Carolina: From the Earliest Times to the Present Day*. Philadelphia: J.B. Lippincott, 1905.

———. *The Reformed Society of Israelites*. New York: Bloch Publishing Company, 1916.

Fein, Isaac. *The Making of an American Jewish Community: The History of Baltimore Jewry from 1773 to 1920*. Philadelphia: Jewish Publication Society, 1971.

Feldman, Egal. "The Social Gospel and the Jews." *American Jewish Historical Quarterly* 58 (March 1969): 308–22.

Finke, Roger, and Rodney Stark. *The Churching of America, 1776–2005: Winners and Losers in Our Religious Economy*. New Brunswick, NJ: Rutgers University Press, 2005.

Fishkoff, Sue. *The Rebbe's Army: Inside the World of Chabad-Lubavitch*. New York: Schocken Books, 2003.

Franklin, Benjamin. *The Autobiography of Benjamin Franklin*. New York: Cosimo Classics, 2007.

Gans, Herbert. "The Origin and Growth of a Jewish Community in the Suburbs." In *The Jews: Social Patterns of an American Group*, ed. Marshall Sklare. New York: Free Press, 1958, 205–48.

Gartner, Lloyd P. *History of the Jews of Cleveland*. Cleveland: Western Reserve Historical Society, 1978.

Gastwirt, Harold. *Fraud, Corruption and Holiness*. New York: Kennikat, 1974.

Glanz, Rudolf. *Studies in Judaica Americana*. New York: Ktav, 1970.

Goebel, Thomas. "The Uneven Rewards of Professional Labor: Wealth and Income in the Chicago Professions, 1870–1920." *Journal of Social History* 29, 4 (Summer 1996): 749–77.

Goldman, Karla. *Beyond the Synagogue Gallery: Finding a Place for Women in American Judaism*. Cambridge, MA: Harvard University Press, 1993.

Goldstein, Israel. *A Century of Judaism in New York: B'nai Jeshurun, 1825–1925*. New York: Congregation B'nai Jeshurun, 1930.

Goldstein, Sydney. *The Synagogue and Social Welfare: A Unique Experiment, 1907–1953*. New York: Bloch, 1955.

Goodfriend, Joyce. *Before the Melting Pot: Society and Culture in Colonial New York City, 1664–1730*. Princeton, NJ: Princeton University Press, 1992.

Gordon, Albert. *Jews in Suburbia*. Boston: Beacon Hill Press, 1959.

Goren, Arthur. *New York Jews and the Quest for Community: The Kehillah Experiment, 1908–1922*. New York: Columbia University Press, 1970.

Grinstein, Hyman. *The Rise of the Jewish Community of New York*. Philadelphia: Jewish Publication Society, 1945.

Gurock, Jeffrey. *Orthodox Jews in America*. Bloomington: Indiana University Press, 2009.

———. *When Harlem Was Jewish, 1870–1930*. New York: Columbia University Press, 1979.

Haber, Samuel. *The Quest for Authority and Honor in the American Professions, 1750–1900*. Chicago: University of Chicago Press, 1991.

Hagy, James. *This Happy Land: The Jews of Colonial and Antebellum Charleston*. Tuscaloosa: University of Alabama Press, 1993.

Hambrick-Stowe, Charles, *Charles G. Finney and the Spirit of American Evangelicalism*. Grand Rapids, MI: William Eerdmans Publishing Company, 1996.

Handy, Robert. "The American Religious Depression, 1925–1935." *Church History* 29 (March 1960): 3–16.

Hapgood, Hutchins. *The Spirit of the Ghetto*. Cambridge, MA: Harvard University Press, 1967.

Hardman, Keith. *Charles Grandison Finney, 1792–1875, Revivalist and Reformer*. Syracuse, NY: Syracuse University Press, 1987.

Hatch, Nathan. *The Democratization of American Christianity*. New Haven, CT: Yale University Press, 1989.

Heller, James G. *Isaac M. Wise: His Life, Work, and Thought*. New York: Union of American Hebrew Congregations Press, 1965.

Hershkowitz, Leo. *Wills of Early New York Jews*. New York: American Jewish Historical Society, 1967.

A History of Congregation Beth El, Detroit, Michigan, Volume II, 1900–1910. Detroit: Winn & Hammond, 1910.

Holifield, E. Brooks. *God's Ambassadors: A History of the Christian Clergy in America*. Grand Rapids, MI: William Eerdmans Publishing Company, 2007.

———. "The Penurious Preacher? Nineteenth-Century Clerical Wealth: North and South." *Journal of the American Academy of Religion* 58, 1 (1990): 17–37.

Howe, Irving. *World of Our Fathers*. New York: Harcourt, Brace and Jovanovich, 1976.

Hudnut-Beumler, James. *In Pursuit of the Almighty's Dollar: A History of Money and American Protestantism*. Chapel Hill, NC: University of North Carolina Press, 2007.

Hyman, Paula. "Immigrant Women and Consumer Protest: The New York City Kosher Meat Boycotts of 1902." *American Jewish History* 70 (September 1980): 91–105.

"Items Relating to Congregation Shearith Israel, New York." *Publications of the American Jewish Historical Society* 27 (1920): 1–125.

Jeffries, C. P. B. "The Provincial and Revolutionary History of St. Peter's Church, Philadelphia, 1753–1783." *The Pennsylvania Magazine of History and Biography* 48 (January 1924): 39–65.

Jewish Community (Kehillah) of New York City. "Report to the Executive Committee of the American Jewish Committee." *American Jewish Year Book* 15 (1913–1914): 444–45.

———. "Report to the Executive Committee of the American Jewish Committee." *American Jewish Year Book* 17 (1915–1916): 378.

Jick, Leon. *The Americanization of the Synagogue, 1820–1870*. Hanover, NH: Brandeis University Press, 1976.

Joselit, Jenna. "Bingo's Sacred History." *The Jewish Daily Forward*, March 14, 2008.

———. *New York's Jewish Jews: The Orthodox Community in the Interwar Years*. Bloomington: Indiana University Press, 1981.

Judson, Dan. "A History of 'Mushroom Synagogues.'" *American Jewish Archives Journal*. Forthcoming.

———. "Money, Schism, and the Creation of American Reform Judaism." *CCAR Journal* 57, 2 (2010): 90–102.

———. "When Jews Chose Their Dues." *Reform Judaism* (Spring 2014): 16–22.

Kahan, Arcadius. "Economic Opportunities and Some Pilgrim's Progress." In *Essays in Jewish Social and Economic History*, ed. Roger Weiss. Chicago: University of Chicago Press, 1986, 101–117.

Kahn, Ava F. *Jewish Voices of the California Gold Rush: A Documentary History, 1849–1880*. Detroit: Wayne State University Press, 2002.

Kammen, Michael. *New York: A Colonial History*. New York: Charles Scribner's Sons, 1975.

Kaplan, Mordecai. "The Future of Judaism." *Menorah Journal* (June 1916): 160–72.

———. *Judaism as a Civilization: Toward a Reconstruction of American-Jewish Life*. New York: Schocken, 1973.

Karp, Abraham. "New York City Chooses a Chief Rabbi." *Publications of the American Jewish Historical Society* 44 (1955): 129–98.

Karp, Jonathan. "It's the Economy Schmendrick: An 'Economic Turn' in Jewish Studies?" *AJS Perspectives* (Fall 2009): 8–11.

Katz, Irving. *The Beth El Story*. Detroit: Wayne State University Press, 1955.

Kaufman, David. *Shul with a Pool: The "Synagogue Center" in American Jewish History*. Hanover, NH: Brandeis University Press, 1999.

Kaunfer, Elie. *Empowered Judaism: What Independent Minyanim Can Teach Us about Building Vibrant Communities*. Woodstock, VT: Jewish Lights Publishing, 2010.

Kindleberger, Charles. *Manias, Panics and Crashes: A History of Financial Crises*. New York: John Wiley & Sons, 2000.

Kirschenbaum, Alan, and Arie Melnik. "Determinants of the Salaries of Rabbis." *Contemporary Jewry* 15 (1994): 157–71.

Kobrin, Rebecca, ed. *Chosen Capital: The Jewish Encounter with American Capitalism*. New Brunswick, NJ: Rutgers University Press, 2012.

Kohn, S. Joshua. *The Jewish Community of Utica, New York, 1847–1948*. New York: American Jewish Historical Society, 1959.

Korn, Bertram. "An American Jewish Leader in 1860 Voices His Frustration." In *Michael: On the History of Jews in the Diaspora*, ed. Lloyd P. Gartner. Tel Aviv: The Diaspora Research Institute, 1975.

———. *American Jewry and the Civil War*. New York: Atheneum, 1970.

———. *A Bicentennial Festschrift for Jacob Radar Marcus*. New York: Ktav, 1976.

———. *The Early Jews of New Orleans*. Waltham, MA: The American Jewish Historical Society, 1969.

———. *Eventful Years and Experiences: Studies in Nineteenth-Century American Jewish History*. Cincinnati: American Jewish Archives, 1954.

———. "A Reappraisal of Judah Touro." *The Jewish Quarterly Review* 45, 4 (April 1855): 568–81.

Krinsky, Carol. *Synagogues of Europe: Architecture, History, Meaning*. New York: MIT Press, 1985.

Lazerov, Y. L. *Der Yiddisher Redner, vol. 2: Oyf Eyn Yaakov*. New York: Y. Z. Bookbinder, 1927.

Lederhendler, Eli. *Jewish Immigration and American Capitalism, 1880–1920: From Caste to Class*. Cambridge, UK: Cambridge University Press, 2009.

Leibowitz, Aryeh. "The Pursuit of Scholarship and Economic Self-Sufficiency: Revisiting Maimonides Commentary on Pirkei Avot." *Tradition* 40, 3 (2007): 31–41.

Lenn, Theodore. *Rabbi and Synagogue in Reform Judaism*. West Hartford, CT: Central Conference of American Rabbis, 1972.

Long, Kathryn. *The Revival of 1857–1858: Interpreting an American Religious Awakening*. New York: Oxford University Press, 1998.

Lytton, Timothy. *Kosher: Private Regulation in the Age of Industrial Food.* Cambridge, MA: Harvard University Press, 2013.

Marcus, Jacob Rader. *The Americanization of Isaac Mayer Wise.* Cincinnati: American Jewish Archives, 1969.

———. *The Colonial American Jew, 1492–1776.* Detroit: Wayne State University Press, 1970.

———. *The Handsome Young Priest in the Black Gown: The Personal World of Gershom Seixas.* Cincinnati: American Jewish Archives, 1970.

———. "The Oldest Known Synagogue Record Book of Continental North America, 1720–1721." In *Studies in American Jewish History: Studies and Addresses.* Cincinnati: Hebrew Union College Press, 1969, 44–53.

Marcus, Jacob Rader, and Abraham Peck, eds. *The American Rabbinate: A Century of Continuity and Change, 1883–1983.* Hoboken, NJ: Ktav, 1985.

Margo, Robert. "The Rental Price of Housing in New York City, 1830–1860." *The Journal of Economic History* 56 (September 1996): 605–25.

Marsden, George. *The Evangelical Mind and the New School Presbyterian Experience: A Case Study of Thought and Theology in Nineteenth-Century America.* New Haven, CT: Yale University Press, 1970.

Martin, Asa E. "Lotteries in Pennsylvania Prior to 1833." *The Pennsylvania Magazine of History and Biography* 47 (1923): 307–27.

———. "Lotteries in Pennsylvania Prior to 1833 [Part 2]." *The Pennsylvania Magazine of History and Biography* 48 (1924): 66–96.

Massachusetts Bureau of Statistics of Labor. *Sixth Annual Report.* Boston: Wright and Potter, 1875.

McCusker, John. *How Much Is That in Real Money? A Historical Price Index for Use as a Deflator of Money Values in the Economy of the United States.* Worcester, MA: American Antiquarian Society, 1992.

Mehotra, Ajay. "Envisioning the Modern American Fiscal State: Progressive-Era Economists and the Intellectual Foundations of the U.S. Income Tax." *UCLA Law Review* 52 (2005): 1793–866.

Mendes-Flohr, Paul. "Werner Sombart's *The Jews and Modern Capitalism*: An Analysis of Its Ideological Premises." *Leo Baeck Institute Yearbook* 21 (1976): 87–107.

Mendolsohn, Adam. *The Rag Race: How the Jews Sewed Their Way to Success in America and the British Empire.* New York: New York University Press, 2014.

Mervis, Leonard. "The Social Justice Movement and the American Reform Rabbi." *American Jewish Archives* 7 (1955): 171–230.

Meyer, Michael. *Response to Modernity: A History of the Reform Movement in Judaism.* New York: Oxford University Press, 1998.

Middleton, Simon. *From Privilege to Rights: Work and Politics in Colonial New York City.* Philadelphia: University of Pennsylvania Press, 2006.

"Minute Book of the Congregation Shearith Israel." *Publications of the American Jewish Historical Society* 21 (1913): 1–171.

Moise, L. C. *Biography of Isaac Harby*. Columbia, SC: R. L. Bryan, 1931.

Moore, Deborah Dash. *At Home in America: Second Generation New York Jews*. New York: Columbia University Press, 1981.

———. *B'nai Brith and the Challenge of Ethnic Leadership*. Albany: SUNY Press, 1981.

Morawska, Ewa. *Insecure Prosperity: Small Town Jews in Industrial America, 1890–1940*. Princeton, NJ: Princeton University Press, 1996.

Mosse, Werner. "Judaism, Jews and Capitalism: Weber, Sombart and Beyond." *Leo Baeck Institute Yearbook* 24 (1979): 3–15.

Mostov, Stephen. "A 'Jerusalem' on the Ohio: The Social and Economic History of Cincinnati's Jewish Community, 1840–1875." PhD diss., Brandeis University, 1981.

Nadell, Pamela, and Jonathan Sarna, eds. *Women and American Judaism: Historical Perspectives*. Hanover, NH: University Press of New England, 2001.

Noll, Mark, ed. *God and Mammon: Protestants, Money, and the Market, 1790–1860*. New York: Oxford University Press, 2001.

Olds, Kelly. "Privatizing the Church: Disestablishment in Connecticut and Massachusetts." *Journal of Political Economy* 102, 2 (1994): 277–97.

Pointer, Richard. "Philadelphia Presbyterians, Capitalism, and the Morality of Economic Success, 1825–1855." *The Pennsylvania Magazine of History and Biography* 112, 3 (July 1988): 349–74.

Polland, Annie. *Landmark of the Spirit: The Eldridge Street Synagogue*. New Haven, CT: Yale University Press, 2009.

Pool, David de Sola. *Portraits Etched in Stone — Early Jewish Settlers, 1682–1831*. New York: Columbia University Press, 1952.

Pool, David de Sola, and Tamar de Sola Pool. *An Old Faith in the New World: Portrait of Shearith Israel, 1654–1954*. New York: Columbia University Press, 1955.

Powell, Luther. *Money and the Church*. New York: Association Press, 1962.

Proceedings of the Committee on Jewish Law and Standards of the Conservative Movement. New York: The Rabbinical Assembly, 1997.

Proceedings of the Rabbinical Assembly of America, 1930–1932. New Rochelle, NY: The Little Print, 1933.

Proceedings of the Rabbinical Assembly of America, 1933–1938. New York: The Ad Press, 1939.

Raider, Mark. "The Aristocrat and the Democrat: Louis Marshall, Stephen S. Wise and the Challenge of American Jewish Leadership." *American Jewish History* 94, 1–2 (March-June 2008): 91–113.

Rainsford, William. *The Story of a Varied Life: An Autobiography*. Garden City, NY: Doubleday, Page & Company, 1922.

Raphael, Marc Lee. "'Our Treasury Is Empty and Our Bank Account Is Overdrawn':
Washington Hebrew Congregation, 1855–1872." *American Jewish History* 84
(1996): 81–98.

"Report of Commission on Social Justice." *Central Conference of American Rabbis
Yearbook.* New York: Central Conference of American Rabbis, 1932, 94–105.

Reznikoff, Charles. *The Jews of Charleston: A History of an American Jewish
Community.* Philadelphia: Jewish Publication Society, 1950.

Rich, Michael. "Henry Mack: An Important Figure in Nineteenth-Century Jewish
America." *American Jewish Archives* 47, 2 (1995): 261–79.

Richin, Moses. *The Promised City: New York's Jews, 1870–1914.* New York: Harper
Torchbooks, 1970.

Rosell, Garth, and Richard A. G. Dupois, eds. *Memoirs of Charles G. Finney.* Grand
Rapids, MI: Academie Books, 1989.

Rosenbaum, Fred. *Visions of Reform: Congregation Emanu-El and the Jews of San
Francisco, 1849–1999.* Berkeley, CA: Judan L. Magnes Museum, 2000.

Rudolph, B. G. *From a Minyan to a Community: A History of the Jews of Syracuse.*
Syracuse, NY: Syracuse University Press, 1970.

Sarna, Jonathan D. *American Judaism.* New Haven, CT: Yale University Press, 2005.

———. "The Debate over Mixed Seating in the American Synagogue." In *The
American Synagogue: A Sanctuary Transformed*, ed. Jack Wertheimer. New York:
Cambridge University Press, 1987, 363–94.

———. "The Democratization of American Judaism." In *New Essays in American
Jewish History*, eds. Pamela S. Nadell, Jonathan D. Sarna, and Lance J. Sussman.
Cincinnati: American Jewish Archives, 2010, 95–108.

———. *A Great Awakening: The Transformation That Shaped Twentieth Century
American Judaism and Its Implications for Today.* New York: Council for Initiatives
in Jewish Education, 1995.

———. *JPS: The Americanization of Jewish Culture, 1888–1988.* Philadelphia: The
Jewish Publication Society, 1989.

———. "Seating and the American Synagogue." In *Belief and Behavior: Essays in the
New Religious History*, eds. Philip R. Vandermeer and Robert P. Swierenga. New
Brunswick, NJ: Rutgers University Press, 1991, 189–206.

Sarna, Jonathan D., and Karla Goldman. "From Synagogue-Community to Citadel
of Reform." In *American Congregations*, ed. James Lewis and James Wind.
Chicago: University of Chicago Press, 1994.

Sarna, Jonathan D., and Alexandra Shecket Korros. *American Synagogue History: A
Bibliography and State-of-the-Field Survey.* New York: Markus Wiener, 1988.

Schappes, Morris. *A Documentary History of the Jews in the United States, 1654–1855.*
New York: Citadel Press, 1952.

Schine, Robert. "'Members of This Book': The *Pinkas* of Vermont's First Jewish

Congregation." *American Jewish Archives* 60 (2008): 51–98.

Schwarz, Jacob. *Financial Security for the Synagogue*. Cincinnati: Union of American Hebrew Congregations, 1935.

Scott, Donald. *From Office to Profession: The New England Ministry, 1750–1850*. Philadelphia: University of Pennsylvania Press, 1978.

Shapiro, Robert. "A Reform Rabbi in the Progressive Era: The Early Career of Stephen S. Wise." PhD diss., Harvard University, 1984.

Sharfman, Harold. *The First Rabbi: Origins of Conflict Between Orthodox and Reform: Jewish Polemic Warfare in a Pre–Civil War America: A Biographical History*. Malibu, CA: Pangloss, 1988.

Silberman, Lou. *American Impact: Judaism in the United States in the Early Nineteenth Century*. Syracuse, NY: Syracuse University Press, 1964.

Silver, Abba Hillel. "The Relation of the Depression to the Cultural and Spiritual Values of American Jewry." *The Jewish Social Service Quarterly* 9 (December 1932): 44–48.

Silverstone, Gedalya. *Sukkat Shalom*, 2 vols. St. Louis, MO: Molnester Printing Co., 1934.

Sklare, Marshall. "Church and Laity Among Jews." *Annals of the American Academy of Political and Social Science* 332 (November 1960): 60–69.

———. *Conservative Judaism: An American Religious Movement*. New York: Schocken Books, 1972.

Sklare, Marshall, and Joseph Greenbaum. *Jewish Identity on the Suburban Frontier*. New York: Basic Books, 1967.

Slobin, Mark. *Chosen Voices: The Story of the American Cantorate*. Urbana: University of Illinois Press, 1989.

Soyer, Daniel. *Jewish Immigrant Associations and American Identity in New York, 1880–1939*. Cambridge, MA: Harvard University Press, 1997.

Starr, Paul. *The Social Transformation of American Medicine: The Rise of a Sovereign Profession and the Making of a Vast Industry*. New York: Basic Books, 1984.

Sussman, Lance. *Isaac Leeser and the Making of American Jewry*. Detroit: Wayne State University Press, 1995.

———. "The Suburbanization of American Judaism." *American Jewish History* 75 (1985): 31–47.

Swichkow, Louis J., and Lloyd P. Gartner. *The History of the Jews of Milwaukee*. Philadelphia: Jewish Publication Society, 1963.

Tarshish, Allan. "The Charleston Organ Case." *American Jewish Historical Quarterly* 54 (1965): 411–49.

———. "The Economic Life of the American Jew in the Middle Nineteenth Century." In *Essays in American Jewish History to Commemorate the Tenth Anniversary of the Founding of the American Jewish Archives*, ed. Jacob Rader

Marcus. Cincinnati: American Jewish Archives, 1958, 263–95.

Temkin, Sefton. "Isaac Mayer Wise: A Biographical Sketch." In *A Guide to the Writings of Isaac Mayer Wise*, ed. Doris C. Sturzenberger. Cincinnati: American Jewish Archives, 1981.

———. *Isaac Mayer Wise: Shaping American Judaism*. Oxford, UK: Oxford University Press, 1992.

United States Department of Commerce, Bureau of the Census. *Historical Statistics of the United States, Colonial Times to 1957*. Washington, D.C.: Superintendent of Documents, 1960.

———. *Religious Bodies, 1906*. Washington, D.C.: U.S. Government Printing Office, 1910.

———. *Religious Bodies, 1916*. Washington, D.C.: U.S. Government Printing Office, 1919.

———. *Religious Bodies, 1926*. Washington, D.C.: U.S. Government Printing Office, 1929.

———. *Religious Bodies, 1936*. Washington, D.C.: U.S. Government Printing Office, 1941.

United States Department of Labor, Bureau of Labor Statistics. *History of Wages in the United States from Colonial Times to the Present*. Bulletin 604. Washington, D.C.: U.S. Government Printing Office, 1934.

Urofsky, Melvin. *A Voice That Spoke for Justice: The Life and Times of Stephen Wise*. Albany: SUNY Press, 1982.

Vorspan, Max, and Lloyd Gartner. *History of the Jews of Los Angeles*. Philadelphia: Jewish Publication Society, 1970.

Weinberger, Moses. *People Walk on Their Heads: Moses Weinberger's Jews and Judaism in New York*, ed. and trans. Jonathan Sarna. New York: Holmes and Meier, 1982.

Weisbach, Lee. *The Synagogues of Kentucky*. Lexington: University Press of Kentucky, 1995.

Wenger, Beth. *New York Jews and the Great Depression: Uncertain Promise*. New Haven, CT: Yale University Press, 1996.

Wertheimer, Jack, ed. *The American Synagogue: A Sanctuary Transformed*. Cambridge, UK: Cambridge University Press, 1987.

Wertheimer, Jack. *Tradition Renewed: A History of the Jewish Theological Seminary of America*, 2 vols. New York: Jewish Theological Seminary, 1997.

White, Ronald, and C. Howard Hopkins. *The Social Gospel: Religion and Reform in Changing America*. Philadelphia: Temple University Press, 1976.

Wischnitzer, Rachel. *Synagogue Architecture in the United States*. Philadelphia: Jewish Publication Society, 1955.

Wise, Stephen. *Challenging Years: The Autobiography of Stephen Wise*. New York: G.P. Putnam's Sons, 1949.

———. *Free Synagogue Pulpit*, vol. I. New York: Bloch, 1908.

Wiznitzer, Arnold. *The Records of the Earliest Jewish Community in the New World.* New York: American Jewish Historical Society, 1954.

Wolf, Edwin II, and Maxell Whiteman. *The History of the Jews of Philadelphia from Colonial Times to the Age of Jackson.* Philadelphia: Jewish Publication Society, 1956.

Wright, Carol. *Seventh Special Report of the Commissioner of Labor: The Slums of Baltimore, Chicago, New York, and Philadelphia.* Washington, D.C.: Government Printing Office, 1894.

Zeligson, Hayim. "The First Jews from Suvalk in America." In *Memorial Book of Suvalk*, ed. Berl Kagen, trans. Ida Schwarcz. New York: The Suvalk and Vicinity Relief Committee of New York, 1961, 567–69.

Zelizer, Viviana. *Pricing the Priceless Child: The Changing Social Value of Children.* Princeton, NJ: Princeton University Press, 1994.

———. *The Social Meaning of Money: Pin Money, Paychecks, Poor Relief, and Other Currencies.* Princeton, NJ: Princeton University Press, 1997.

Zola, Gary. *Isaac Harby of Charleston, 1788–1828.* Tuscaloosa: University of Alabama Press, 1994.

Zunz, Olivier. *Philanthropy in America: A History.* Princeton, NJ: Princeton University Press, 2011.

Index